THE WORLD OF TRAVEL

First published in 1986 in four volumes Travel by Water, Travel by Road and Rail, Travel by Air, Space Travel

Published by
Macmillan Children's Books
A division of
MACMILLAN PUBLISHERS LTD
Houndmills, Basingstoke, Hampshire RG21 2XS
and London
Companies and representatives
throughout the world

Designed and produced by BLA Publishing Limited,

British Library Cataloguing in Publication Data

The world of travel
1. Transport for children
I Title
380.5

ISBN 0 333 51139 5

Printed in Hong Kong

Photographic credits

t = top b = bottom l = left r = right

cover: ZEFA, Yachting World, Japan National Tourist Organization, The National Motor Museum, Beaulieu

8*b* ZEFA; 9*b* Yachting World; 11*b* Philip Sauvain; 23 "Trustees of the Science Museum" (London); 25*t* The Mansell Collection; 25*b* National Maritime Museum London; 27*t* The Mansell Collection; 27*b* National Maritime Museum London; 28*t* ZEFA; 28*b* Mystic Seaport Museum; 31 ZEFA; 33*t*, 36 University of Liverpool; 37*t* British Caledonian; 37*b* Norwegian Caribbean Lines; 38*t*, 38*b*, 39, 42, 43*t* ZEFA; 44 British Petroleum; 45 ZEFA; 46 Racal-Decca Company; 47*t* ZEFA; 47*b* Royal National Lifeboat Institution; 48 Boeing Company; 49*t* British Hovercraft Corporation; 52*t* Mansell Collection; 52*b*, 57*b* ZEFA; 59 The Bridgeman Art Library; 62*t* ZEFA; 62/63, 64*t* The Bridgeman Art Library; 65 Mansell Collection; 67 ZEFA; 69*t*, 69*b*, 70, 71*t*, 71*b*, 72, 73 The National Motor Museum, Beaulieu; 75 Victor Hand; 77*t* Canadian Pacific; 77*b* Australian Information Service, London; 78 ZEFA; 79*t* Loek Polders; 79*b* ZEFA; 80*t* Austin Rover; 80*b* Loek Polders; 81*t* Porsche Cars; 81*b* General Motors (Cadillac); 82, 83*t*, 83*b* ZEFA; 84, 85*t*, 85*b* L.A.T. Photographic; 86 ZEFA; 87*t* SNCF French Railways; 87*b* Japan National Tourist Organization; 90 SNCF – French Railways; 91*t*, 91*b* General Motors (Adam Opel AG); 92 Loek Polders; 93*b* Japan National Tourist Organization; 96, 97 Flight International; 97*b* Australian Information Service, London; 101 Flight International; 102 RAF Museum; 105*t* James Gilbert; 105*b* McDonnell Douglas; 108 DPR Marketing and Sales; 109 RAF Museum; 110, 112 Boeing Company; 113 Civil Aviation Authority; 114 KLM Royal Dutch Airlines; 115 British Airways; 115*t* British Caledonian; 115*b* British Airways; 119 Cathay Pacific; 120 ZEFA; 121 British Caledonian; 122*t* KLM Royal Dutch Airlines; 122*b* McDonnell Douglas; 123*t* British Airports Authority; 123*b* ZEFA; 124 British Airports Authority; 125 KLM Royal Dutch Airlines; 125*b* British Airports Authority; 126*t* ZEFA; 126*b*, 127, 128 British Caledonian; 127*t* DPR Marketing and Sales; 129*b* Flight International; 130 Boeing Company; 131 ZEFA; 132 Flight International, 133 British Airports Authority; 135 Civil Aviation Authority; 136*t*, 136*b*, 137 Lockheed – California Company; 145*b* ZEFA, 145, 149*t*, 149*b*, 150, 151*t*, 153*b*, 156, 157*b* NASA; 158 ZEFA; 159*t* NASA; 159*b* ZEFA; 162*t*, 162*b*, 163*b*, 163*t*, 166 NASA; 167 ZEFA; 167*b* NASA; 169*t*, 169*b*, 170*t* NASA; 174*t* ZEFA; 175, 176*b* NASA.

Note to the reader
In this book there are some words in the text which are printed in **bold** type. This shows that the word is listed in the glossary on page 182. The glossary gives a brief explanation of words which may be new to you.

THE WORLD OF TRAVEL

M
MACMILLAN

Contents

Travel by air

Space travel

TRAVEL BY WATER

Michael Pollard

Introduction

This book tells the story of sailors and the sea. Two thirds of the surface of the Earth is covered by seas and oceans. The land is broken up into masses. The large masses of land are called **continents**. The small ones are called islands.

When the first sailors went to sea, they did not know what they would find at the end of their journeys. There were no maps to help them. No one knew what lands lay beyond the **horizon**. Every journey was an adventure. People went to sea to find new places to live. They traded goods from their own countries with goods from others. Sometimes they just took what they found.

When they came home, they told stories about what they had seen. People began to know about the world. Sailors brought back new kinds of food and new ideas. They learned to find their way from one place to another by using the stars to guide them. They drew maps of where they had been.

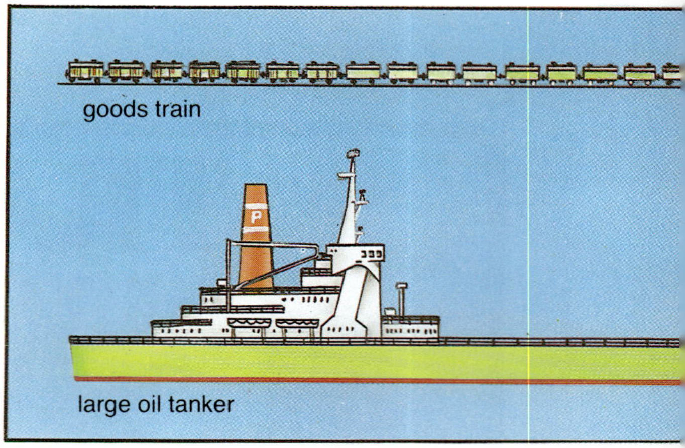

▼ A road and railway run along the valley of the River Rhine in West Germany. Railways, roads and rivers all carry people and goods.

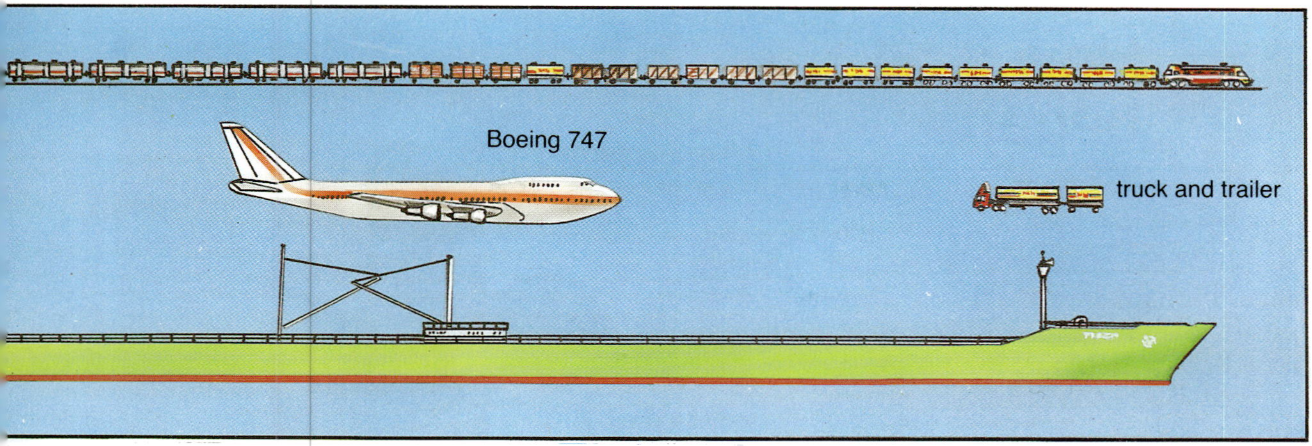

▲ **Ships carry more goods than trains but are slower. Trains carry more than planes but are slower. Planes carry more than heavy trucks and are faster.**

Sailing the seas

Life has never been easy for sailors. Strong winds and gales could blow them off course. Ships could be wrecked on rocky coasts or on rocks hidden under the water. In the oceans, large waves could swamp and sink their small boats. But if there was no wind, sailing ships could be **becalmed**. As their ships had no engines, they might be unable to move for weeks.

At first, people used their muscles to paddle their boats along. Then they began to use sails to catch the wind. It is only in the past 150 years that engines have been used to do the work.

Now there are thousands of ships at sea. Some carry people. Others are for **cargo**. Travel by sea is slower than by land or air. But ships can carry heavier cargoes. They can also carry more people than aircraft or even the longest train.

Moving through water

It is quite hard work making a boat move through water. As a boat moves forward, the water in front of it slows it down. Because of this, the smallest boats and the largest ships all have pointed **bows**. This helps them to cut their way through the water. In many other ways people have tried to make travel by water easier.

▼ **Sailing boats are used for fun and sport. They do not need engines. They use the power of the wind.**

How it all began

The first people to travel by water probably found out how to do so by chance. Perhaps they lived near a river. Someone may have seen a floating log and climbed on to it. Later, the people may have used the log to fish from, or to cross a river.

The next stage was to hollow out a log to make a simple boat. This could be done with flint tools or by fire. These boats were called **dugouts**. Another piece of wood was shaped to make a paddle.

Dugouts must have been heavy and difficult to handle. Soon, other kinds of boats were made. Smaller logs were tied together to make rafts. These could be steered and pushed along with a pole long enough to reach the river bed.

The first people found that they could use a log to travel by water. They sat astride the log and used a piece of wood to paddle the log along.

Floating

Have you ever wondered why some things float in water, and some sink? If an object is made of something heavier than water, it will sink. If it is lighter, it will float. That is why a piece of iron or stone will sink, but a piece of wood will float.

The first real boat was a long tree trunk with some of the wood carved or burnt out of it. This kind of boat is called a dugout canoe.

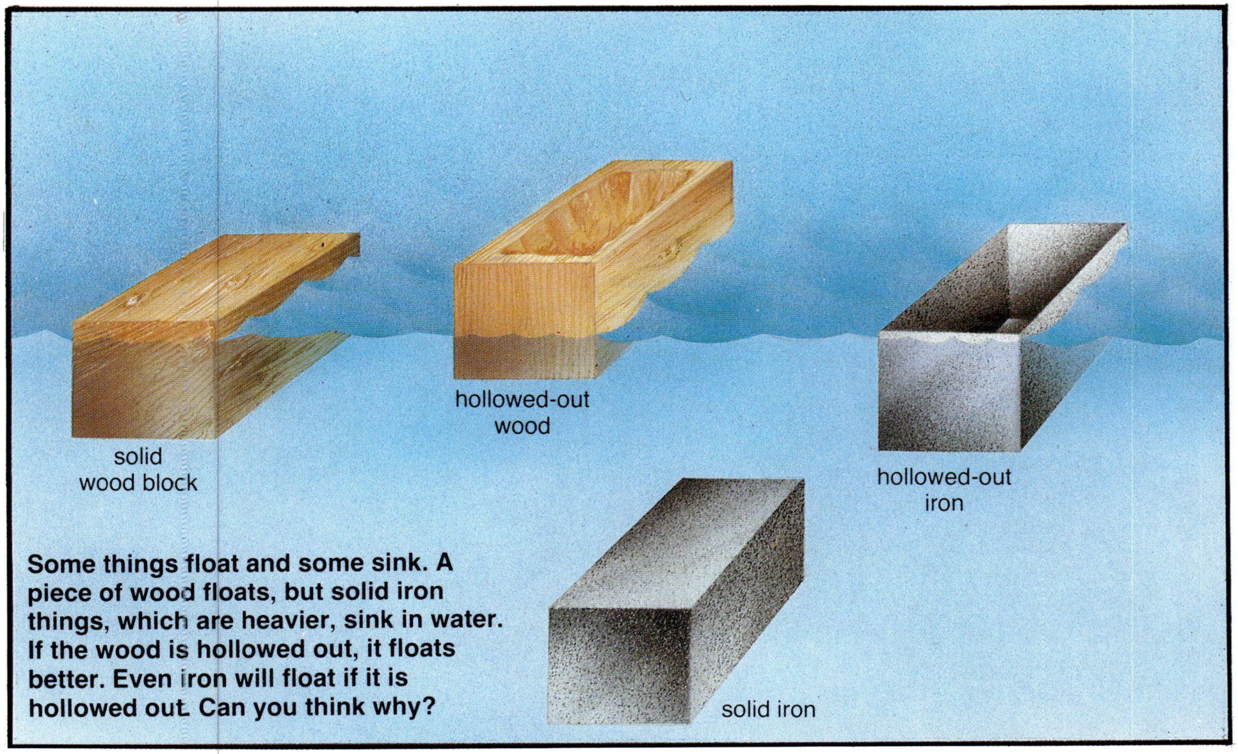

Some things float and some sink. A piece of wood floats, but solid iron things, which are heavier, sink in water. If the wood is hollowed out, it floats better. Even iron will float if it is hollowed out. Can you think why?

Anything put into water will take up some space. Because of this the water level rises. This is called **displacement**. When you get into the bath, your body displaces some of the water. Sit up in the bath and look at the water level. Now lie down. You will see that the water level has risen. If you have put too much water in the bath, some of it will spill out.

If you put a solid block of wood in water, it will float. But most of it will be under the water. The wood displaces its own weight of water. If you hollow out the piece of wood to make a dugout, it will float better. There is less weight to be displaced.

Iron does not float. But if a ship is built of thin sheets of iron, it does. This is because it displaces only the weight of the thin sheets. This weight is spread over a large area of water. But if a ship is filled with too much cargo, it will displace too much water and sink.

▼ Fill a bowl with water right to the top. Now lower something into the water. The water overflows. It is displaced. Try this with something that floats, like an orange. The further things sink the more water they displace.

The River Nile

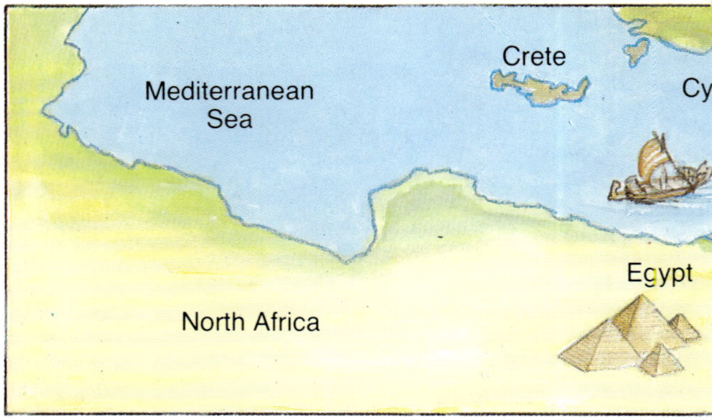
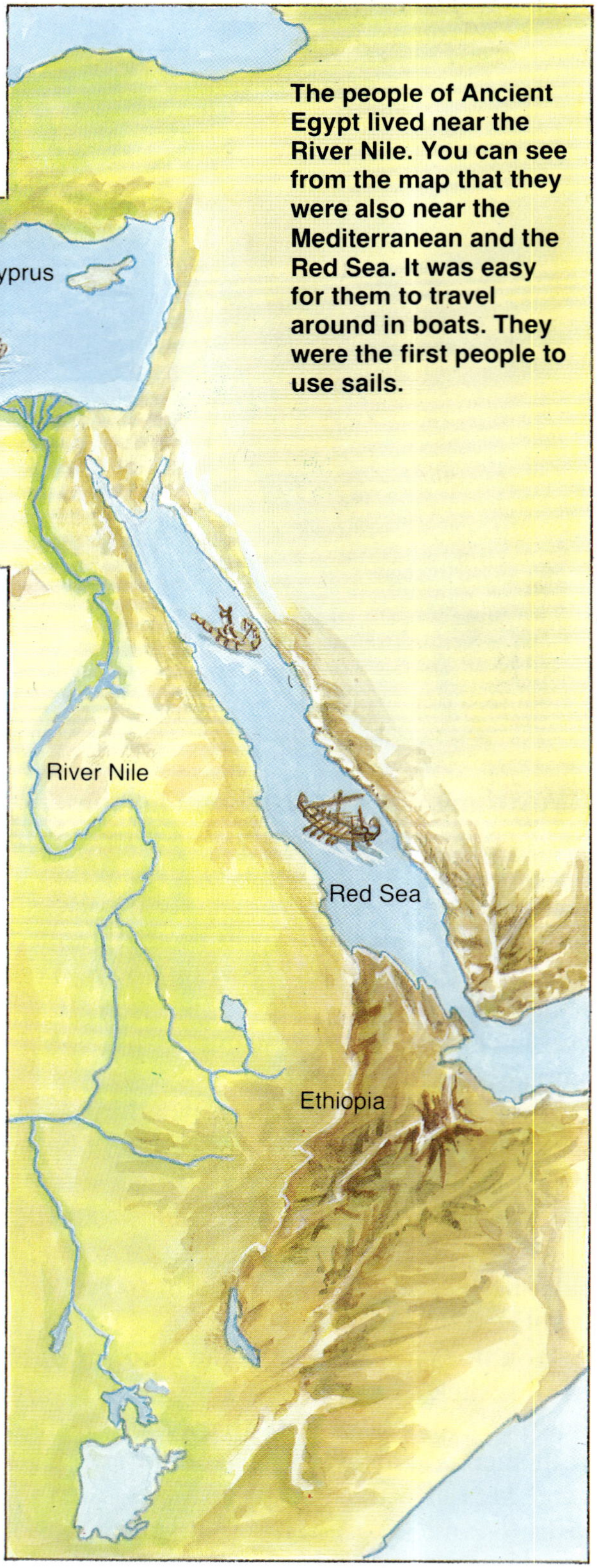

The people of Ancient Egypt lived near the River Nile. You can see from the map that they were also near the Mediterranean and the Red Sea. It was easy for them to travel around in boats. They were the first people to use sails.

We believe that the first people to build real boats lived in Ancient Egypt. This was about 5000 years ago. They lived near the banks of the River Nile. You can see that it was easy for them to travel from one place to another by water.

Their first boats were made of bundles of **reeds** tied together. They were small boats and could carry only one or two people. A paddle was used to move the boat through the water.

The boat builders

The Egyptians wanted to build larger boats. They needed something stronger than reeds. There were no large trees in Egypt. But there were plenty of small **acacia** trees. So they began to use the wood from small trees to build their boats.

The wooden boats were stronger and larger than those made of reeds. But even so these boats were quite small and not very strong. They had to be made of short planks cut from the small trees. Also, there were no trees tall enough to provide a long **keel**. The keel is a beam that goes along the bottom of a boat. It gives the boat strength, and is like a backbone.

► The Egyptians made their boats with short planks of wood. The boards were curved at both ends. While the boat was being built, the ends were tied together by a long rope. Then the rope was tightened to give the boat strength.

The Egyptians were also the first people to use the wind to push their boats along. They grew cotton and wove it into **sailcloth**. Their boats had one large square sail. With ropes, the sailors were able to turn the sail. This way they could catch the wind. If there was no wind, the sailors used paddles instead.

A boat needs a **rudder** so that it can be steered. The Egyptians fixed a paddle near the back of the boat, known as the **stern**. When the rudder was turned in one direction, the boat turned the same way.

About 4000 years ago the Egyptians were using their ships to take goods up and down the River Nile. Some sailors went further and took their ships to sea. They discovered other lands.

Egypt began to trade with other countries. Ships carried corn and cotton across the sea. They brought back jewels, spices, wood and metal.

There was a great queen of Egypt whose name was Hatshepsut (*Hat-shep-sut*). She sent sailors to explore new lands and find treasure. They sailed down the Red Sea to the land we call Ethiopia. They went across the Mediterranean Sea to the island of Crete. The sailors brought back gifts for the queen. They brought her cattle and monkeys, as well as jewels.

▼ Queen Hatshepsut's boats were large. Each boat had a mast and one large square sail. The mast was held in place by ropes. There was a large paddle at the stern. They used this paddle to steer the boat.

The Phoenicians

One of the lands Egyptian sailors went to was Phoenicia (*Fe-nish-ia*). This is now called Lebanon. The Phoenicians began to build ships of their own. They had tall **cedar** trees which they could use. Their ships had long, straight keels. These ships were strong and could sail in rough seas. They had large, square sails. There were also teams of men with oars. On some of their ships there were two or three banks of oarsmen, one bank above the other.

The Phoenicians built two kinds of ships. They used **longships** for battle. These were long, narrow ships with **rams** at the bow. The rams were used to sink enemy ships. With their two or three banks of oarsmen, longships could travel fast. They were the first warships. Other countries soon began to build their own. Another kind of Phoenician ship was called the **round ship**, because of its shape. It was

Phoenician longships travelled very fast. They had sails but they also carried many oarsmen. You can see the two banks of oars and the oarsmen, one above the other.

wider and travelled more slowly. This kind of ship was used for carrying cargo.

The Phoenicians were brave warriors and sailors. They fought many sea battles around the Mediterranean Sea. They were also explorers. They sailed out of the Mediterranean into the Atlantic Ocean. They set up trading posts wherever they went. One of these was at Carthage in North Africa. Carthage became a great city. Ships from Phoenicia also went down the Red Sea and right around Africa. Others sailed to England and northern Europe.

Greek and Roman ships

Phoenician sailors went to Greece and Rome. The Greeks and Romans copied their ships. Their long ships were known as **galleys**. A Roman galley was like a Phoenician longship, but the Romans improved them. They put a second sail at the bow. They put a paddle on each side of the stern. This made it easier to steer. Just in front of the stern, they built a **deckhouse**. On warships this looked like a castle. The Romans conquered most of western Europe. They used their ships to bring goods and treasure back to Rome.

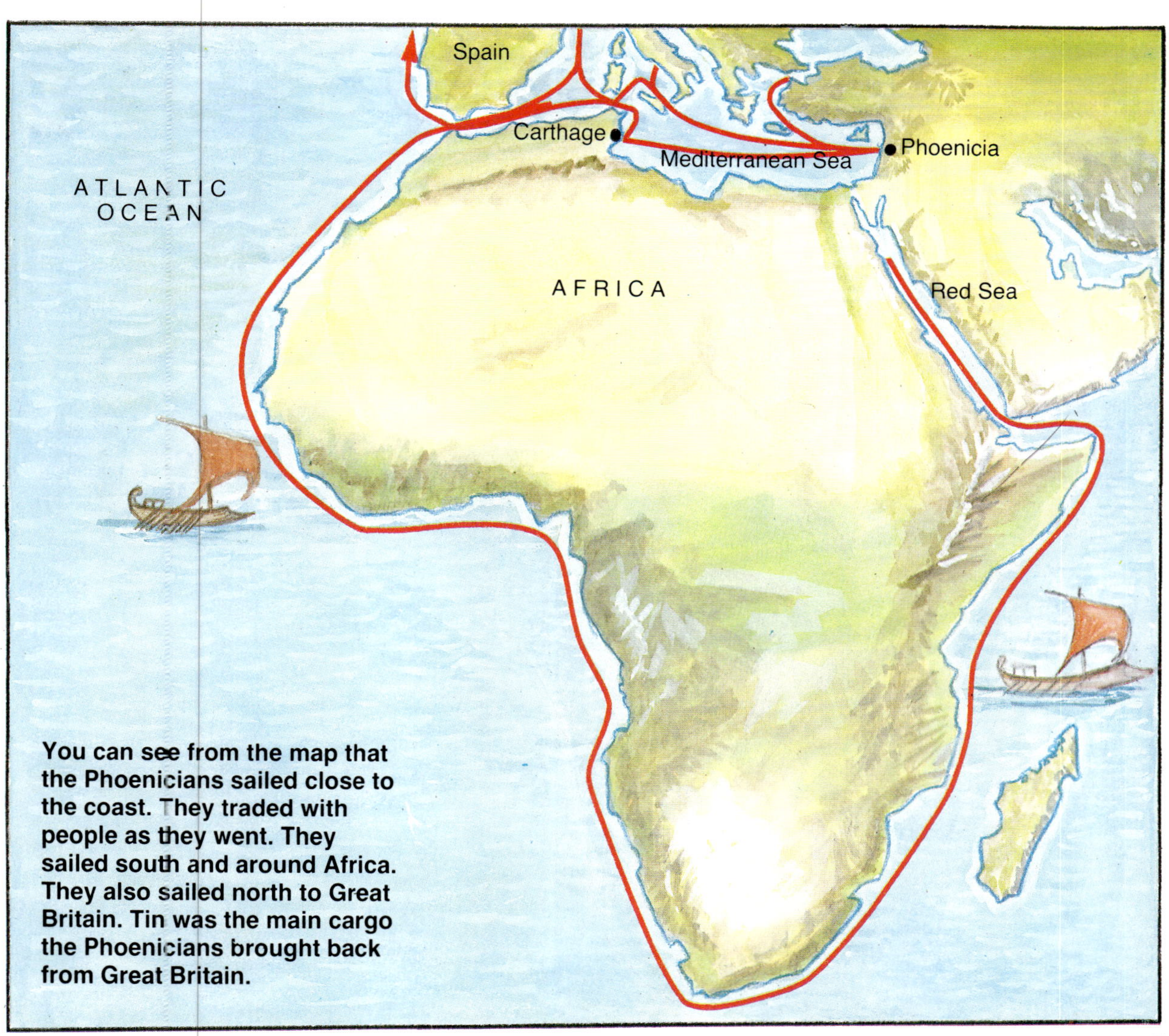

You can see from the map that the Phoenicians sailed close to the coast. They traded with people as they went. They sailed south and around Africa. They also sailed north to Great Britain. Tin was the main cargo the Phoenicians brought back from Great Britain.

The Vikings

The Vikings lived in northern Europe about 1000 years ago. They were fierce warriors and good sailors. They loved the sea, and they enjoyed exploring new lands.

The Vikings found a new way to build ships. They used long planks of wood. Each plank overlapped the one below. This type of ship is called **clinker built**. We know exactly what Viking boats were like. When a leader died, his ship was buried with him. Some of these Viking ships have been dug up and restored.

There were many different types of Viking ships. Short, wide ships were used to carry cargo. The Vikings built longships for fighting and exploring. Their longships were curved up at the bow and stern. On the bow there was often a **figurehead**. This was a carving of the head of a dragon or a snake.

▼ Viking longships were long and narrow. Each ship had one brightly coloured sail. The Vikings stood up in their open boats when they rowed. Although they were not protected from the weather, the Vikings made voyages to Iceland and Greenland. They also travelled as far as North America in longships like this one.

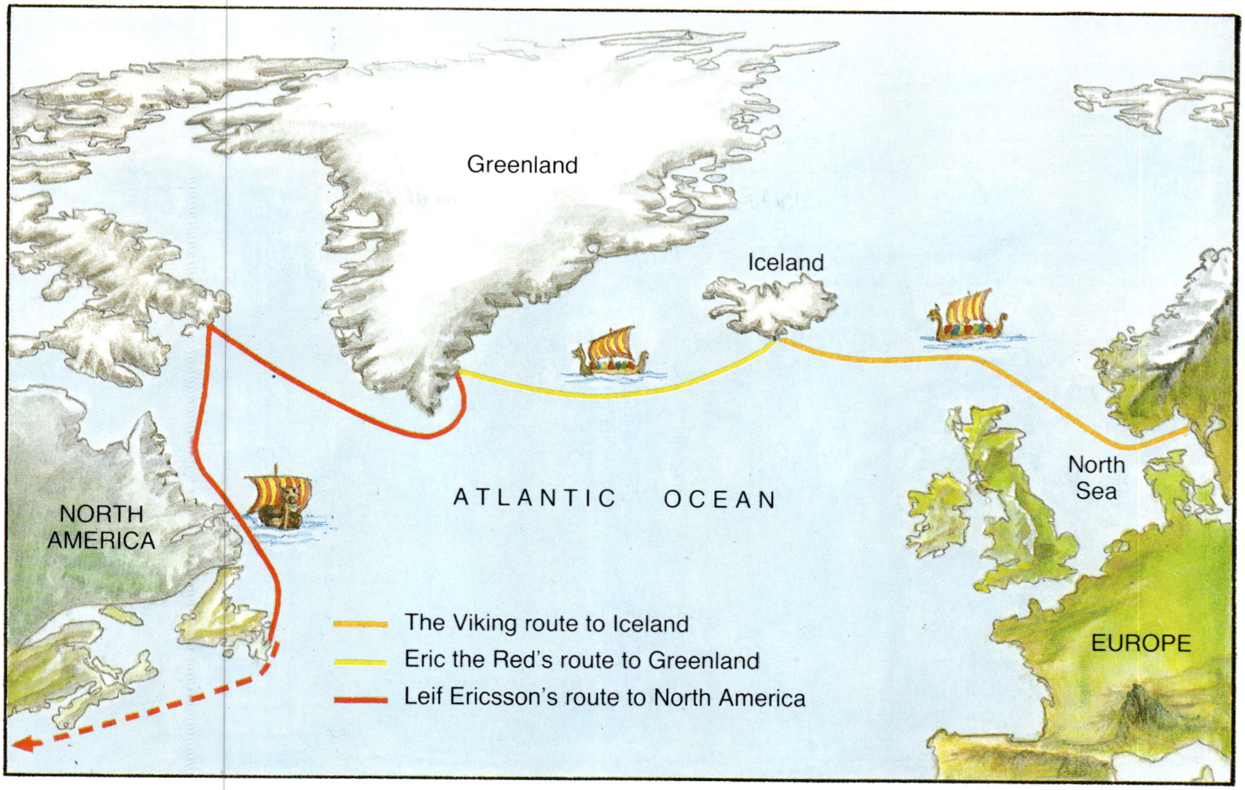

▲ Nearly 1000 years ago, Leif Ericsson sailed on from Greenland. He found a place which he called Vinland. There were vines and grapes growing there. Some people think Vinland was near New England, USA. He may have been the first person from Europe to discover America.

The biggest longships had as many as 80 oarsmen. They had large, square sails in bright colours. Viking ships had one steering oar, or rudder. It was fixed to the right side of the stern. This 'stern board' gave sailors the word **starboard**. Starboard means the right hand side of a ship. The sailor's word for the left hand side is **port**. When longships were in port, they tied up on that side. This way they did not damage the rudder.

The Vikings sailed all around Europe. They went across the Baltic Sea to Russia. At first, they explored other lands. Later, Viking families settled in the lands they had visited.

Leif Ericsson

The Vikings also sailed west into the Atlantic Ocean. They discovered Iceland. Viking families settled there. Sailors went out from Iceland to look for other new lands.

One of the sailors was called Eric the Red. He sailed west from Iceland and found Greenland. Eric the Red settled in Greenland and had a son whose name was Leif Ericsson. Leif Ericsson became an explorer like his father.

One day, Leif Ericsson's ship was blown off course in a gale. The wind blew it westwards. He landed at a place where he saw grape vines growing. He called the new land Vinland because of the vines. Vinland may have been on the coast of New England, USA, but we are not sure.

The Vikings did not settle in Vinland. It was another 400 years before sailors from Europe found America again.

Using the wind

The Arabs were the first people to use a lateen sail. This sail was in the shape of a triangle. A lateen sail works better than a square sail when the wind is blowing from the side. Arab dhows today still use lateen sails.

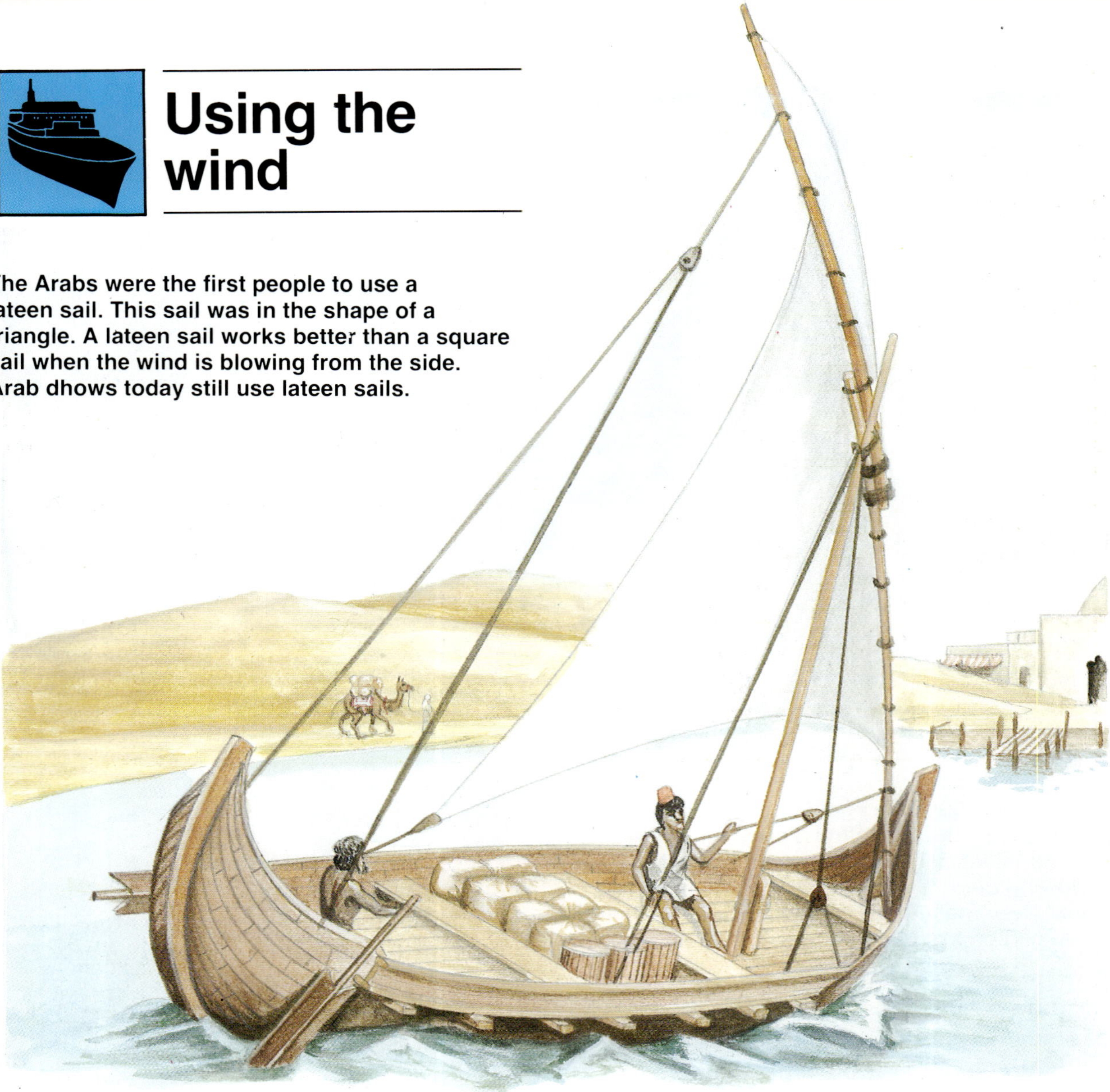

All the ships you have read about so far had square sails. Square sails worked well if there was a **following wind** from behind the ship. The sails were no use if the wind was blowing from any other direction. That is why square-sailed ships needed oarsmen. The men provided the power to push the ship forward if the wind was not right.

Arab seamen in the Red Sea and the Indian Ocean used another kind of sail. They sailed in light boats called **dhows**. These boats had one sail in the shape of a triangle. One side of the sail was fixed to the mast. The opposite corner was fixed to the side of the boat. The Romans copied this idea. They built boats with two or more triangular sails. These came to be called **lateen** sails.

Lateen sails were set along the ship instead of across it. Because of this, lateen sails were better than square sails when the wind was blowing across the ship. This was called a **beam wind**.

Catching the wind

If a boat with lateen sails heads straight into the wind, the sails do not pick up any air. The boat will not move. But, unlike square sails, lateen sails can be **trimmed**. This means moving them from side to side so that the wind catches them. The boat can then go forward by **tacking**. When a boat tacks it moves forward on a zig-zag course.

When a boat tacks, the sails are trimmed to catch the wind first on one side and then on the other side. So the boat can sail on either side of the wind. Tacking takes longer because the boat is not moving in one straight line. But the boat can move forward when sailing against the wind.

The Romans used ships with both kinds of sails. They had large, square sails for use in a following wind. They also had lateen sails for use when the wind was across or in front of them.

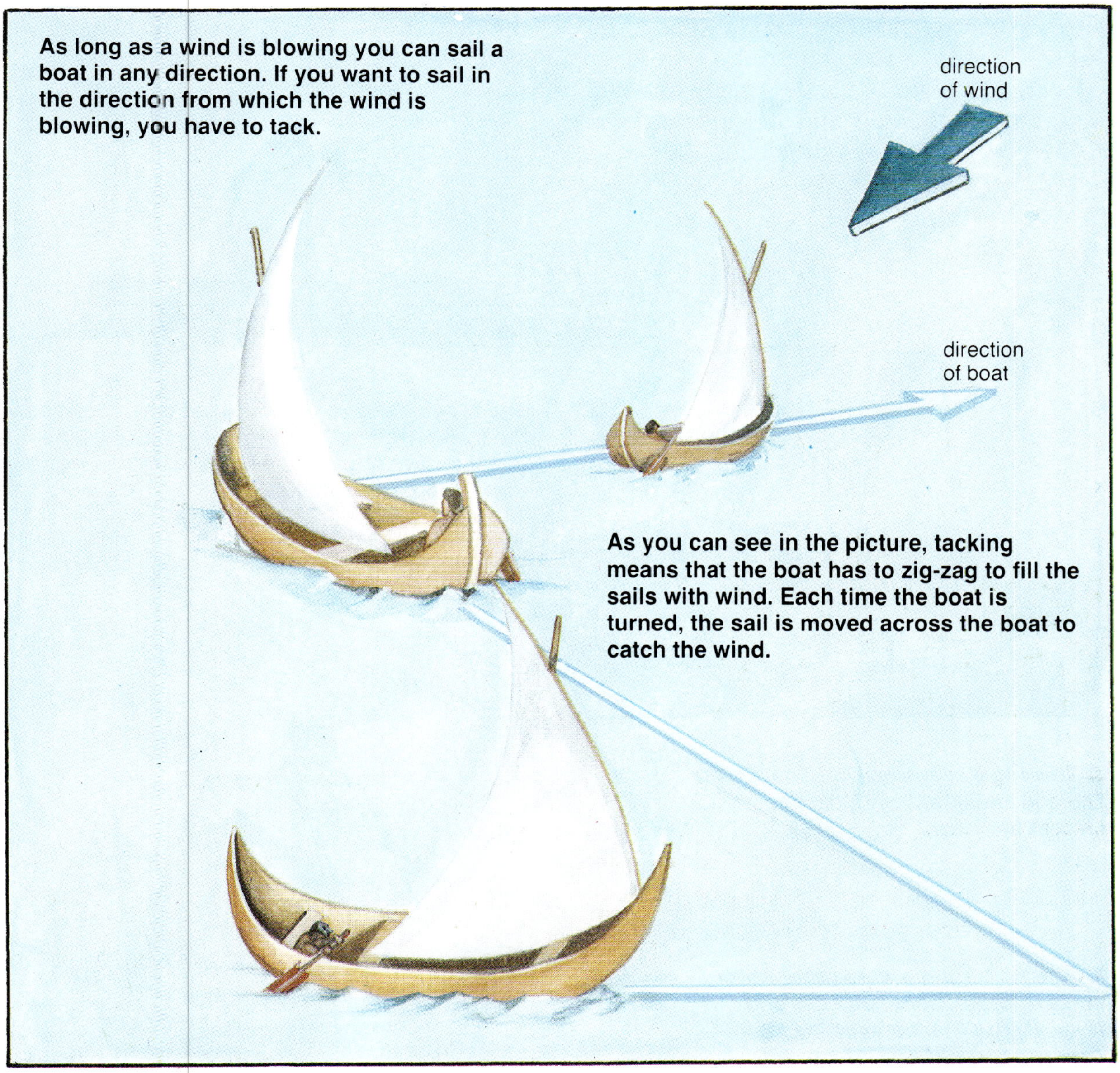

As long as a wind is blowing you can sail a boat in any direction. If you want to sail in the direction from which the wind is blowing, you have to tack.

As you can see in the picture, tacking means that the boat has to zig-zag to fill the sails with wind. Each time the boat is turned, the sail is moved across the boat to catch the wind.

How ships changed

After the Vikings, the boatbuilders of the Mediterranean countries had new ideas. They added more masts and sails to give their ships extra speed. They used some square and some lateen sails. A rudder fixed to the stern was used to steer, instead of a paddle. They made their ships out of stronger wood. These ships were safer in rough seas. 'Castles' made of wood were built at the bow and stern. The deck at the bow of a ship is still called the fo'c'sle, or **forecastle**.

There were pirates at sea in those days. They attacked merchant ships to take their goods. Merchant ships, like warships, were given 'castles' to protect the crew.

At first, warships fought by ramming each other. Sailors fought with **pikes** or poles if they were close enough. Later, around 1400, ships carried heavy guns. Special gun decks were built into warships. The guns were fired through gun ports – holes cut in the ship's sides. About this time, a **crowsnest** was fixed at the top of the **mainmast**. There, a lookout would keep watch for land, pirates or enemy ships.

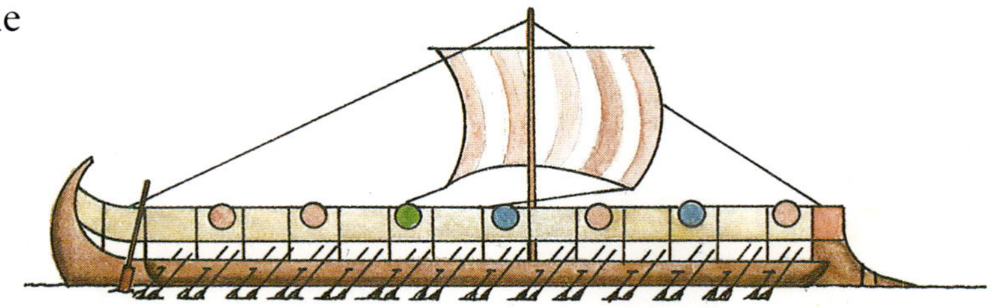

▲ Galleys like this one were used as warships in the Mediterranean for many years. Sometimes they had two square sails. There was a steering oar at the stern of the galley.

▲ The cog was a small merchant ship. The cog was fitted with 'castles' to protect the crew.

► The Portuguese were great sailors and explorers. They built the first caravel. The first caravels had two square sails and one lateen sail.

▼ The galleass was the last warship to have oars as well as sails. It had three lateen sails. The galleass was last used in a battle in 1571.

▲ Galleons stood high out of the water. They had 'castles' at the bow and at the stern. They carried heavy guns on three or more decks.

▼ Spanish sailors used their galleons as merchant ships as well as for war. Galleons were strong and safe for long ocean voyages.

▲ Carracks were very large ships. Some could carry several hundred passengers. Carracks were used as warships and as merchant ships.

Christopher Columbus

▼ Christopher Columbus reached the West Indies after a voyage of 69 days. During the next 10 years Columbus made three more journeys looking for a way through to the Indian Ocean. People from Spain travelled with him. They settled on the islands of the West Indies.

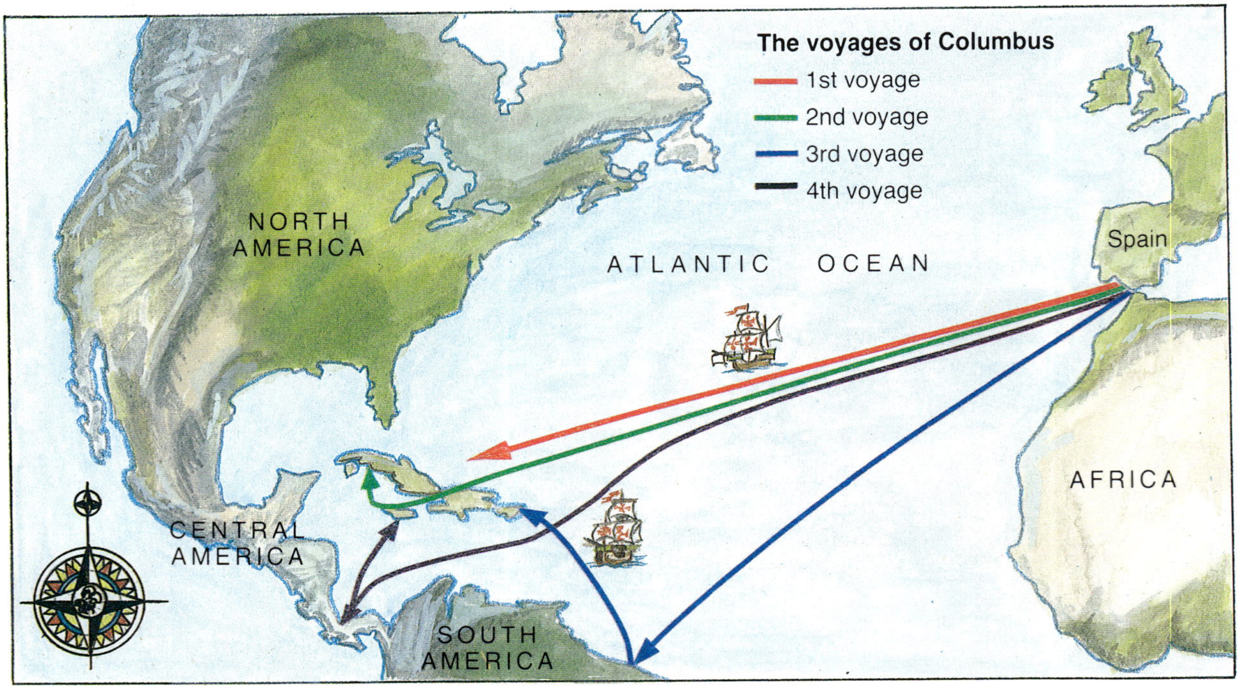

Many of the goods that people in Europe wanted came from Asia. Silk came from China and spices from India. They were brought by land. Explorers thought that if they sailed west from Europe they would reach Asia more quickly. It would be easier to bring back goods by sea than by land.

Christopher Columbus was one man who thought this way. He was a sailor from Genoa in Italy. He studied books and maps, and planned his **voyage**. But he had no money to buy ships.

He went to Portugal, hoping that the king would help. But he would not, so Columbus went to Spain. It took four years before the king of Spain said he would pay for the voyage.

Sailing west

In 1492, Columbus set sail. He had 88 men and three ships. He sailed in a **carrack** called *Santa Maria*. The other two ships were **caravels**. Their names were the *Pinta* and the *Nina*. They sailed west across the Atlantic.

▼ The *Santa Maria* was only about 35 m long. A large oil tanker is about ten times as long.

After six weeks, they had seen no land. The sailors began to be afraid. How would they get back home? Would their voyage ever end? But Columbus took no notice. 'Sail on!' he ordered.

Then, when they had been at sea for two months, they saw the branch of a tree floating in the water. Land must be near. The next night, a lookout in the crowsnest of the *Nina* called, 'Land ahoy!' The long voyage was over.

Columbus thought it must be India. But it was not. It was the island of San Salvador in the Bahamas. Columbus landed there. Then he explored some of the other islands nearby. He called them the Indies because he thought they were part of India. We call them the West Indies to this day.

Later voyages

Columbus sailed across the Atlantic four times. He put settlers on some of the islands in the West Indies. On his third voyage he found South America. On his fourth he got as far as Panama. He was still sure that he was close to India and that if he sailed on he would get there. But he was thousands of miles away. There was no way through from the Atlantic to the Pacific. Columbus had found Central America, but he still thought he had found a part of Asia.

▼ This picture shows a model of the *Santa Maria*. As well as a square mainsail, the ship carried a smaller topsail.

Around the world

Columbus was just one of the men who tried to find a way to Asia by sailing west. Another was John Cabot. He was from Genoa, like Columbus. In 1497 he set sail from England. There were only 18 men on one small carrack. After 53 days he sighted land. He was sure he had reached China. But he was wrong. He landed at Cape Breton Island, on the east coast of Canada.

Next year, he sailed west again. He went up the coast of Labrador. Then he sailed south as far as Chesapeake Bay. But supplies ran short and he had to go back to England. John Cabot was the first explorer since the Vikings to land on the mainland of North America.

East and west

At this time, Spain and Portugal had the best ships. They sent sailors from Europe to explore other lands. Amerigo Vespucci, an Italian, led several explorations for Spain and Portugal. In 1501 he sailed west and discovered South America but he did not land there. Vespucci realised that America was not part of Asia. America is named after him.

Other sailors went east from Europe. Vasco da Gama was from Portugal. He set out to sail to India. He went around South Africa and crossed the Indian Ocean. In 1498 he reached India. He was the first European to get there by sea.

▼ The map shows the routes of the main sea voyages made by six of the great explorers. Columbus discovered the West Indies. Magellan was the first explorer to sail around the world. Sir Francis Drake made the same voyage around the world 58 years later.

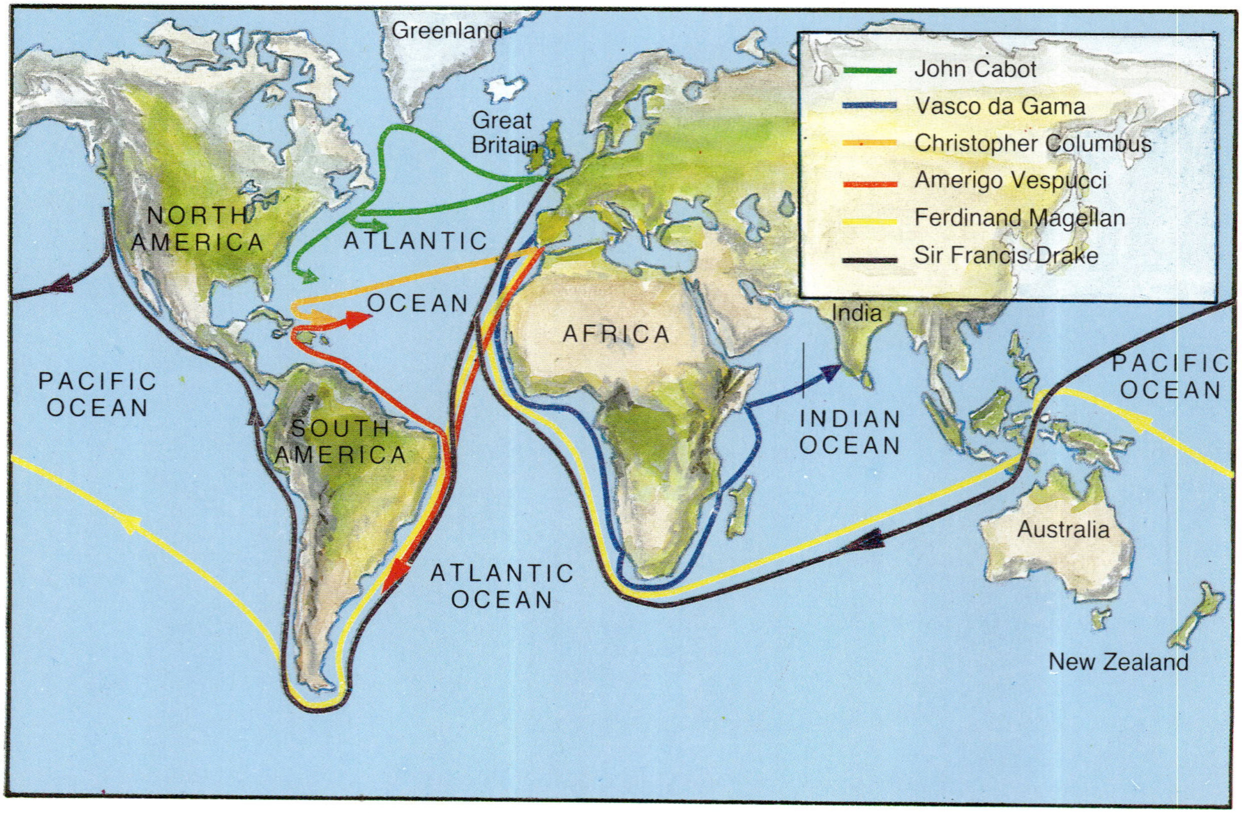

▲ This old picture shows Magellan's ships passing through the channel of water between the Atlantic and Pacific Oceans. It was named the Magellan Straits after him.

Ferdinand Magellan

Ferdinand Magellan was the first man to sail right around the world. He came from Portugal. He wanted to try to find a westward route to China. The king of Portugal would not help. But the king of Spain gave him five ships.

They set sail in 1519. The ships sailed west to Brazil. Then they went south. It was a terrible voyage. The men quarrelled and fought. Food was short. One ship was wrecked, and another went home. But Magellan went on. At last he sailed around Cape Horn into the calm Pacific Ocean.

There was more trouble to come. They saw no land for months. They were short of food and drink. Some of the sailors died. They found an island called Macta and landed on it. Magellan was killed in a fight. One of his captains finally reached home with only one ship and 17 men.

▼ Sir Francis Drake was the first Englishman to sail around the world. He sailed from England in his ship the *Golden Hind* in 1577. He arrived home three years later in 1580.

Australasia

Cook was the first person from Europe to discover Australia.

1st voyage
2nd voyage
3rd voyage

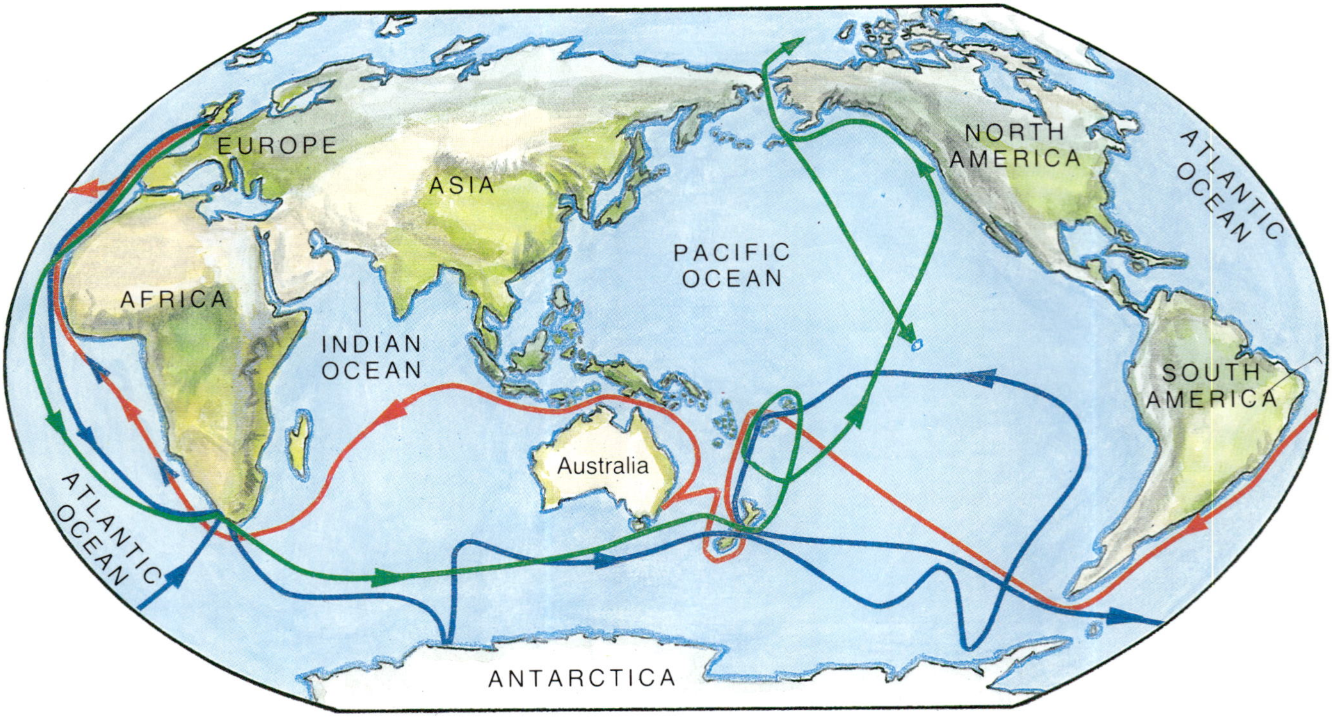

People had sailed west from Europe and found America. Some thought that there was another continent in the south. They called it the 'South Land'.

A Dutch sailor, Abel Tasman, set out to find it. In 1642 he discovered Tasmania and New Zealand. Two years later, he found the north coast of Australia. He thought these were all parts of the 'South Land'. But he could not make them fit together into a map. So far, the map of the 'South Land' showed just a few bits of coast.

James Cook

In 1768, an English sailor set out to find out more about the 'South Land'. His name was James Cook. He joined the navy as a seaman. Then he worked his way up to command his own ship. He was an expert at making **charts**, the maps that sailors use.

Cook did not want to find gold or treasure. He wanted to make a chart of the 'South Land' if he could find it. He took two scientists with him. His ship was a converted coal ship called the *Endeavour*.

Cook sailed west across the Atlantic, and around Cape Horn. He explored the South Sea island of Tahiti. Then he sailed south to look for the 'South Land'. He did not find it. So he sailed on to New Zealand. There he made a chart of the coast.

He decided to sail west and reach home that way. He came to the east coast of Australia. His men landed in a place where there were large numbers of wild flowers. They decided to call it 'Botany Bay'. **Botany** is the science which deals with flowers. This was the first landing in Australia by people from Europe.

Cook set sail on his last voyage in 1776. He sailed around Africa and across the Indian Ocean. He went across the Pacific. When he reached the coast of North America, he turned north. There is a **channel** between Asia and America. It is called the Bering Strait. Cook sailed up this channel. Soon, he could go no further. In front of the ship was a wall of ice. There was no way through. He returned to Hawaii in the Pacific Ocean.

The people who lived there had been friendly on Cook's previous visit. This time they stole a small boat. He tried to punish them, and they started fighting. During this fight, six chiefs were killed and James Cook was stabbed to death.

▲ **Captain James Cook, who was born in 1728 and died in 1779.**

▼ **James Cook chose the *Endeavour* for his voyage round the world, because it was a very strong ship. At one time the *Endeavour* had been used for carrying coal. Two lower decks were put in. You can see that the crew lived on the first deck. Food and drink were stored on the second deck.**

Clipper ships

Settlers from Europe went to live in the 'new lands' that had been discovered. They hoped to make a freer and better life for themselves and their families. Many of them became farmers.

Ships were needed to take the settlers out and bring back the goods they produced. A new kind of fast ship was built for this trade. It was called a **clipper**. The first clipper was built in 1832. She was called the *Ann McKim*. She sailed between America and China.

Clippers were long and narrow. They had sharp, pointed bows which cut through the waves. Their three tall masts had up to six sails on each. There were deep **holds** for the passengers or cargo. Clippers made regular trips across the Atlantic. They took passengers westwards. On the way back, they carried cargo. Because they were so fast, they were given the job of carrying mail.

▲ This ship, the *Pride of Baltimore*, is a clipper.

▼ The *Ann McKim* was the first Baltimore clipper. She was built in 1832 for a local merchant, Isaac McKim, and was named after his wife.

The rush for gold

In 1849, gold was found on the west coast of the United States, in California. People hurried there to join in the 'gold rush'. The quickest way from the east coast of America was by sea. A clipper took three months to sail from New York around Cape Horn. No one had travelled so fast by sea before. Then there was a gold rush in Australia. Thousands sailed there by clipper from Europe.

The tea races

Steamships were soon to take over the passenger and mail trade. But clippers went on being used for cargo. Some goods spoil if they spend too long on their way to the shops. One of these is tea. It goes dry and loses its flavour if it is kept in boxes for very long.

Fast ships were needed to bring the new crop of tea from China to London. The clipper ships were just right for the job. Steamships would have had to stop to take on coal or wood. Clippers could sail all the way without stopping.

Every year there was a race to bring the first new tea to London. Tea merchants gave a prize to the fastest clipper. The *Cutty Sark* was one of the most famous tea clippers. It once sailed 363 miles in one day. No other clipper ever beat this record. Later, the *Cutty Sark* brought wool from Australia. It took 69 days. The usual time was 100 days.

► **The *Cutty Sark* was a British tea clipper, built in 1869. She is now a museum ship at Greenwich, near London. In this picture you can see the full cargo of tea stored below deck.**

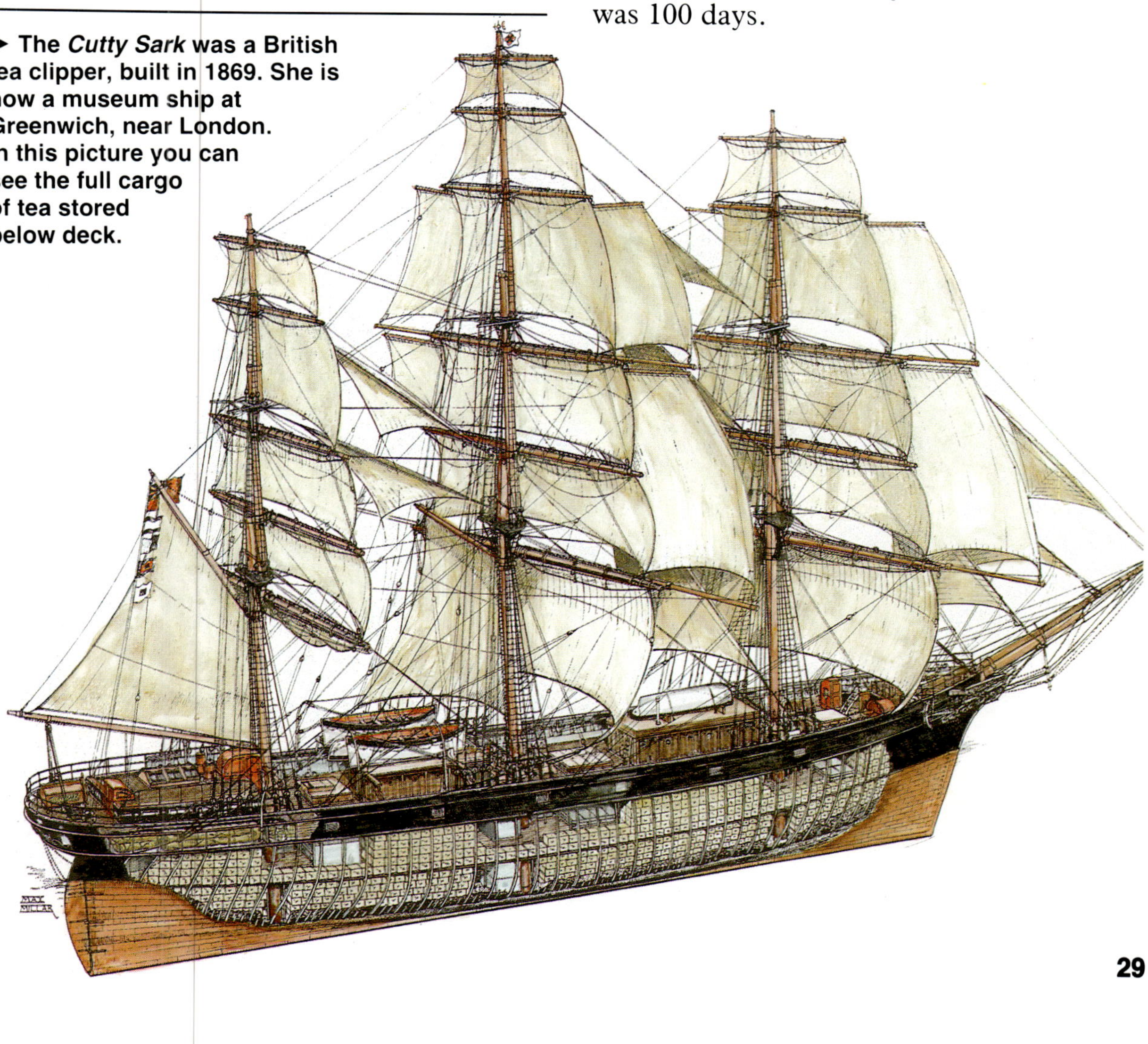

The coming of steam

The steam engine was invented around 1770. It was not long before someone thought of using one to drive a ship. The first steamships were used on rivers.

The steam in a steam engine is made by boiling water. Wood or coal is needed to stoke the fire. The first steamships could not go very far without stopping for more fuel. They could not carry enough to take them across the Atlantic Ocean.

▲ **John Fitch's steamboat, *Experiment*, was driven by three large oars at the stern.**

The first steamships

An American, called John Fitch, ran the first steamship service in 1790. It was on the Delaware River, USA. His ship, called the *Experiment*, had a number of large oars at the stern. They were driven to and fro by a steam engine. But John Fitch lost money and had to stop this service.

Another American, Robert Fulton, built a ship called the *Clermont*. This ship had two paddle wheels, one on each side of the **hull**, like the wheels of a water mill. The engine pushed the wheels around. When the paddles went into the water they drove the ship forward.

In 1807, Robert Fulton ran a service between New York and Albany. The

The *Clermont* made her first journey in 1807. She steamed up the Hudson River from New York to Albany and back in 62 hours. This was a distance of about 400 km.

▲ **The sternwheeler, *Delta Queen*, at work on the Mississippi River near Alabama, USA. The man standing at the stern looks very small next to the huge paddle wheel.**

Clermont steamed at about the same speed as a person can walk. It could carry about 100 people.

At that time in America there were no railways. The roads were poor but there were many rivers. The best way to travel a long distance was by river. This was why so many steamships were built in America. By 1822, there were 35 steamers on the Mississippi alone.

Sternwheelers

Most paddle steamers had a wheel on each side of the hull. But on the Mississippi a new type of ship was built. It was called a **sternwheeler**. It had one large paddle wheel at the stern. Only a small part of the wheel went into the water. Because of this, sternwheelers could be used in shallow waters.

These boats carried people, cargo and mail up and down the great rivers of North America. They helped to open up the country. There are still some sternwheelers on American rivers today. Of course, it is quicker to travel by road or air. But it is much more fun to go by river.

Paddles and propellers

The Atlantic was first crossed by an American steamship in 1819. The ship was the *Savannah*. She was a sailing ship fitted with paddles. She took 21 days to sail from New York to Liverpool. But she used her sails most of the way. The first ship to steam all the way was the *Royal William*. She steamed from Canada to England in 1823.

The first ocean steamships had sails as well as engines. Sails were used if the engines broke down or ran out of fuel. So much fuel was needed that there was little room for cargo or passengers. Steamships lost money on the Atlantic run. Sailing ships were less expensive to run.

In 1838, a race was planned between two British steamships across the Atlantic Ocean. One of the ships was not ready in time for the race. The *Sirius* took part instead. Although she was not built to race across the Atlantic, she did very well. The *Sirius* took 18 days to steam from Liverpool to New York. She did not use her sails at all. On the way the *Sirius* ran out of coal. Cabin doors, furniture, planks and one mast were used as fuel to keep her going. The other ship was the *Great Western*. She was built to cross the Atlantic Ocean. The *Great Western* made the crossing in 15 days and still had plenty of coal left at the end of the journey.

The paddle-steamer *Britannia*.

Samuel Cunard

One man found a way of making money with steam. He was Samuel Cunard. He had owned a share in the *Royal William*. Now he started up on his own. He won the **contract** to carry mail between Britain and Canada. Mail did not take up much space.

Cunard built four paddle steamers for the job. The first was the *Britannia*. Her first voyage was in July 1840. She took just 14 days to steam from England to Canada. This was a record. Cunard's company became one of the great Atlantic shipping lines.

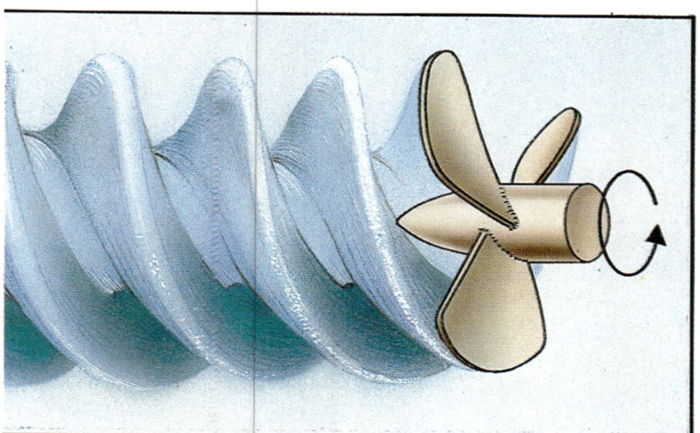

Brunel

Isambard Kingdom Brunel was a British **engineer**. He had built the *Great Western*. She was the first steamship to provide a regular service across the Atlantic. Now he decided to build a larger ship. She was called the *Great Britain*. She was made of iron and was the biggest ship ever built at that time. The *Great Britain* was the first ocean steamship to have a **propeller** instead of paddles. There were also six masts of sails.

Sadly, she ran aground on her fifth voyage. Brunel sold her. After many adventures, she ended up as a wreck in the Falkland Islands. In 1970, she was brought back to Britain and is now on show in Bristol. She lies in the same dock where she was built in 1843.

◄ The ship's engine makes the propeller turn around. As the propeller turns, its curved blades 'bite' into the water. They force the water backwards, so that the ship moves forwards. The first propellers had two very long blades. They often broke. Today, propellers have three, four or more very strong blades.

Passage to America

In the 1800s, millions of people went from Europe to live in North America. Most of them were poor. They had just enough money to pay for their tickets.

This was good business for ship owners. All kinds of ships – steam, sail, large and small – were used. They carried as many passengers as they could.

A few rich people had cabins. The rest lived and slept close together in the holds. It was not an easy voyage. Ships **pitched** and **rolled** in rough seas. Waves crashed over the decks. Passengers had to stay below deck. They had about 45 cm of space each to live and sleep in. They lay in bunks, one row above the other. They had to cook their own food. Often they were too seasick to eat anything.

Seven million **emigrants** crossed the Atlantic like this. Some never reached the end of the voyage. Many ships sank in storms. Sometimes, people died of illness on the way.

The emigrants travelled below deck. They were crowded together like cattle.

Life on board ship was no better for the crew. They had very little space to live in and their food was poor. Captains wanted to cross the Atlantic as fast as they could. They took risks with their ships. At the end of the trip, the captain would often try to cheat the crew out of their pay.

The cabin trade

Not everyone who crossed the Atlantic was poor. Not everyone was an emigrant. More and more people went to see their families, or on business.

The voyage was no safer for them than for the poor. There was no hope for anyone if a ship went down in the middle of the ocean. But people who had cabins had a little more comfort. Their food was cooked for them. They had more room to sleep and to move about.

There were separate sleeping cabins for men and women. In the daytime they used the space between decks. They would read, talk or play cards. But they would all be longing for the voyage to end. In those days, crossing the Atlantic was no fun.

Rich people travelled in cabins or in open saloons like this.

Ocean liners

In 1894, a British engineer, Charles Parsons, built a new kind of steamship engine. It was called a steam **turbine**. The steam drove a set of blades round and round. The blades were fixed to the **propeller shaft**. The shaft turned, and so did the propeller.

Ships with turbines used less fuel and went faster. Parsons' turbine ship was called the *Turbinia*. It was a small boat but went at about 56 kph.

The first steam turbine ship crossed the Atlantic in 1904. She was called the *Virginian*. Soon all the Atlantic shipping lines started to build bigger and faster turbine ships.

These new ocean **liners** were like huge hotels on water. They had ballrooms, swimming-pools, shops and restaurants. There were dances, shows and concerts to help fill in the time. The great days of ocean travel had arrived.

The Blue Riband

The United States and many European countries had liners on the Atlantic run. They competed with each other to make the crossing in the shortest time. The fastest ship won the Blue Riband (or Ribbon) of the Atlantic.

In 1907 the Blue Riband was won by a Cunard ship. She was the *Mauretania*. She held the record for 22 years. Then it went to Germany, and then to France.

The *Queen Mary* was a new Cunard ship. She made her **maiden voyage** in 1936. She crossed the Atlantic in under four days and won the Blue Riband. In 1952, it was won by a new US liner, the *United States*. She crossed in ten hours less than the *Queen Mary*, at a speed of 66 kph. But by that time fewer people wanted to travel by sea.

▼ In 1938, the *Queen Mary* crossed the Atlantic Ocean in 3 days, 20 hours and 42 minutes. Her average speed was nearly 59 kph.

▲ Cunard's liner, *Queen Elizabeth II*, was launched in 1967. The QE2 is now a luxury cruise liner and carries 2000 passengers.

Cruise liners

Forty years ago, there were 60 liners on the Atlantic run. Now there are none. But ship owners have found a new way to use their ships. They use them for cruises, which are really 'holidays at sea'. Cruise ships are even more like hotels than the Atlantic liners.

If you have the time and the money, you can cruise around the world. Or you can take a short cruise of a few days. Cruise liners often travel fast at night. Then the passengers can go ashore each day at a new and interesting port.

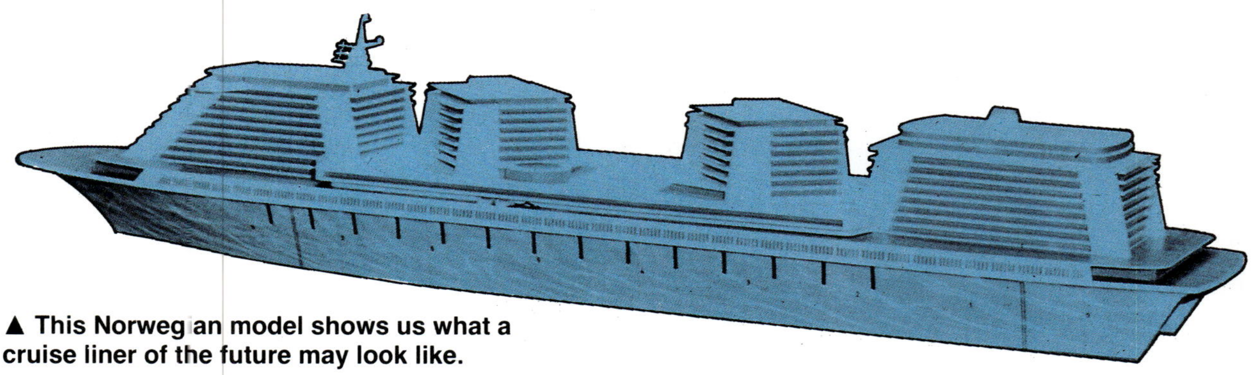

▲ This Norwegian model shows us what a cruise liner of the future may look like.

The busy seas

There are many thousands of ships at work throughout the world. Most of them are **freighters**, ships that carry mainly cargo. Over half of them carry a mixture of goods. They might carry machines or timber, wheat or fruit. There may be up to four decks in the hold of a freighter. These decks are divided by steel walls called **bulkheads**. This makes it easier to load and unload a ship with cargo for different places. Some of these ships carry a few passengers as well.

▲ 'Roro' ferries are built to carry cars and trucks on short sea routes or across wide rivers. Roro stands for 'roll on, roll off'. These ferry boats have a bow and a stern that can open up to make a ramp. People can drive cars and trucks straight on board. They can drive off again at the end of the voyage. This means that the ferry boats can be loaded and unloaded very quickly. A large ferry boat can carry 350 cars or about 60 large trucks. Before roro ferries were used, cars and trucks had to be loaded and unloaded by crane.

◄ The trailer of a milk carrier is being unloaded by crane. This harbour is in Miami, Florida, USA.

▲ **Freighters are docked at Kowloon harbour, Hong Kong. The ship with the yellow funnel is empty. She is high out of the water. The river boats alongside have cargo for loading. There are also containers on the dockside.**

Loading and unloading

It is important to load and unload quickly when a ship is in port. A cargo ship earns money only when it is on the move. Many of these ships have deck cranes, called **derricks**. These are used to lift the cargo out of the hold.

Ships are loaded with great care. Heavy freight must be spread evenly. Ships must not be overloaded. On the side of every ship there is a painted line called the **Plimsoll line**. When the water level touches the line, it shows that the ship is fully loaded.

The smallest cargo ships are called **coasters**. These are the small delivery trucks of the sea. They can use almost any port. They go from one to another and pick up any cargo they can. Coasters stay fairly close to the land. Often, they have a crew of only three or four people.

Coming into harbour

Ships do not come into harbour like cars driving into a car park. They cannot stop quickly. They do not turn easily. Docking a ship is a skilled job.

It is usually the job of the harbour **pilot**. He is a captain who knows the harbour well. He goes out to meet the ship in a pilot boat. This is a small motor boat. He joins the captain on the **bridge**, and guides the ship into harbour.

When the ship sails again, it may be towed out of the harbour by tugs. These are small ships with very powerful engines. They pull the ship out to the open sea.

Inland waterways

Not all travel by water is across the sea. Boats travel inland as well. Sometimes they use **canals** made by people. Sometimes they use wide rivers. Rivers and canals used for shipping are called **inland waterways**.

Canals do not all pass over flat country. Boats using canals may have to cross high ground. When they do this they go through **locks**. Then they can move from one level to another. A boat going 'uphill' goes into the lock. The gates close behind it. Water is pumped into the lock until it is at the higher level. Then the gates in front are opened and the boat can move on.

Most of the cargo on inland waterways is carried by **barge**. A barge is a flat-bottomed boat specially built for inland waterways. Some have engines, but most do not. Those without engines are called **dumb barges**. Sometimes they are towed by a tug. Sometimes push-boats are used to push a string of dumb barges, one behind the other.

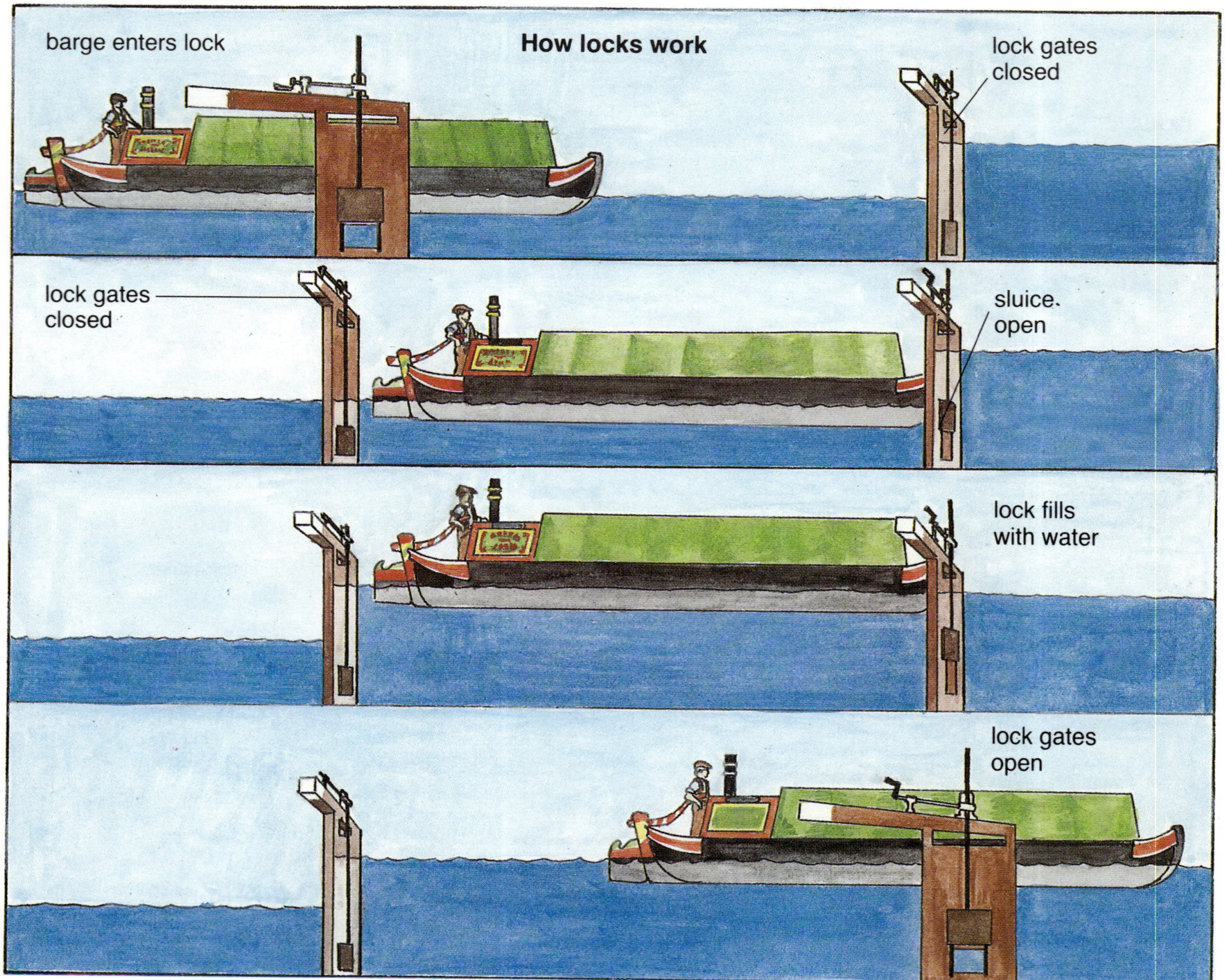

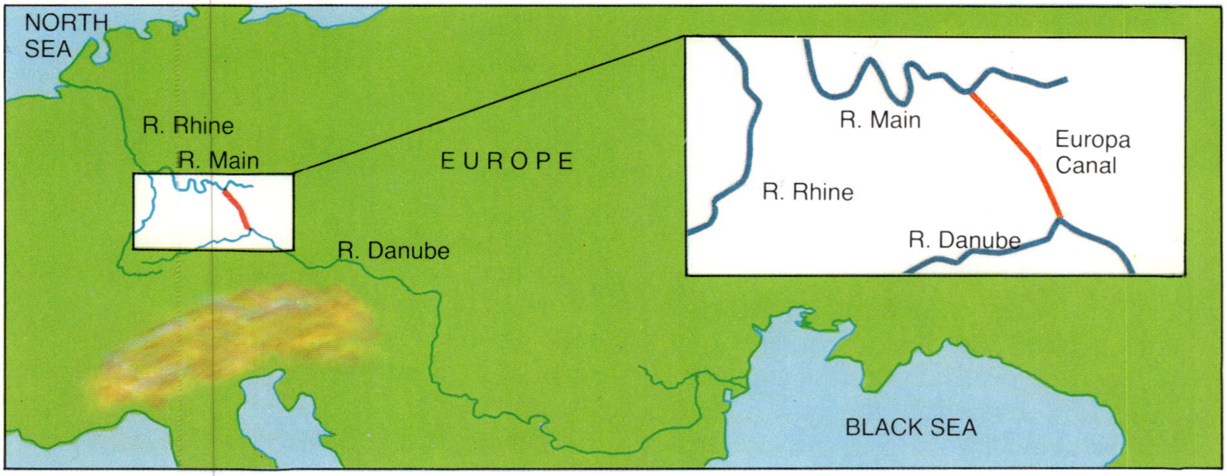

▲ **The Europa Canal will soon be finished. The Main and the Danube rivers will be joined by a canal.**

▼ **The map shows the world's largest inland waterway system. The Missouri joins the Mississippi at St Louis. The length of these two rivers together is 6000 km.**

The Europa Canal

Work is going on in Europe to make a new inland waterway. It will join up the North Sea and the Black Sea.

The Rhine, the Main and the Danube are three of Europe's longest rivers. They have been used as inland waterways for many years. But there is a strip of land between the Main and the Danube. It is about 160 km long. The plan is to dig a canal through this strip. Then the rivers can be used all the way from The Netherlands to southern Russia. The first part of the route was opened in 1970.

The Mississippi

The Mississippi is the longest river in the United States. It flows south to the Gulf of Mexico. On the way it is joined by other large rivers. They make up the world's largest inland waterway system.

Goods come from Tulsa in the west and Pittsburgh in the east. A canal links the Mississippi with Chicago. River travel is slow, but it is cheaper than road, rail or air.

The Mississippi is so wide that barges are tied together to make rafts. There may be as many as 40 barges in one raft. Then the raft is pushed along by a push-boat at the back.

The great canals

There is a thin strip of land separating the Red Sea from the Mediterranean. It is only 160 km wide. At one time, goods brought by sea from Asia had to be unloaded at the northern end of the Red Sea. Camels then carried the goods north to Port Said in Egypt. From there, ships sailed across the Mediterranean to Europe. This took a lot of time, but it was easier and quicker than sailing all the way around Africa.

The Suez Canal

In 1859, it was decided to build a canal, or channel, along the old camel route. This was a huge task. The canal would link the Red Sea with the Mediterranean. The journey from Asia to Europe would be much quicker. A French engineer, Ferdinand de Lesseps, was in charge of the work. The work took much longer than he had expected. Britain and France had to give more money so that the work could go on.

Ten years later, the Suez Canal opened. A great fleet of 68 ships steamed through it. The leading ship was French. Flags flew and bands played. There were parties and fireworks.

You can see that the Suez Canal was dug out of the desert. The canal, which is 162 km long, goes from Port Said to Suez.

The Panama Canal

A narrow strip of land joins North and South America at Panama. Before the canal was dug, ships had to sail around South America to get from the Atlantic to the Pacific Ocean. In the 1880s de Lesseps started work on the canal but he ran out of money. It was completed by American engineers in 1915. The Panama Canal is 68 km long.

The St Lawrence Seaway

The five Great Lakes of North America lie between the United States and Canada. All the water from these lakes flows out into the Atlantic Ocean along the St Lawrence River. On the way, the water goes through rapids and over waterfalls. At one time, ships could use only some parts of the waterway.

The United States and Canada worked together to build larger locks and new canals. In 1959, the work was completed. The St Lawrence Seaway is made up of lakes, canals and locks on its journey to the sea. It stretches over about 3700 km from Thunder Bay, Lake Superior, to the Atlantic Ocean. All but the largest ships can use this seaway.

▲ Ships cannot use their engines in the locks on the Panama Canal. Electric engines are used to tow the ships through each lock. You can see the rails and the engine on the left hand side of the lock.

During the winter months, parts of the seaway are iced up. For the rest of the year ships ply to and fro all the time. They carry grain, iron ore and other goods to Europe and the world.

► The St Lawrence Seaway is a great water highway linking the Great Lakes with the Atlantic Ocean. Large bulk cargo ships load up at Thunder Bay, Lake Superior, and at other ports on the Great Lakes. They carry grain and iron ore along the seaway. When they reach the Atlantic Ocean, the ships go to countries all over the world.

Giant carriers

Loading and unloading a cargo ship has to be done quickly. The faster it can be done, the sooner the ship can set off on its next voyage. Many ships are built to carry just one type of cargo. It might be grain, or sugar, or coal. These ships are called **bulk carriers**. They carry their cargo loose in their holds.

Oil tankers

Tankers are specially built to carry oil and liquid fuels. Tankers are long low ships with engines at their sterns. The rest of the space is taken up with oil tanks. The largest tankers of all can carry over 350 000 tonnes of oil. They can be more than 340 m long. Sometimes the crew use bicycles to get from one end to the other. Walking takes too long.

Although oil tankers are very large, they have small crews. But each crew member is highly trained. For safety reasons they have to take great care. Oil burns easily. There is always a risk of fire. Because they are so large, tankers take a long time to slow down or alter course. They have computers to help them.

Like all ships, tankers sometimes have accidents at sea. When they do, oil may be spilled. This **pollutes** the sea. As a result, the oil can kill birds and fish. The oil may be swept ashore by the sea. When this happens it spoils the beaches for the people who use them.

Container ships

Another new kind of ship is built to carry cargo in **containers**. These are very large metal boxes. Containers are all the same shape and size. So they fit neatly into the ship's hold. Some are stacked on deck. The first container ship went to sea in 1964.

Containers are filled at a factory. Then they are taken to the port by road or rail. Containers are quicker and easier to load than bulk cargo. The containers can carry liquids as well as solid cargo. Liquids are carried in large plastic bags inside the containers. Special ports have been built to handle these ships. They are called **container terminals**.

◀ The *British Trent* is owned by the British Petroleum (BP) Oil Company. She is a large tanker that carries oil.

► On the right, you can see a ship being unloaded at a container terminal. The containers are all the same size. They fit easily on top of each other. They can be put in the hold and on the deck of a container ship.

SEA-LAND
SEA-LAND

Safety at sea

One night in 1912, a liner was steaming across the Atlantic from Southampton to New York. It was her maiden voyage. She was the largest ship at sea at that time. There were over 2200 passengers and crew on board. The ship's name was *Titanic*.

In the spring, icebergs float down to the Atlantic from the north. The *Titanic* hit one. She sank. About 1500 people were drowned.

There were not enough lifeboats on the *Titanic*. Even if all the boats had been full, only half the people on board could have been saved.

It was the worst sea disaster ever. After this accident the safety rules at sea were changed. Now, ships must have enough lifeboats or life-rafts for all the people on board.

The *Titanic* could have steered clear of the iceberg if the crew had known where it was. After the sinking, a **patrol** was set up to watch for icebergs and report them. This is done today by **satellites** in space.

Radar

Many things have changed since those days. Now, all ships have **radar**. Radar shows a picture of the sea around the ship. It shows the possible dangers. These could be other ships, icebergs, rocks, or the coast. Radar goes on working at night and in fog.

Lights and signals

Some stretches of water are very busy. One of these is the English Channel, between France and England. In these places, ships have to keep in shipping lanes. The lanes are marked by **buoys** which send out radio and radar signals. Lightships and lighthouses also help to guide ships through dangerous waters. They have flashing lights and foghorns as well as radio and radar.

◄ In this picture a ship's officer is looking at the radar screen. You can see that it is like a round TV screen. It works both night and day. The radar screen lights up to show the position of other ships, rocks and land. The officer can tell by looking at the screen how far away these objects are from his ship. He can alter course or slow the ship down to avoid hitting them.

Sea rescue

Near the coast there are special services to help ships in trouble. In the USA, boats from the Coastguard Service **patrol** these waters. There are also coastguard stations on shore. They have rescue boats. In Britain, the Lifeboat Service keeps rescue boats at shore stations, ready for any **emergency**.

Helicopters are often used for sea rescue work. The helicopter crew lowers ropes to pick people out of the water. Sometimes the helicopters are used to pick up people from ships at sea. They can be brought ashore if they are ill or injured.

◀ This is a lighthouse in Maine, USA. Ships can work out where they are when they see the light.

▼ This British lifeboat has been built so that it does not sink if it turns over in a stormy sea.

New kinds of ship

The ships of today are quite different from those of 100 years ago. They are much larger and their engines are more powerful. They use oil as a fuel rather than coal. What about the future? Are there likely to be more changes?

Shipbuilders are trying out new ideas all the time. In 1958, the United States built a cargo ship driven by **nuclear power**. It was called the *Savannah*, and could travel for three years without refuelling. But the ship cost too much and no more were built.

The Japanese have gone back to an old idea. They have fitted an oil tanker with sails. Like the early steamers, it has engines as well. The sails are used only when the wind is right. They are controlled by a computer.

Even the fastest ships are slow compared with land or air travel. Ships cannot go much faster than 55 kph. This is because they have to force their way through water. If they can skim over the top of the water instead of through it, they can go much faster.

Hydrofoils

The **hydrofoil** has **foils** beneath the hull. They are like small aircraft wings and work in the same way. They are curved on top and flat underneath. As the hydrofoil gathers speed, the foils lift the boat out of the water. It skims the surface of the water.

▼ **As the hydrofoil gathers speed the foils make it lift above the water.**

The British hovercraft is starting on its journey. Air is pumped down below the hovercraft. This lifts it above the water. Four giant propellers drive it forward. The hovercraft can skim over the waves like a very low-flying plane. It can move over land as well as over water.

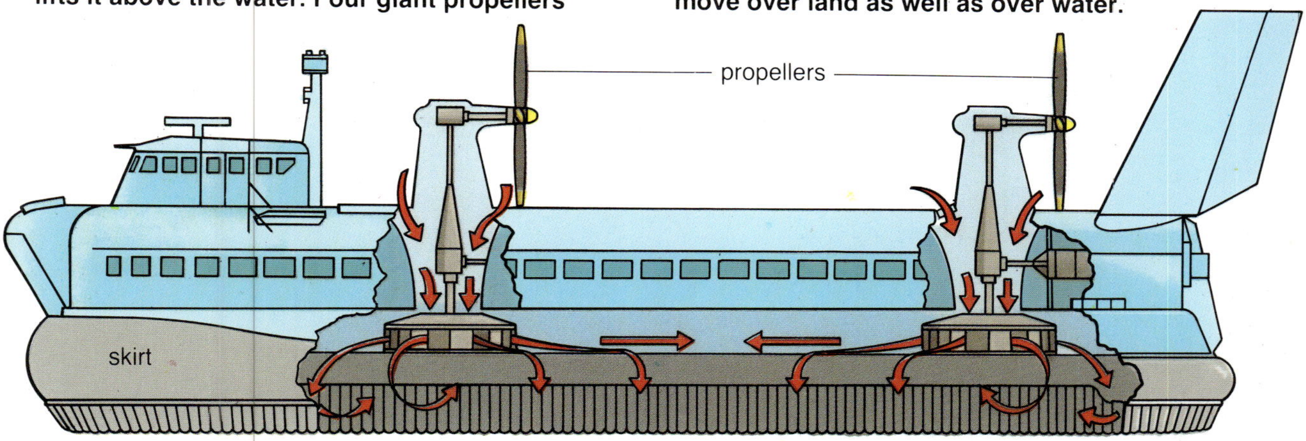

Hovercraft

The **hovercraft** floats on a cushion of air. This lifts it above the water. Large pumps suck in air and pump it down to the **hull**. There, it is kept in by a plastic or rubber 'skirt'. The air cannot escape and it makes a cushion. The hovercraft is driven forward by propellers. These spin in the air like aircraft propellers.

Hydrofoils and hovercraft can go two or three times faster than ships. But they can only be used in calm seas. In rough seas they are easily damaged or overturned. Also, they give a bumpy and noisy ride. But maybe these problems will be solved one day. Then giant hydrofoils and hovercraft may be used on the oceans.

TRAVEL BY ROAD AND RAIL

Michael Pollard

Introduction

What would it be like if you had to walk everywhere? You can only walk at about six kilometres per hour. It would take you two-and-a-half hours to go 16km. You would be quite tired by the end of your walk. If you went this distance by road or rail the journey would soon be over.

Today, we travel by road and rail for many reasons. Children often go to school by car or bus. Adults sometimes **commute** to work on trains. We go to visit friends or relatives, or we take a holiday. Some people go away from home on **business**. Trucks and trains carry goods and mail. Road and rail travel makes it possible for all of us to live the way we do.

▲ This old picture shows a train passing through an American city in the 1880s. As the train moved slowly through the streets, it made a lot of noise. The wheels clanked on the rails, and a bell rang all the time to tell people that the train was coming. At crossings, a man with a flag warned people to keep out of the way.

Road and rail

Moving around was not always so easy as it is today. Until about 150 years ago the roads were poor and there were no cars. Some people travelled about on horseback, or in a cart or **carriage** pulled by horses. Most people walked to work and children walked to school.

There was no rail travel before 1825. No one had ever travelled at a speed of 50 kph. Many people, even doctors, thought that travelling at this speed would be bad for their health.

In the 1830s, the first railways came to towns and cities. They caused a great change in people's lives. Someone could post a letter one day which would arrive many kilometres away on the next day. For the first time the people who lived in cities could have fresh food because it could be brought in from the countryside by train. People could travel far and wide if they had money for the **fare**.

For many years, trains were the main means of transport on land. The kind of engines used in cars and trucks were not invented until 100 years ago. At first, there were only a few cars on the roads. Then more cars and trucks were made and the roads were improved.

Now we have a choice if we want to travel or send goods by land. We can use roads or railways. We can travel part of the way by road and part by rail. This book tells the story of how people travel by land.

◀ In Tokyo, Japan, some trains run along a special kind of railway track. The trains sit astride a single rail called a monorail. Electric motors turn the driving wheels. There are monorails also in France and Germany.

▶ The wheel was invented nearly 5000 years ago. Wheels have been used for transport ever since. Trains were invented only 150 years ago. Cars were invented after trains. They have been used for only 100 years.

before 3000 BC	**The first wheel** Solid wooden wheels found in Russia date from before 3000 BC 
about 2000 BC	**The first ox-cart** We know that the Sumerians used an ox-drawn sledge about this time 
about 1300 AD	**Pack animals** These were used very widely in Europe in the Middle Ages, and earlier in Asia 
about 1500 AD	**The first carriages** These were only used by nobles and rich people 
1804 AD	**The first railway locomotive** This was built by Richard Trevithick, a Cornish engineer 
1863 AD	**The first motor car** This was built by a French engineer in Paris 

Wheels and chariots

▲ Tree trunks were used as rollers to move heavy objects like this huge block of stone.

The first carts did not have wheels. They were like **sledges**. They had wooden runners and were pulled by oxen. When a load is pushed or pulled along the ground, a force called **friction** tries to hold it back. Friction made sledges very hard to use on the rough ground.

Long ago, people used tree trunks to help them with their building. When they wanted to move a heavy block of stone they used tree trunks as rollers. This idea led to another one. They began to use slices of tree trunks as solid wheels.

Then they made a simple **barrow**. This was just a wooden box with solid wooden wheels on each side. The barrow had two handles so that a person could wheel it along. Even now, it is far easier to wheel a load in a barrow than to drag it along the ground. This is because the wheel is round, and only a tiny part of it touches the ground. So there is less friction and you use less effort to do the work.

There were no roads in early times. The tracks that people used were rough and bumpy. Wheels were often knocked off. Then people had another idea. They found that they could join two wooden wheels with a wooden **axle**. The axle made the wheels last longer.

► Solid wooden wheels were first used for simple hand carts or barrows. The wheels were made by slicing through tree trunks.

Animal power

Oxen were used to pull ploughs and sledges. They were also used to pull carts with wheels. When the load was heavy, two or more oxen were used. Oxen and ox carts are still used today in some parts of the world. They are strong, but they are very slow. Horses are much faster. Wild horses from central Asia were used to pull light carts called **chariots**. These had two wheels and were built for speed. Chariots were first used for war, and later for hunting.

The Romans lived in a part of the world that is now called Italy. They found another use for chariots. The Romans used them for racing round a track. Thousands of Romans watched the chariot races. The winners of the races were treated as heroes.

▲ About 4000 years ago, people began to use wheeled carts drawn by oxen. The wheels of the carts were joined by an axle. The body of a cart was shaped like the letter A.

▼ The racing chariots had two wheels. The Romans stood up when they drove the chariots.

Roman roads

The Romans ruled most of Europe and North Africa for about 400 years. They were very good builders and **engineers**. The Romans built the first real roads. They needed the roads so that soldiers could be sent quickly to any part of their **empire**. They built forts along the road to guard the troops from attack.

There were no maps to help the Romans plan their roads. They had to mark out the **route** on the ground as they went along. The engineers did this by looking from the top of one hill to the next hill. Between the hills they lit fires. They moved the fires until they were all in line with each other. Then the engineers marked out the route with posts.

The Roman roads ran in a straight line for a great distance because of this way of working. Many of the modern roads in Europe follow the same routes used by the Romans more than 1500 years ago. The Romans thought they would keep their empire for ever. That is why they built their roads to last a long time.

Building a road

The Roman roads were eight metres wide. They were built on raised banks called **aggers**. These sloped down on each side so the water ran off them. The aggers were made of chalk or clay which was packed very tightly. This was covered by a layer of **flints** or stones. The top layer of the road was laid with **gravel** or large stone blocks. These roads were so good that the Roman soldiers could march 50 km in a day.

▼ The Romans built the first good roads about 2000 years ago. First they built up banks of earth and stone. Then they laid the surface of the roads on top.

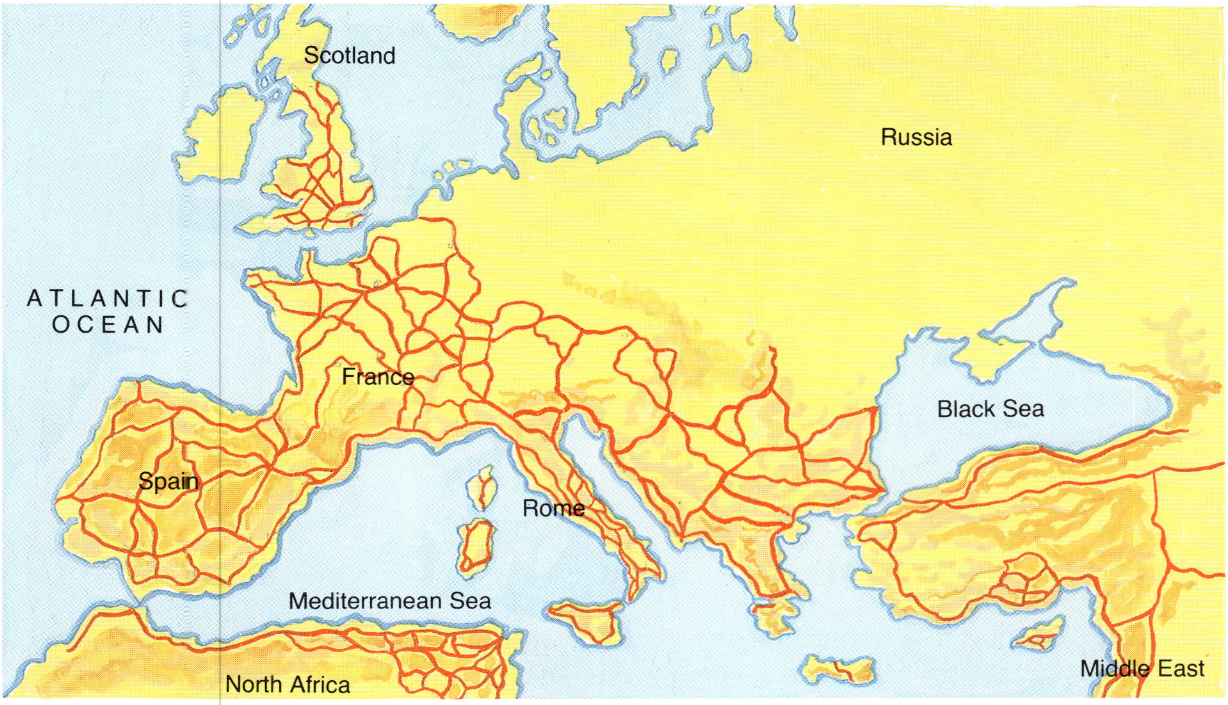

▲ **The map shows some of the main roads built by the Romans. You can see that the Romans controlled most of western Europe and part of North Africa and the Middle East. The Romans went as far north as Scotland. They built good, straight roads wherever they went.**

▲ **This Roman road looks the same today as it did 2000 years ago. It is part of the main highway between Rome and Ostia. Ostia was the port from which Roman galleys sailed to North Africa and other parts of their empire. The road was called the Decumanus Maximus.**

Water supplies

As well as making roads, the Romans built towns, farms and large houses called **villas**. These houses had hot and cold water. They even had a kind of central heating. It was important for the Romans to have a good supply of fresh water. This often meant bringing it a long distance.

The Romans built huge **aqueducts** to bring the water to their towns. Aqueducts were channels made of stone. If an aqueduct had to cross a valley, the Romans built it along a line of pillars. They joined the pillars with curved **arches**. They used the same idea to make their road bridges. Some of these Roman bridges can still be seen in parts of Europe.

Carriages and coaches

The Roman Empire did not last. By about 400 AD the Romans had left most of the countries they had occupied. Their fine villas and forts, towns and roads fell into ruins. No one bothered to mend the roads.

The people of Europe travelled less after the Romans had gone. If they had to travel, they went on horseback. They used old tracks and paths. These were too rough and narrow for carts. Goods were carried by pack animals. These were horses, donkeys or mules, with baskets or packs slung over each side. Up to nine of them would be roped together and led by one driver.

In towns, where there were rough roads, wagons were used. The wagons had four wheels and four horses to pull them. They had canvas tops and looked rather like the wagons of the American West.

▲ The roads in Europe became too bad for carts to use after the Romans left. People used pack animals instead of carts. The animals were led along old paths and tracks.

▼ The first carriages were splendid things. They were very heavy and had four large wheels. A carriage was drawn by four or six horses.

▲ **A stage coach carried about nine passengers. Some sat inside the coach and some sat outside with the driver. Stage coaches stopped often at inns where the horses were changed. Sometimes the passengers had a meal at the inn.**

The most comfortable way for people to travel in towns was by **sedan chair**. This was a covered, box-like chair. Servants carried it, using **shafts** at the front and the back. Only rich people could afford to travel this way.

Carriages

About 350 years ago horse carriages were built to carry people. The bodies of these carriages were slung on iron **springs**. This gave the passengers a smooth ride on the rough town roads. If you could not afford to own a carriage, you could hire one.

Slowly, the roads between towns were improved. Carriages began to use them. They often got stuck in the mud or snow. Sometimes, the wheels were smashed by holes in the road. There was another danger. There were often **highwaymen** waiting in the woods to rob rich travellers.

The stage coach

About 1700 the first stage coaches ran. These took people from one place to another for a fare. The horses were changed every 16 km or so. A trip of 100 km could take up to twelve hours. Bit by bit the roads were improved and the stage coaches went faster. Until the railways came, this was the main way people travelled on land.

When roads were built in the USA, stage coaches began to run there too. They carried mail as well as people from town to town. As in Europe, stage coaches were no longer used once the railways came.

The great trails

The people who travelled by sea to America from Europe began by settling on the east coast. Later, many of them wanted to find new land to farm. They went in trains of ox-drawn wagons to the great plains of the mid-west. Dozens of wagons would set out together. It was a time of great adventure.

On these long journeys, people would have to take with them all the things they would need. They took food, clothes, bedding and tools. For months on end, the wagons were their homes on wheels.

▲ **At night a camp was made. The wagons were put in a circle. This way people felt safer. In the centre of the circle they lit a camp fire. Here they cooked their food. Then they settled down for the night.**

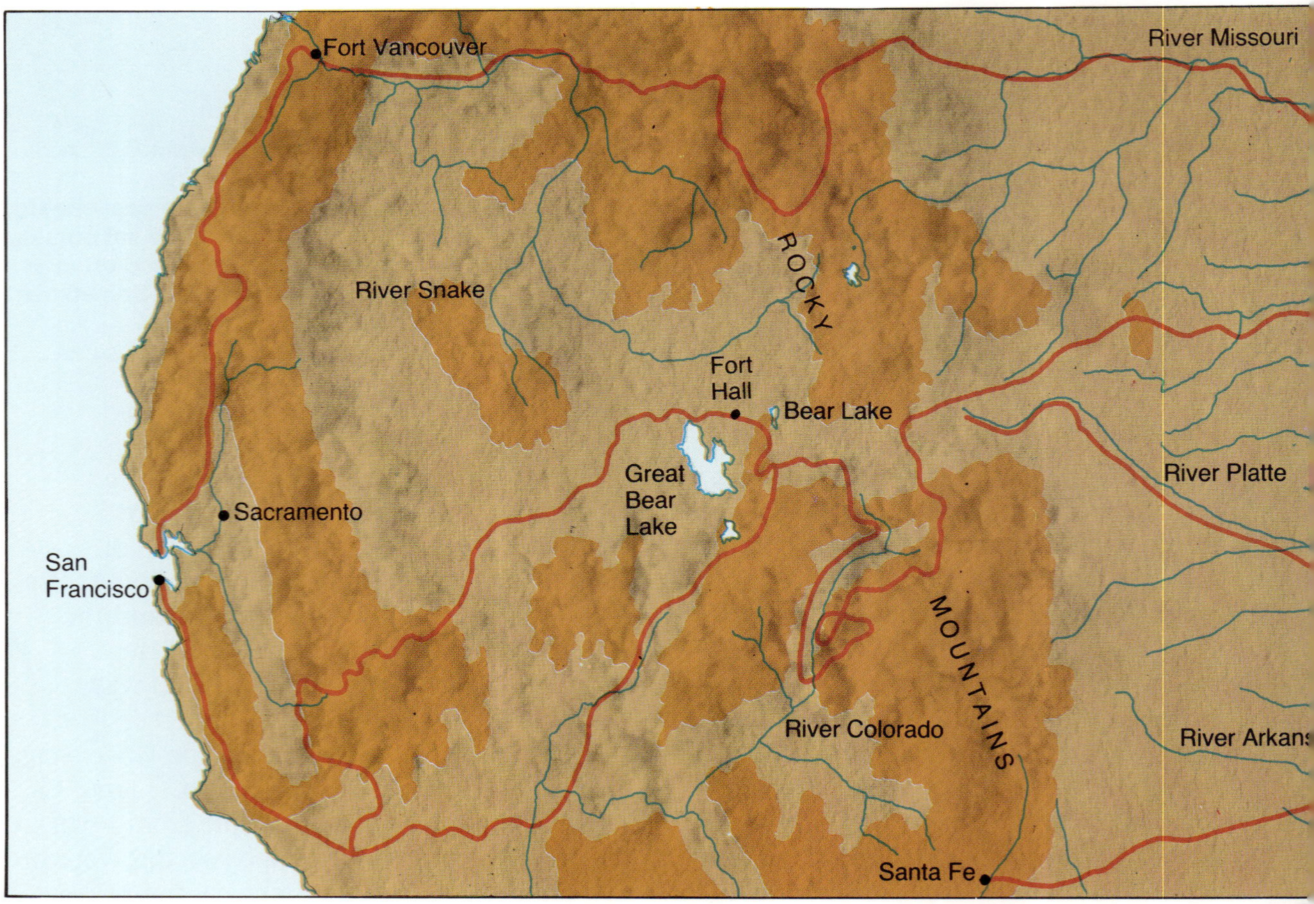

The journey

The wagon trains set out from Independence in Missouri. The first great **trail** across the United States was to Santa Fe. It was made in 1822. Twenty years later, the first wagon trains crossed the Rocky Mountains to Oregon on the west coast.

Each wagon train had a captain in charge. There was a guide to lead the way. Most days they only went about 16 km. Sometimes a wagon train would take a whole day crossing a river. Wagons would sink up to their axles in mud as their drivers looked for a shallow **ford** to cross the river.

Each night they found a good place to camp. The wagons were put in a circle for safety. In the Rockies the trail was rough and full of danger. Sometimes the wagons had to go along narrow ledges. There was often a steep drop on one side. When a wagon wheel broke, the whole train had to stop while the wheel was mended.

▲ It was always dificult taking a wagon train across a river. Sometimes the wagons had to go over rocks and stones. Wheels would be broken. Often the wagons got stuck in the mud.

The gold rush

The last great trail was to California. Gold was found there in 1848. The news spread fast. The next year, thousands of people set out. Most men went on their own, but some took their families with them.

They went on the Oregon trail as far as Fort Hall in the Rockies. There they headed west and had to find their own way. Crossing the mountains was a difficult and dangerous journey. The 'Forty-niners', as they were called, hoped to make their fortunes out of gold. Very few did, but many people settled in California rather than travel back across the Rockies.

Wagons went on being used in the United States for many years. But the crossing of the **continent** by rail was soon to come. Then the days of the great wagon trains were over.

The first railways

Tracks with rails were first used at coal mines. These tracks had rails of wood laid on edge. Wagons filled with coal were pulled along the tracks by horses. The wagon wheels kept on rubbing against the rails, causing friction. This made it hard for the horses to pull the wagons.

The answer was to use iron rails instead. Also, wheels were made with a raised edge, called a **flange**. The flange inside the wheels then kept the wheels on the iron track. Today, all railway wheels have flanges.

▲ George Stephenson's Rocket was built in 1829. You can see the flanges on the huge front driving wheels.

Steam locomotives

Steam engines had been used at mines to pump out water, and to lift coal or tin to the top of the mine. Richard Trevithick was the engineer at a Cornish tin mine. In 1804, he built the first steam **locomotive**. This was the first steam engine to run on an iron track.

George Stephenson was also an English mine engineer. He built steam engines to use at his coal mine in north-east England.

The first passenger railway

Stephenson was asked to build an engine for the first passenger railway. It was to run between Stockton and Darlington in north-east England. He built the engine and it was named Locomotion.

In 1825, Locomotion pulled the first train to carry passengers. It ran all the way from Darlington to Stockton, a distance of 65 km. On the trip, Locomotion reached a speed of 24 kph.

◀ **The Best Friend of Charleston was built in 1830. It had a large upright boiler. The tall chimney channelled smoke and sparks high into the air. This helped to stop sparks from setting light to fields and woods by the side of the track.**

Stephenson was soon asked to build a new railway. This one went from Liverpool to Manchester. The owners offered a prize for the best locomotive. Stephenson's was called The Rocket. It reached a speed of 46 kph, and won the prize.

The South Carolina Railroad

The next year, a steam locomotive was built in New York. It was called The Best Friend of Charleston, and used wood for **fuel**. The South Carolina Railroad opened on Christmas Day, 1830.

The Best Friend of Charleston ran a service from Charleston each day for five months. This was the United States' first rail service. Then, one day, the driver wanted more speed. The boiler blew up and the driver was killed. The locomotive was rebuilt. This time it was called The Phoenix. The railway continued to run. Two years later the South Carolina Railroad was the longest in the world.

▼ **This old print shows the first passenger train to travel on the Stockton to Darlington Railway.**

Railways worldwide

By 1850, there were nearly 10 000 km of track in Britain. The railways spread fast. Lines ran from London to all the main cities. The Great Western Railway opened in 1841. It ran 190 km from London to Bristol. This was the finest railway of them all. The lines were level and straight so the trains could go very fast. The Great Western Railway was built so well that its bridges and tunnels are still used today.

► Between 1835 and 1841, Isambard Kingdom Brunel built the Great Western Railway from London to Bristol. This picture shows the entrance to a tunnel on this railway. The tunnel was built so well that it is still used today.

▼ The Lafayette was one of the first American locomotives. It was built in 1837 and ran on the Baltimore and Ohio Railroad. Coal was carried in the tender behind the locomotive. The driver stood on the footplate near the huge boiler.

Railways in Europe

At first, people in Europe were afraid of railways. Then France and Germany bought engines made by Stephenson. The locomotive for the first German railway was called Der Adler (The Eagle). It arrived from England, complete with its English driver, William Wilson. He wore a top hat when he drove the train. Wilson spent the rest of his life driving trains in Germany.

The first Russian railway also used a Stephenson locomotive. It opened in 1836 at St Petersburg, now known as Leningrad.

The Golden Spike

Railways spread quickly in the United States, too. By 1850, there were nearly 5000 km of track. Ten years later there were 15 000 km of track. At first, most of the lines were in the eastern part of the USA.

Then two companies set out to build a railway right across the USA. The Central Pacific Railroad built east from Sacramento. The Union Pacific worked west from Omaha. There were 3200 km of track to be laid. The route went across the **prairies** , the desert and the Rocky Mountains.

The work began in 1864. Five years later, the two tracks met at Promontory Point, Utah. It had been five years hard work. There was snow in winter and fierce heat in the summer. The workmen were often attacked by robbers. They also had to fight off herds of wild buffalo.

At last, it was time to drive in a spike to hold the last rail in place. A special 'golden spike' was used. Everyone cheered and clapped. Bells rang all over the USA.

Canada's east to west railway opened in 1886. It was called the Canadian Pacific. Before it was built, it took five months to travel across Canada from east to west. The train took only five days.

This American train of the 1880s has broken down on the line. You can see the 'cowcatcher' grill on the front of the locomotive.

Building railways

▼ The new railways built across the United States had to cross many rivers and valleys. The massive trestle bridges were made of timber cut in nearby forests. These wooden bridges have now been replaced by trestle bridges made of steel.

Trains pick up speed slowly. They cannot brake sharply. They cannot climb steep slopes or turn sharp bends. A railway track has to be as level as possible. The curves must be gentle.

Millions of tonnes of earth and rock had to be moved to make the railways. If there were hills in the way, **cuttings** or tunnels had to be made. **Embankments** were built up to take the lines across low-lying ground. Bridges and **viaducts** had to be built to cross rivers and valleys.

No one had ever done work like this before. The first railway builders had to find out how to do it as they went along. They had no drills or trucks. People used picks, shovels and barrows to build the first railways.

Explosives were used to make tunnels. First earth and rock was blasted out to make a hole. Then all the **rubble** had to be cleared away. At each blast the tunnel became deeper. At the same time the work became more dangerous. The blasts and falls of rock caused many injuries. Some of the people were killed.

Bridges

Before the railways, road bridges only had to take the weight of horses and wagons. Trains were much heavier. The bridges built to carry railways had to be stronger than any road bridge that had been built before. Road bridges were mostly quite short. Some of the railway bridges had to be hundreds of metres long.

Building bridges cost a great deal of money. One way of cutting costs was to use materials that were close at hand. On the great east-to-west railways in North America, timber was easy to find. The track was carried across rivers on **trestle** bridges made of wood.

In Europe, stone or brick was used more often. Some bridges were made of stone or brick arches. Some had brick or stone supports, with frames of iron to carry the track. Other bridges were made completely of iron.

Stations

Railway companies spent large sums of money on the main line stations. Some of these were built to look important, like castles or **cathedrals**. The smaller stations were less grand. In many parts of the world, the 'station' is just a hut beside the line.

▼ One of the largest bridges in the world is the Forth rail bridge in Scotland. Built in 1890, it carries a railway track over the Firth of Forth. It has three huge spans made of steel girders.

The first cars

For 50 years after the railways began horse-drawn carriages were still used on the roads. No wonder that the trains had become so popular! They were faster and more comfortable than horse carriages. There were no cars or trucks.

Road wagons

A few people had tried building 'horseless carriages' to use on the roads. The first of these carriages had steam engines. The water to make steam was carried in tanks. Coal or wood was the fuel for the engines.

In 1769, a Frenchman, named Cugnot, built the first steam wagon. It was very heavy and was slow. It was also hard to steer. A person could walk as fast as this steam wagon could move.

Some of the later steam engines worked better. They were, however, still slow and hard to drive. Large numbers of steam wagons were built to carry heavy goods, such as logs and coal. Some of these steam wagons were still in use 50 years ago.

Steam rollers worked very well on the roads. It did not matter that they were slow and heavy. They did their job better because of this. In some parts of the world, steam rollers built 100 years ago are still in use.

A new kind of engine

A lighter engine was needed for cars. Engineers tried using other fuels. In 1876, a German called Nicholas Otto made a new kind of engine. It used gas as a fuel. In 1885, another German, Gottlieb Daimler, made the Otto engine work better by using petrol.

Daimler and another German, called Benz, built cars with Otto engines. The Daimler car had four wheels. It could take four people. The Benz was lighter. It had three wheels and carried two people.

Soon, many other people were making cars. Some great names are among the early car makers. Henry Ford built his first car in 1896. Three years later, Robert E. Olds made the first Oldsmobile. For many years the Oldsmobile was the best-selling car in the United States.

▼ Cugnot's steam wagon had three large cartwheels. The frame was made of great wooden beams. It had a boiler in the front which worked two cylinders. The top speed was about 3 kph.

◀ The first petrol-driven car was built by a German, Karl Benz. It was a three-wheeler and carried two passengers. Like a bicycle, its frame was made of steel tubes, and the wheels had wire spokes. The Benz could travel at 13 kph.

▼ By 1899, cars like this smart Fiat were seen on the roads. The wheels had solid rubber tyres. The Fiat could seat four people, two of them facing backwards.

Motoring for the rich

The first cars were sold to people who were rich enough to own horses and carriages. Many of the makers of carriages began to make car bodies. This is why many of the first cars looked like carriages. After about 1900, cars began to have a shape of their own.

In those days you could not go to a showroom and buy one of the cars on display. You had to order your car. Then it was made for you. These early cars were made to last a long time. They had strong wooden frames. The body of the car was made of metal. It was heavier than the metal used in cars today. The seats were made of the best leather. The door handles and other **fittings** were made of brass which shone like gold.

The car drivers

In most cars of that time, the driver sat in front on his own. The first cars did not have windscreens. The driver often had no roof over his head. The passengers who sat in the back seat were protected from the weather.

Some rich people liked to do their own driving, but most had **chauffeurs**. Chauffeurs had to clean and mend the car as well as drive it. Often these were men who had worked as coachmen with horses. Some cars had speaking tubes so that owners in the back seat could give orders to their chauffeurs as they went along the road.

▼ This Mercedes was made in Germany in 1904. It could carry four people in great comfort. The passengers had some protection from the weather, but there was no windscreen. The four brass headlamps were fed by gas. They had to be lit one at a time. Each lamp could be twisted around in any direction. Two spare tyres were carried next to the driver's seat.

▲ **This Napier was built in England in 1907. It had a huge six-cylinder engine and was very fast. The Napier was made for long-distance touring.**

► **The Cadillac was, and still is, one of America's finest makes of car. This four-seater was built in 1903.**

Motoring around

In open cars you had to wrap up well when you went for a drive. Men wore leather coats, goggles and gloves. The women wore dust coats made of linen. They had veils tied around their hats. Goggles and veils were needed because the roads were so dusty.

In wet weather, you might get stuck in the mud and have to push the car out. If you ran out of fuel, you were in real trouble. There were no petrol stations. Drivers would have to look for a shop which sold petrol.

The laws about speed then were very strict. Until 1896, the speed limit in Britain was four miles per hour (6 kph). A man with a red flag had to walk in front of each car. In the United States, cities had their own speed limits. Sometimes they were as low as five miles per hour (8 kph). Drivers who drove too fast were called 'road hogs'.

Henry Ford

One man thought that more people would buy cars if the price could be brought down. He was an engineer called Henry Ford. He built his first car in his spare time. That was in 1896. Six years later Henry Ford started his own company to make cars. He built a factory in Detroit, USA.

In 1908, a new Ford car was made. It was called the Model T. The Model T was built for hard work. You could drive it almost anywhere. Spare parts were cheap and easy to fit.

Over 15 million Model Ts were sold. Ford went on making them until 1927. Each year he was able to lower the price. The last Model T to be made cost only one-third of the price of the first one. This was because Henry Ford had worked out a new way of making cars.

Mass production

Before 1908, cars were built one at a time. A team of men would finish one car and then start work on the next one. Working in this way was slow and costly. Ford saw that the work of building a car could be split up into a number of different jobs. If each man did just one job on each car, the work would be done faster. This way of working is called **mass production**. The more cars that were made this way, the less each one cost to make. As Henry Ford made more and more cars he was able to put his prices down.

Ford put **conveyor belts** in his factory. These slow moving belts carried the cars along at a steady speed. As the cars moved along each worker did one special job on every car. At the end of the line, the cars were finished and ready for sale.

The Model T Ford and Henry Ford's production line.

Other car makers copied Ford's ideas. They too started mass production. Henry Ford, however, had a big headstart. The others had a long way to go to catch him up. By 1926, the Ford company was the biggest producer of cars in the world. It had factories in Britain and in other countries. Two million Ford cars were made each year.

No more Model Ts were made after 1927. Spare parts can still be bought. There are some people who collect these cars. Some of these collectors are still driving their Model Ts.

▶ **After World War 2, the Ford Company made a number of sports cars, as well as cars for the family. This 1955 Ford Thunderbird had a large eight-cylinder engine, called a V8. In the 1960s, the Ford Mustang was the first 'pony' car. This was a smaller sports car which was popular with younger people.**

'The Century'

New York and Chicago are two of the largest and busiest cities in the United States. They are almost 1600 km apart. People who travel on business between the two cities want to travel in comfort so that they can get some work done on the way. They will travel regardless of what it will cost them to do so. Today, business people travel by plane between New York and Chicago, but 50 years ago they travelled by train.

Back in time

Let's go back in time. It is 2.45 in the afternoon. We are at Grand Central Station in New York. The train conductor shouts 'All aboard!' Up at the front of the long train the locomotive whistles in reply. All the doors are closed, and The Twentieth Century Limited begins to move. 'The Century', as travellers call it, moves off on its journey. We are on the way to Chicago on one of the most comfortable trains that has ever been built.

▲ **The Twentieth Century Limited, 'The Century' as it was called, ran daily from New York to Chicago. In 1930, the train was made up of 13 massive cariages. Together these carriages weighed 1000 tonnes.**

A 'Limited' train has a fixed number of seats on it. If you buy a ticket, you are sure of a seat. When all the seats are taken, no more tickets are sold. 'The Century' was like a first class hotel on wheels. It had fine dining cars and **saloons**. There was plenty of room to read or work. There was even an office where people could have letters typed.

▲ After World War 2, 'The Century' was pulled by a diesel locomotive. Sometimes, as seen here, there were three diesel units to pull one train.

▼ This huge 4–6–4 Hudson steam locomotive was used to haul 'The Century' in the 1930s. It was 'streamlined' so that it could go faster.

Speeding up

The Twentieth Century Limited first ran in 1902. In those days the whole journey took about twenty hours. The train went at a speed of about 80 kph. It travelled through five states and there were eight stops on the way.

The New York Central and Hudson River Railroad built new and better engines for the train. By 1938, the journey time had been cut to 16 hours. You could do a morning's work in New York. Then you could catch the train, and be in Chicago in time for an early morning meeting the next day.

Now it takes less than three hours to fly from New York to Chicago. No one needs 'The Century' any more, so it no longer runs. For 50 years it was one of the most famous trains in the world. Now it has become a part of railway history.

Railways of the world

The Twentieth Century Limited was just one of the world's great trains. It does not run any more, but many others do.

Railways have always liked to give names to their **luxury** trains. These trains cover long distances at speed. The passengers travel in great comfort. **Attendants** do all they can to help the passengers.

Across the continents

The world's great continents have famous trains running across them. The Indian Pacific runs from Perth to Sydney in Australia. Perth is on the Indian Ocean. Sydney is on the Pacific. That is how the train got its name. The Indian Pacific has the longest stretch of straight track in the world. It runs without a bend for 475 km.

The Canadian is Canada's great east-to-west train. It runs across Canada from Montreal to Vancouver. On the way it passes through the Rockies. Some of the coaches have clear, **domed** roofs. From these, the passengers can look at the mountain scenery as they speed on their way.

Europe's most famous train was the Orient Express. It passed through ten countries on its way from Paris to Istanbul in Turkey. This train first ran in 1883. The coaches had fine furniture and thick carpets. There were showers on board. Stories have been written and films have been made about the Orient Express.

The Flying Scotsman

Each morning, a train leaves Kings Cross Station in London. It is bound for Edinburgh in Scotland. This is Britain's most famous train, the Flying Scotsman.

The distance from London to Edinburgh is 640 km. The journey takes less than five hours. Today it is drawn by a **diesel** locomotive. Until 1952, the Flying Scotsman was drawn by a steam locomotive. One day in 1938 it reached a speed of 202 kph. It still holds the world record for the fastest steam train.

Some Famous Trains

Train	*Country/Continent*	*Route*	*Distance (km)*	*Average Speed (kph)*
Canadian	Canada	Montreal to Vancouver	4800	70
Flying Scotsman	United Kingdom	London to Edinburgh	640	128
Indian Pacific	Australia	Perth to Sydney	3970	62
Mistral	France	Paris to Nice	1090	120
Orient Express	Europe	Paris to Istanbul	3000	44
Russia	USSR	Moscow to Vladivostok	9438	48
Shinkhansen Hikari	Japan	Tokyo to Osaka	517	162
Twentieth Century Limited	USA	New York to Chicago	1540	96

▲ This Canadian Pacific train is crossing a viaduct in the Rocky Mountains. In this picture you can see three of the special domed coaches. Passengers can sit in these coaches to get a better view of the scenery. The coaches, coloured silver and red, glisten in the sun.

► The Indian Pacific is seen here leaving Kalgoorlie in Western Australia.

Modern roads

The old road **networks** in most countries were made when people travelled by horse and cart. They were not built for fast and heavy traffic. One way to think of road networks is to imagine a tree. The trunk roads are the main roads, and the branch roads are the smaller, side roads.

Motorways

Most countries of the world have now built new, wide roads for motor traffic only. These new roads avoid towns and villages. They are linked to the main cities by wide **feeder** roads.

These **motorways** have gentle slopes and curves so that traffic can keep up a steady speed. There are only a small number of entry and **exit** points. Slow vehicles such as farm tractors and bicycles are not allowed to use the motorways.

The first people to build roads like these were the Germans. In the 1930s, they opened their first fast motorway. They called it an **autobahn**. These roads were designed for speed. They were also built to take the German army swiftly from one place to another.

In France, the new high speed roads are called **autoroutes**. The Italians call them **autostrada**. Names used in other countries are freeway, highway or expressway.

Motorways are very costly to build. In some places, part of the cost is paid back by the drivers who use the roads. They pay a **toll** to travel on them. The roads are called **toll roads** or **turnpikes**. Some new roads in the United States, France and Italy are paid for in this way.

◀ The junction between two roads or motorways is sometimes called an interchange. They are designed so motorists can change from one highway to another at a steady speed without any danger. This interchange is at San Diego, California, USA.

► There are tollgates on many of the French autoroutes. In this picture you can see several tollgates. A green light above the gate tells motorists which gate they can use. Gates with a red cross above them are closed.

All these large new roads have more than one lane of traffic going in each direction. Traffic going one way is kept apart from traffic going the other way. Two or three lanes are the usual number in Britain. In the United States, roads may have as many as six lanes of traffic going in each direction.

▼ Many of the German autobahns have 'cloverleaf' junctions. You can see from this air photo why they are called cloverleaf junctions.

Changing direction

Fast-moving traffic needs to be able to join or leave a motorway safely. Each **junction** is built in such a way that traffic can leave or join without crossing other lanes of traffic. Exit and entry lanes may be carried over the motorway on **flyovers** or underneath on **underpasses**. The pattern of some of these junctions looks like the outline of a giant four-leaved clover. These are called 'cloverleaf' junctions.

Cars today

There are well over 200 million cars on the world's roads today. There is a type of car to suit everyone. Some people choose cars which are cheap to run. Others want speed and comfort. People's needs change from time to time. Then they change their cars for new ones.

Every year the car makers bring out new **models**. They change the **design** to make the cars look better. New fittings are added to keep the new models up-to-date. By doing all these things they hope to sell more cars. Each car maker hopes that people will buy their cars and not those produced by other car makers.

Economy cars

Some small cars can go 18 km on one litre of petrol. These are known as **economy** cars. British Leyland's Mini Metro and the Renault 4 are two such models. Economy cars are popular in Europe. People take shorter trips than in the USA. Economy cars are cheap to run and easy to park because they are small. They are not as comfortable to drive on longer journeys as larger cars are.

Family cars

There are more family cars on the road than any other type. They can seat four or five people in comfort. Plenty of baggage can be carried in family cars.

Large companies like Ford and Nissan keep their **production lines** going by making cars to suit the family. In Europe, these cars are mostly smaller than those used in the USA. In the USA the distances are longer and the fuel is cheaper than in Europe. Saving fuel is not quite so important.

▲ The Mini Metro is a small car made in Britain. It is very cheap to run and easy to park.

► The Citroen BX is a medium-sized family car made in France. Some of the body panels are made of plastic. This makes the Citroen lighter and easier to repair.

▶ The Porsche 911 is made at Stuttgart in West Germany. The Porsche Company only build sports cars. They have fairly small engines but they go very fast. They hold the road well on corners. These cars got their name from Dr Ferdinand Porsche who was a racing car designer.

Luxury cars

Luxury cars are often owned by people with a lot of money, or by companies. The engines are larger and they use much more petrol. Luxury cars like Rolls-Royce and Cadillac are often used by important people. Cars like these are sometimes driven by chauffeurs.

Sports cars

Many people dream of owning a sports car. Sports cars, like Ferrari, Alfa Romeo and the Corvette are exciting to drive. They are sleek and low — and very fast. They use a lot of petrol. Most of us would like to own a sports car at some time in our lives.

◀ This photograph shows a 1985 Cadillac, a Fleetwood Brougham. It is a very large luxury car and uses a lot of petrol. Cars that use a lot of petrol are sometimes known as 'gas guzzlers'.

Giants of the road

▼ **American truck drivers like to keep their trucks clean and bright. This large Peterbilt truck has a rest cabin behind the driving compartment. The two exhaust pipes channel the fumes high in the air. This keeps the fumes away from people on the ground.**

As the new high speed roads were built, trucks became larger and larger. Now trucks have taken much of the **freight** trade away from the railways. Giant trucks carry goods right across the USA. Long distance trucks cross Europe from Britain to the Middle East.

Most of these huge trucks are **articulated**. This means that they are built in two parts. In front is the **tractor unit**. The large engine and the driver's cab make up the tractor unit. This links up with the trailer behind. In some countries, but not in Britain, a second trailer can be added on to make a train of trailers.

Articulated trucks are easier to drive and park than trucks made in one piece. They can unhitch and start the next job before the trailer is unloaded. In the USA, some drivers own the tractor unit, but not the trailer. With just one tractor unit they can keep busy and earn a good living.

The sleeping quarters are in the cab, behind the driver's seat. These have bunk beds. Some have a cooker and a TV set.

Juggernauts

Juggernaut is an Indian word. It means a huge cart. The word is used in Europe for giant trucks. Like American truckers, British drivers can sleep in their cabs when they need to.

If drivers start out from Britain, they have to cross the English Channel. They go by sea ferry. Large ferries can carry up to 60 juggernauts. Then a long trip to the Middle East may take the drivers through ten countries. They have to learn the rules of the road for each country. The British drive on the left side of the road. They have to drive on the right once they cross the Channel.

The outback

In the middle of Australia is desert land called the **outback**, or back country. There are few towns and farms. The largest trucks in the world are used to carry goods through the outback. One truck may have three or more trailers. The distances between the few towns are so great that the drivers may take days to get from one town to the next.

▲ Containers are brought by sea to Tilbury Docks, London. You can see the hoist on the right of the picture. This is used to lift the containers off the ship and on to the trucks.

▼ This picture shows a line of heavy trucks, or 'road trains', moving across the Australian outback. Trucks often travel in groups in case one truck breaks down in the desert.

Grand Prix

The first motor races were held on public roads. The races were noisy and dangerous. There were many accidents. It was soon decided that motor races must take place on special tracks.

'Grand Prix' is French for 'big prize'. The first Grand Prix was held at Le Mans in France in 1906. The roads were closed to the public for two days while the race was on. The cars had to complete 1250 km in the two days. It was not just a sporting event. Car makers put their cars in the race to make people talk about their names. They used the race to test and improve their cars.

In 1907, the first motor racing track was built at Brooklands near London. It was used for the British Grand Prix. At that time, people thought that nothing on Earth could go faster than 130 mph (209 kph). The curves on the track were **banked**. As the cars went round the track they went up the banking. Later, when cars went faster than 130 mph (209 kph), many of them went over the top, and the drivers were killed.

Indianapolis

The most famous race in the world was the Indianapolis 800 km race. It was first run in 1911. Ray Harroun won it in a Marmon Wasp. His speed was 120 kph. The Indianapolis race now counts as the Grand Prix in the USA.

▼ A pit-stop at Indianapolis, USA. Every second counts. All the wheels can be changed and the car can be back in the race in under ten seconds.

▲ This photo shows motor racing in the 1930s, at Brooklands. The faster cars went higher up the banked track. The cars in the picture are, from left to right, Austin, Riley, Bentley and MG. They are travelling at about 160 kph.

▼ The start of the Portugal Grand Prix, 1985.

Formula 1

Early racing cars were very heavy. They had huge engines. Very often the car with the largest engine won the race. So it was decided to group cars in classes. Each class is called a **formula**. The Formula rules limit the size of the engine and the width and weight of the car. Formula 1 is the top class of racing cars. They are the fastest racing cars. Only Formula 1 cars can take part in Grand Prix races.

Ten countries throughout the world have Grand Prix races which count in the world championship. This began in 1950. The top drivers take part in all the races. They earn points for their finishing places in each race. The driver with the most points is named world champion for the year. Britain's first champion was Mike Hawthorn in 1958. The first American winner was Phil Hill in 1961.

High speed trains

High **S**peed **T**rains are called HSTs. They should really have special track to run on. HSTs need long, straight stretches with very gentle curves. In most countries of the world the old track is improved by 'smoothing' it out so the HSTs can use it.

In Britain, the HSTs are called '125s'. They can reach a speed of 200 kph. The first service started running from London to Bristol in 1976. An even faster British train is called the **A**dvanced **P**assenger **T**rain, or APT. It can reach a speed of 250 kph. The engineers have had trouble getting the APT ready for use.

America's first HST is called the Metroliner. It goes from New York to Washington in three hours, at a speed of 120 kph. Once the track is smoothed out, it will be able to reach 260 kph. Canada's HST is called the Turbo Train. The coaches **tilt** to help the train go round curves. The Turbo runs from Montreal to Toronto. It takes just over four hours to do the 536 km journey.

▼ The Canadian HST runs between Montreal and Toronto. It is called the Turbo, or LRC. The letters stand for Light, Rapid and Comfortable. The LRC has a top speed of about 200 kph.

French HSTs

The French State Railways built a special track for their HST. It runs from Paris to Lyons – 425 km – in just two hours. Their train is called the TGV. *Train Grand Vitesse* is French for high speed train. The top speed of the TGV is 300 kph.

The Tokaido Express

Japan's HST also runs on a special track. Most people call the Tokaido Express the 'Bullet Train' because of its shape and speed. The Bullet Train takes about three hours to cover the 517 km from Tokyo to Osaka. It has a top speed of 250 kph.

The Japanese are now building a Bullet Train network all over their country. There are plans to build a line right up to the north of Japan. It will run under the sea to the island of Hokkaido.

▲ This picture shows the French TGV at speed. The TGV travels on the fast stretches of track at a speed of 269 kph.

▼ Japanese Bullet trains have a total weight of 880 tonnes. There are 16 coaches to each train.

The record breakers

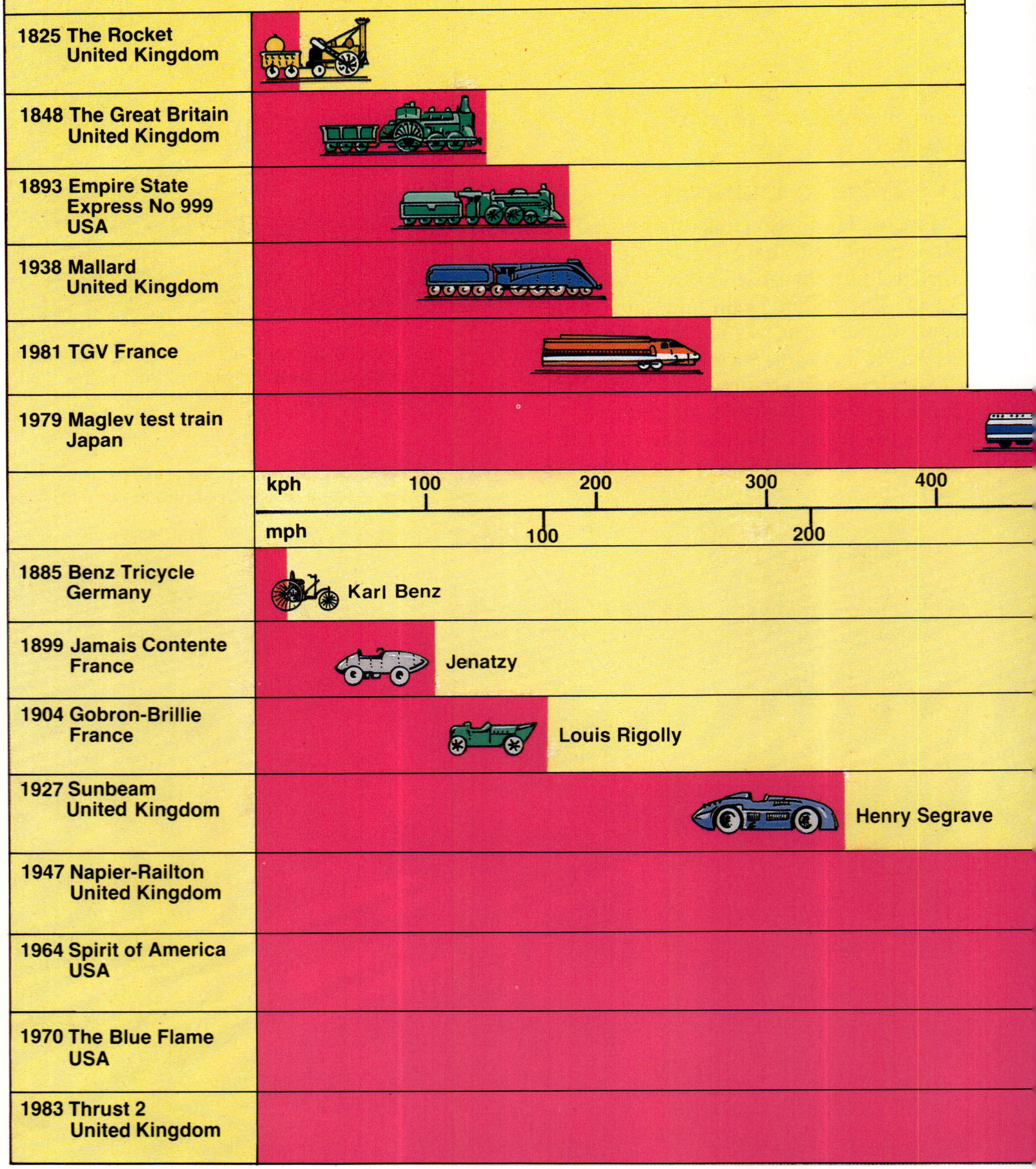

Who is the fastest on road and rail? Makers of cars and locomotives have always wanted to see their names at the top of the list. For many years, trains went faster than cars. By the time the first car was built, trains had reached a speed of 112 kph. The first cars had a top speed of 16 kph. Even then, people thought they were dangerous. However, cars soon became faster than trains. They have stayed ahead ever since.

Railway records

The passengers who have travelled fastest by rail are the Japanese. In 1979, a train on a test track in Japan went over 514 kph. The fastest regular train service is also in Japan. It is the Bullet Train. France holds the record for the fastest train on a normal track.

Land speed records

All the holders of land speed records drove cars which had to be specially built for that purpose. They are only able to carry one person, the driver. In 1970, an American, Gary Gabelich, drove at 1016 kph. His car, Blue Flame, had a rocket engine. Then, in 1983, Richard Noble drove his Thrust 2 at a slightly higher speed of 1019 kph. Thrust 2 was powered by a jet engine.

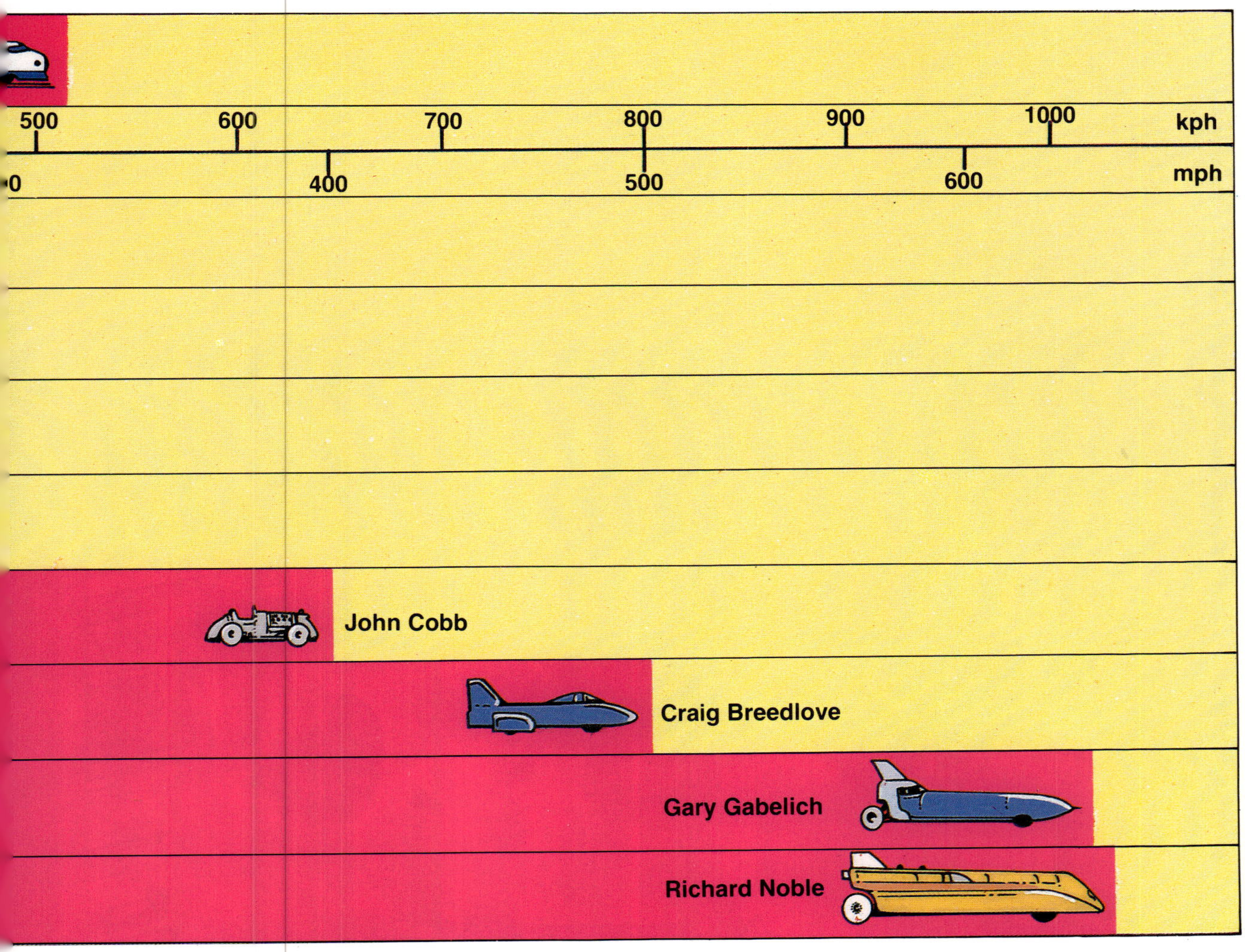

Safety on road and rail

A train weighs several hundred tonnes. Trains travel at very high speeds. They cannot stop suddenly or swerve. Yet travel by rail is safer than travel by road.

Railway signals

The speed of the first railways frightened people. From the start safety signals had to be used. The first idea was to keep trains apart from each other by a time interval. A second train would not set off until a fixed time after the first. This did not work if the first train broke down.

The 'block' system was better. It is still used on most lines today. Each line is divided into sections or blocks. Only one train is allowed in one section at a time. A signal warns the driver if there is a train in the section ahead. Then he must stop until the signal shows 'all clear'.

Many trains are also fitted with **automatic** warning systems. These sound a hooter or buzzer in the cab as the train passes each signal. If a train passes a signal set at 'danger', the brakes of the train go on automatically. The same sort of system can be used to slow a train down if it is going too fast at any point on the track.

Many modern trains are fitted with the 'dead man's handle'. This is a metal lever which the driver holds down to keep the train moving. The moment he lets go the train stops. This way the train is not able to move if the driver collapses or dies.

▼ The French rail system is up-to-date. Information about the trains is fed into computers at the traffic control centres. There are many of these centres throughout France. A large plan shows the railway track. This lights up to show where each train is, and where it is going.

▲ **New car models are tested with dummy people inside them. The car is made to crash head-on into a wall. In this picture, the front of the car has crumpled, but the passengers are safe.**

Safety on the road

It is not easy to make road travel safe. There is little to stop car drivers from breaking the rules of the road. There are not enough traffic police to watch every driver.

Even if the drivers cannot be made to drive more safely, the cars can be made safer to drive. When car makers make a new model they test it by crashing it. They make the car run into a wall at different speeds. There are dummy people inside. The car makers can see what happens to the dummies when the crash takes place.

Most new cars are now built with 'safety shells' around the passengers. The shell will take the first shock in a crash. In most countries, people in the front seat have to wear safety belts. In some countries, people in the back must wear safety belts as well.

▼ **The steel frame at the front and at the back of the car is designed to crumple and absorb the shock from a crash. The passengers are protected by a strong, rigid steel frame around them.**

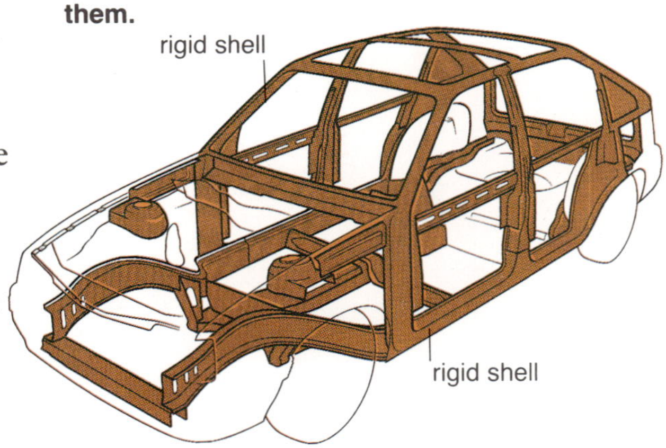

Looking ahead

As we look back through the history of travel by road and rail, we come across 'milestones'. Each milestone marks an event where the human race has made a big stride forward. The invention of the wheel, the steam locomotive and Otto's new engine were all great events in transportation.

Some people think that the year 2000 may bring another great event. This is because the world's oil supplies will soon run out. The shortage of oil will force us to find a new way of making cars work. Cars are a part of our lives. We would not want to do without them.

New cars for cities

Many people think that the electric car is the car of the future. For many years, people have been trying to build a car that would run a long way on electric **batteries**. Up to now, electric cars cannot go very fast or very far. Their batteries are too heavy. Electric batteries need to be re-charged every 32 km or so. What is needed is a small, long-lasting battery.

It may be that one day you will go to work by electric car. The batteries will be charged at home while you sleep. Where you work there will be a place for you to re-charge your battery. Then your car will be ready to take you home again.

It may be that in the future someone will invent a new kind of battery, or even a new kind of engine. Then there will be no noise and no exhaust fumes to spoil our towns and cities.

◄ **The electric car is still a thing of the future in most parts of the world. Dutch people, however, are already driving these cars. In Amsterdam small two-seaters can be rented for use inside the city. They run on batteries and are kept in special parking areas.**

Trains of the future

The trains of the future may be here already. We may see many more trains like the Japanese Bullet Train and the French TGV. One new idea for faster and more efficient trains is the **levitation** train. Most people call it the **maglev** train. This word stands for **mag**netic **lev**itation, which means raised by **magnets**. This train has no wheels. It uses a special track which is fitted with magnets. There are magnets on the train too. When the magnets are switched on, the train is pulled along. Some maglev test lines have been built. There is one short line in use in Britain. It links Birmingham Airport with the National Exhibition Centre nearby.

The maglev idea works well on lines with no junctions. It has not yet been worked out how a maglev train could switch from one line to another.

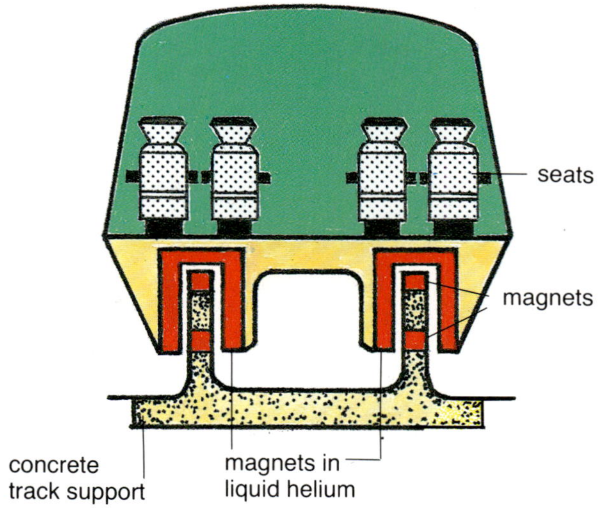

▲ **Maglev trains, like this new Japanese test model, can travel very fast. However they need to have a special track which is costly to build.**

▼ **By the year 2000, we may see maglev trains like this one in many of the world's cities. They will be quiet, and will cause no pollution.**

TRAVEL BY AIR

Michael Pollard

Introduction

Why are aeroplanes so important to us all? Air travel is easy, fast and safe. It is much safer than going by car or crossing the road. Aeroplanes can carry **freight** as well as people. Letters and packages can go by air freight and large things too. Planes can even carry cars and horses.

A farmer in Africa needs a spare part for a tractor. It can go to the farmer by air. This way the tractor is soon back at work again. People can travel by air from America to Europe in just a few hours.

Airports

Almost every city in the world has its own airport. Day and night aeroplanes land and take off. Some of the flights may be to nearby cities. These are called **short haul** or internal flights. They use small aeroplanes which can land or take off on short **runways**.

Other flights from the airport go to cities in other countries. For these **long haul** flights larger aeroplanes are used. They carry hundreds of people and fly thousands of kilometres without stopping.

Famine relief

When people are in trouble, aeroplanes can help them to stay alive. In parts of Africa and Asia, rain may not fall for a number of years. Crops will not grow, and thousands of people may starve. They will die unless food and help are brought to them quickly.

▼ This Boeing 747 has an extra large top deck to take more people. The cargo door is open. Goods are loaded into the plane by a lift.

▲ **This picture of Heathrow Airport, London shows planes from eight different countries.**

▶ **Out on a farm in Australia a man has hurt his leg. The flying doctor will fly him to hospital.**

Aeroplanes from many countries bring in food. Doctors and nurses are also flown in to help. Sometimes, food is dropped from the air if there is no place for a plane to land. Planes can also take people from dry places to areas where there are good stores of food. Many lives can be saved in this way.

Flying doctor

In parts of Australia, some farmers live and work in **remote** places. They are a long way from the nearest town and have to keep in touch by radio. If a doctor is needed, a radio call is made. The flying doctor comes in by a small plane and lands on a nearby field. When people have to go to hospital, they are taken there by plane.

How do planes fly?

People have always wanted to fly like birds. But human beings do not have wings and they are far too heavy. If you spring into the air, your strength gives you the **lift** to get you off the ground. But the **weight** of your body soon brings you down again. Aeroplane wings are designed to give lift. In flight, they give more lift than the weight of the plane.

Take a sheet of paper and move it through the air. The air bends the paper backwards. It is causing **drag**. Once a plane is in the air, like a bird, it has to keep moving forward. The faster it goes the more drag there is. Modern planes are shaped like birds. This helps to reduce the drag. It is called **streamlining**. Even so, there is still plenty of drag. The engines of an aeroplane give it forward **thrust** and this overcomes the drag.

▼ A plane is shaped like a bird for a good reason. It has to pierce the air as it flies. The air slows the plane down. It causes drag. But the engine pulls the plane forward. It gives enough thrust to cancel out the drag.

The weight of the plane pulls it towards the ground. In the air, the wings give the plane lift. This lift cancels out the weight. So the plane is able to keep flying.

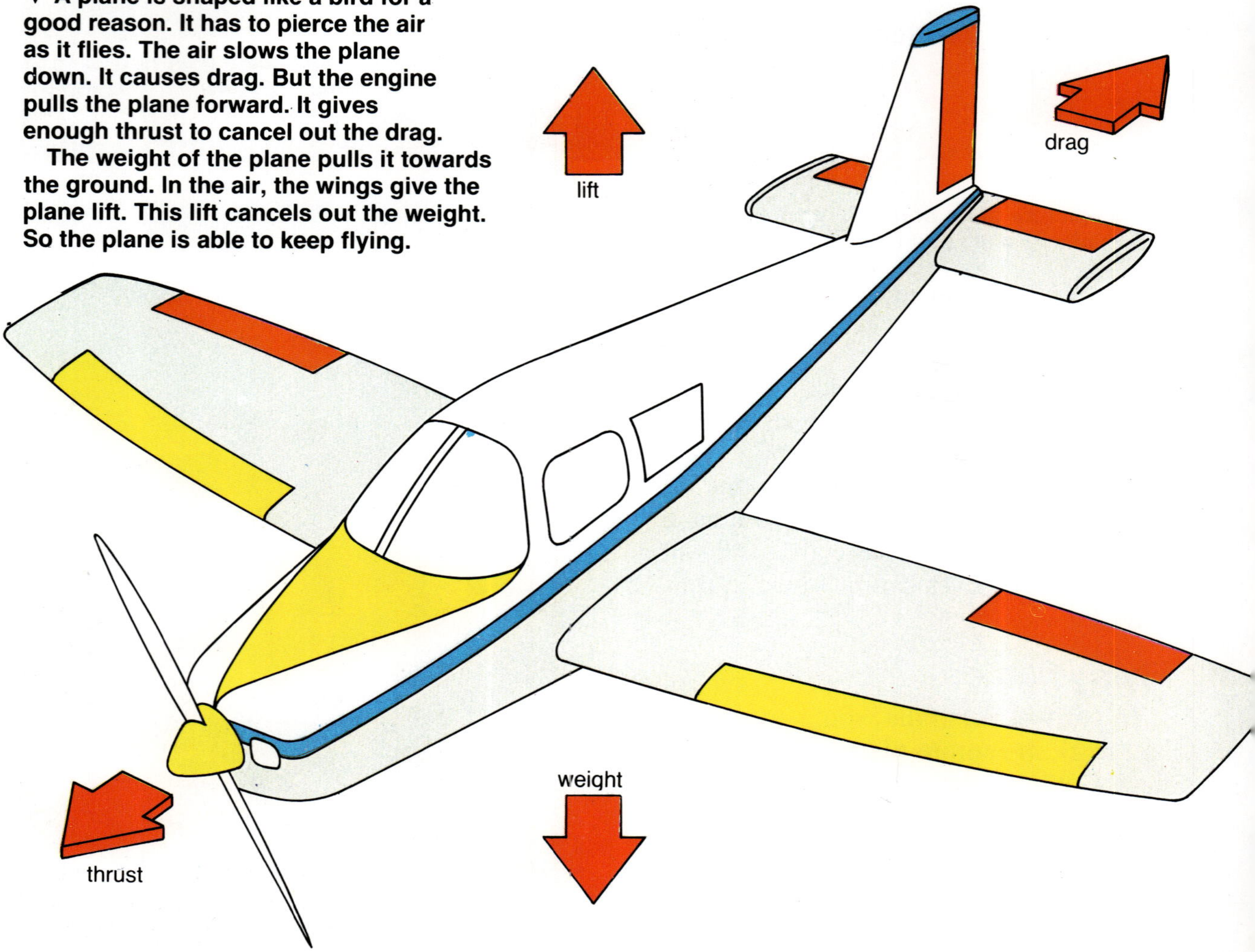

The aerofoil

Aeroplane wings are shaped in a special way to give as much lift as possible. If you could cut a slice through a wing you would see this special shape. It is called an **aerofoil**.

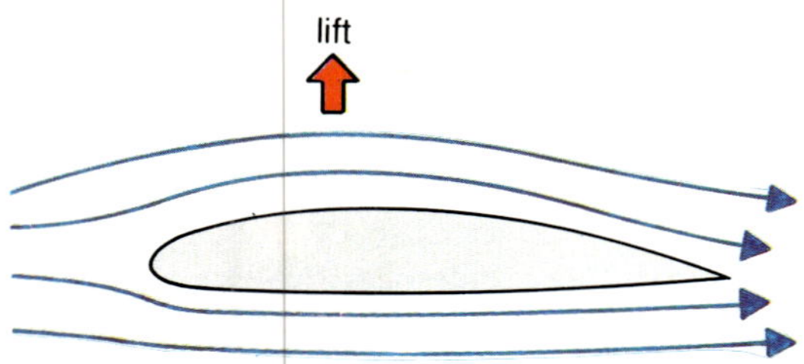

Wings are curved on top and almost flat underneath. When a plane is flying, the air passing over the top of the wing has further to go than the air underneath. In flight, the air under the wing pushes the wing upwards. This gives the plane lift.

Changing direction

In the air, the pilot must be able to change the height and direction of the plane. The **ailerons** on the back edge of each wing help to turn the plane left or right. As one aileron goes up, the other goes down. The **rudder** is part of the tail unit. It moves to the left or the right. The pilot uses the rudder with the ailerons to make a turn or to **bank**. The pilot moves the rudder with foot controls.

The **elevators** are on the rear edge of the tailplane. They are moved up or down to make the plane climb or dive. The pilot pushes the **control column** forward to dive, and pulls it back to climb.

▼ In the picture you can see the elevators. They are moved down to make the plane dive, and up to make it climb. The rudder is used to make the plane turn left or right. The wings must be tilted at the same time. The ailerons on the wings make them tilt. This is called banking.

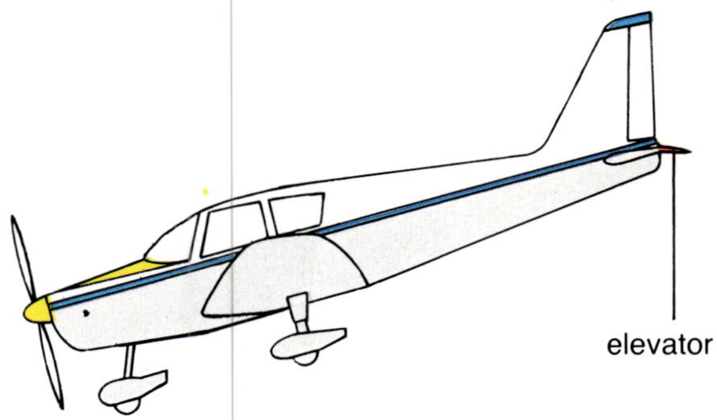

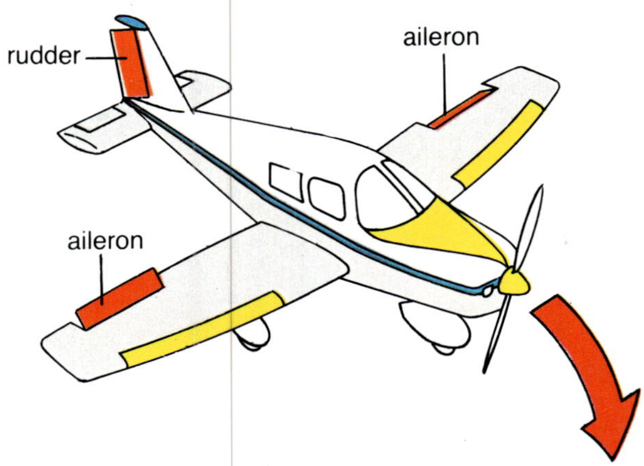

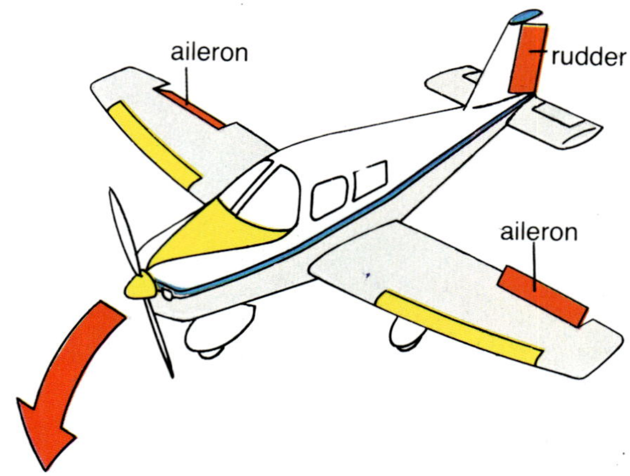

The first people to fly

Nearly 200 years ago people made their first attempts to fly with **gliders**. These were planes without engines. Gliders then had to take off from high ground before they could fly. The large wings of gliders help them to stay in the air.

The first gliders flew without a pilot. But in 1849 the British **inventor** Sir George Cayley built a glider that carried a boy for a short distance. Four years later he made one strong enough to fly a man over a small valley.

Otto Lilienthal

In 1891 a German, Otto Lilienthal, built and flew the first **hang glider**. He flew the glider by hanging beneath the large wings. He could control the direction of the glider by swinging his body in the air. He made about 2000 flights from a hill near Berlin. One day in 1896 his glider was blown by a sudden strong wind. It crashed to the ground. Sadly, Lilienthal was killed.

The Wright brothers

In the United States, around 1900, Wilbur and Orville Wright started to make gliders. First, they worked out ways of controlling their gliders in the air. The wings could be twisted to help steer the glider. There was also a rudder which the pilot could move in flight.

No one had been able to fit an engine to a glider with any success. Some attempts had been made with steam engines but they were too heavy. The Wright brothers made their own petrol engine. This was lighter than a steam engine. They fitted this engine to a glider and called their plane *Flyer I*.

Otto Lilienthal wanted to learn how to steer his glider in the air. He did this by twisting his body about. He could move the wings with his arms. But in his clumsy attempts to fly he always thought that the birds were laughing at him.

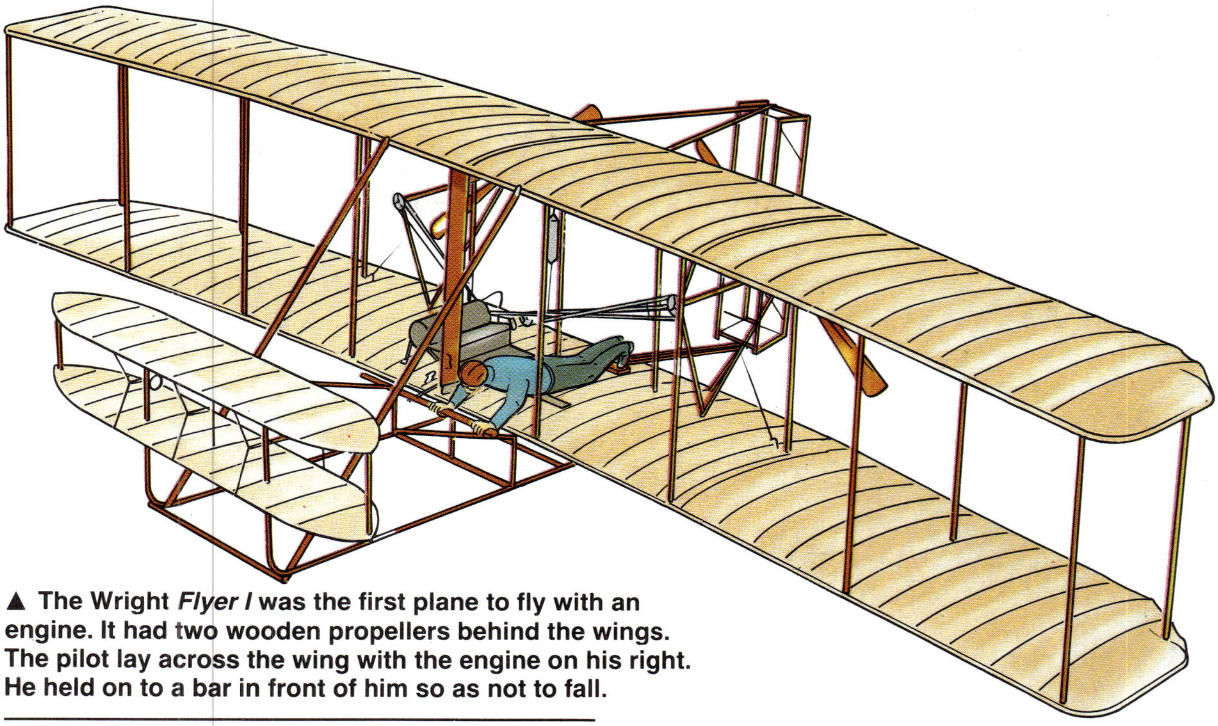

▲ The Wright *Flyer I* was the first plane to fly with an engine. It had two wooden propellers behind the wings. The pilot lay across the wing with the engine on his right. He held on to a bar in front of him so as not to fall.

On 17 December 1903, at the Kill Devil Hills, near Kitty Hawk, USA, Orville Wright made the first **powered** flight. It lasted just 12 seconds and he flew 120 ft (42 m). Later the same day, his brother Wilbur made a flight of 59 seconds and covered 852 ft (280 m). Next year, they built *Flyer II* and *Flyer III*. Each new plane was better than the one before.

By 1908, there were many other pilots and planes taking to the air. But no one could stay in the air so long or travel so far as Orville and Wilbur Wright.

▼ This photograph shows Orville Wright making the first powered flight in *Flyer I*.

World flights

At the end of World War I, there were plenty of spare planes. There were also pilots to fly them. Some of them were keen to find out how far planes could fly. Also they wanted to prove that flight could be made safely across oceans.

No one had flown across the Atlantic Ocean. In 1919 two British men, John Alcock and Arthur Whitten Brown, made the flight. Their plane was a Vickers Vimy **bomber**. It had two engines and extra petrol tanks. They set off from Newfoundland and landed in Ireland 16 hours later.

Lindbergh

The first person to fly the Atlantic **solo** – on his own – was an American, Charles Lindbergh. He took off from New York for Paris on 20 May 1927. His plane was called *The Spirit of St Louis*. It had one engine and very large petrol tanks.

Lindbergh sat in the cramped **cockpit** behind the huge main petrol tank. This meant he could not see straight ahead. For much of the time he was flying in the rain and in the dark. To make matters worse, he had no radio to help him. When he landed in Paris he had flown 5800 km. The flight took over 33 hours, so his main problem was staying awake.

▼ **On 31 May 1927 Lindbergh flew on from Paris to Gosport in southern England. There he was greeted by Royal Air Force officers.**

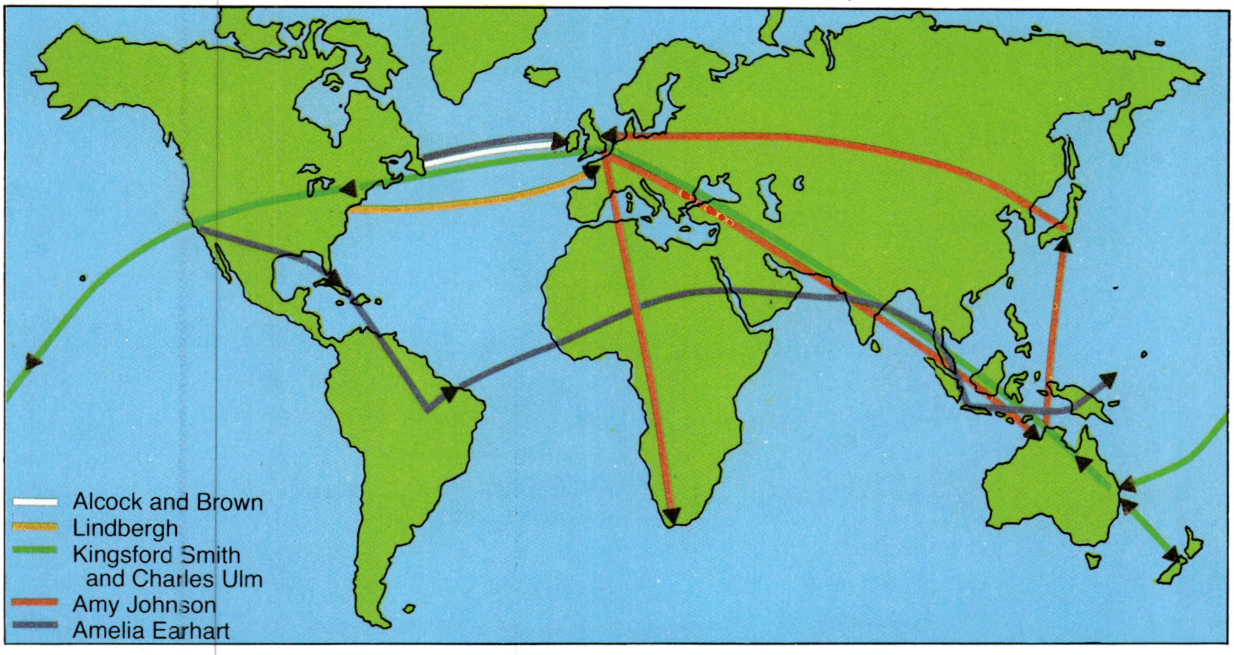

▲ **The arrows give you some idea of the routes taken by the first pilots. Can you imagine just how Amy Johnson and Amelia Earhart felt in their lonely flights across the oceans?**

Around the world

Two Australians, Kingsford Smith and Charles Ulm, were the first people to fly across the Pacific Ocean in 1928. They had to make stops on the way. Their plane, a three-engined Fokker, was called *The Southern Cross*.

Among the first pilots was an English woman, Amy Johnson. She was the first woman to fly solo from England to Australia, in 1930. When she made this flight she had only done 100 hours solo flying. It took her 19½ days to make the flight in her small plane *Jason*.

Another great woman flier was Amelia Earhart, an American. In 1932 she became the first woman to fly the Atlantic. She made the flight solo in a Lockheed Vega.

In 1937 she planned to fly from California, USA, around the world. Near the end of her journey her luck ran out. She was flying from New Guinea to a tiny island in the Pacific. Perhaps she lost her way, or ran out of petrol. No one knows what went wrong. Her plane was not found and she was never seen again.

Key dates in air travel

1853	Sir George Cayley built the first glider to fly with a man on board.
1891	Otto Lilienthal made the first controlled gliding flights.
1900	The Wright brothers flew their No.1 glider.
1902	The Wrights flew No.3 glider, using a rudder to steer it.
1903	The world's first flight of an aeroplane with an engine and propeller, by Wilbur and Orville Wright.
1907	The first flight in Europe lasting over one minute, by Henri Farman.
1919	Alcock and Brown made the first flight across the Atlantic.
1927	Charles Lindbergh made the first solo flight across the Atlantic.
1928	Kingsford Smith and Charles Ulm made the first flight across the Pacific Ocean.
1930	Amy Johnson was the first woman to fly solo from England to Australia.
1932	Amelia Earhart was the first woman to fly the Atlantic solo.

The first airlines

▲ **The Handley Page Hannibal first flew in 1930. Eight of these planes were built as a fleet for Imperial Airways. They flew from Croydon Airport, London, to Europe and Africa.**

The first **airlines** to carry passengers and mail began soon after World War I. Many of them used wartime aeroplanes fitted with seats. In 1920, the first US air mail flight left San Francisco for New York. Many of the airlines we know today started around this time. They grew very rapidly in the years that followed.

The first airliners

The old bombers were replaced by airliners. These were specially built to carry people. The Handley Page Hannibal was a famous early airliner. Because of its shape it was sometimes known as the flying banana. It could carry 38 passengers in great comfort, and was able to fly at about 160 kph.

Only eight of these four-engined **biplanes** were made. Between them they flew more than 16 million km. No one flying in them was ever killed in a crash.

Soon, there were flights between many of Europe's large cities. Air **routes** linked the cities of the United States. People could fly all over the world. Planes had to land every few hundred kilometres to take on more petrol. Because of this long flights had to be made in **stages**.

Flying boats

After 1930, airlines began to use a new kind of plane. This was the flying boat which took off and landed on water. It could carry more petrol so the plane did not have to land so often.

Most flying boats had four engines and carried about 30 people. But the German Dornier Do X was a huge flying boat with 12 engines. It could carry 150 passengers and a crew of ten. On one flight the Dornier carried nine **stowaways** as well.

▼ This photograph of a DC3 was taken on 3 November 1936. The Gooney Bird had a thin outer skin of polished metal. Most other planes at that time were made of wood and fabric.

Still flying today

In 1936, American Airlines bought a new airliner. It was the Douglas DC3, sometimes known as the Gooney Bird. It was streamlined like a bird. The DC3 carried 21 passengers and flew at about 270 kph. By 1939, nine out of every ten airliners in the world were DC3s. Five years later over 10 000 DC3s had been built. Some are still used by airlines today. The Gooney Bird just keeps on flying.

Power for planes

Aeroplane engines have to be powerful. They need to give enough thrust for take off, and for flight through the air. Engines must not break down at any time. They have to be **reliable**.

There are two main types of aeroplane engines. One type of engine is used to turn a **propeller**. The other uses a jet of hot gas to thrust the plane forward. All aeroplane engines need **fuel** to keep going. Propeller engines use petrol as a fuel. Most jet engines use **kerosene**.

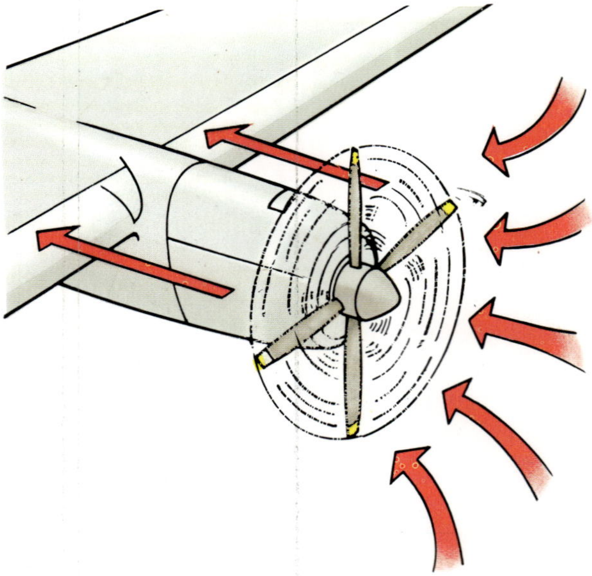

▲ A plane's propeller has two or more blades made of metal. At one time the blades were made of wood. Each blade is very slightly twisted. As the blades spin they force the air backwards. This fast stream of air thrusts the plane forward.

Planes with propellers

Propeller engines burn petrol. They work the same way as car engines. In a car, power from the engine drives the road wheels. In a plane, the engine turns the propeller.

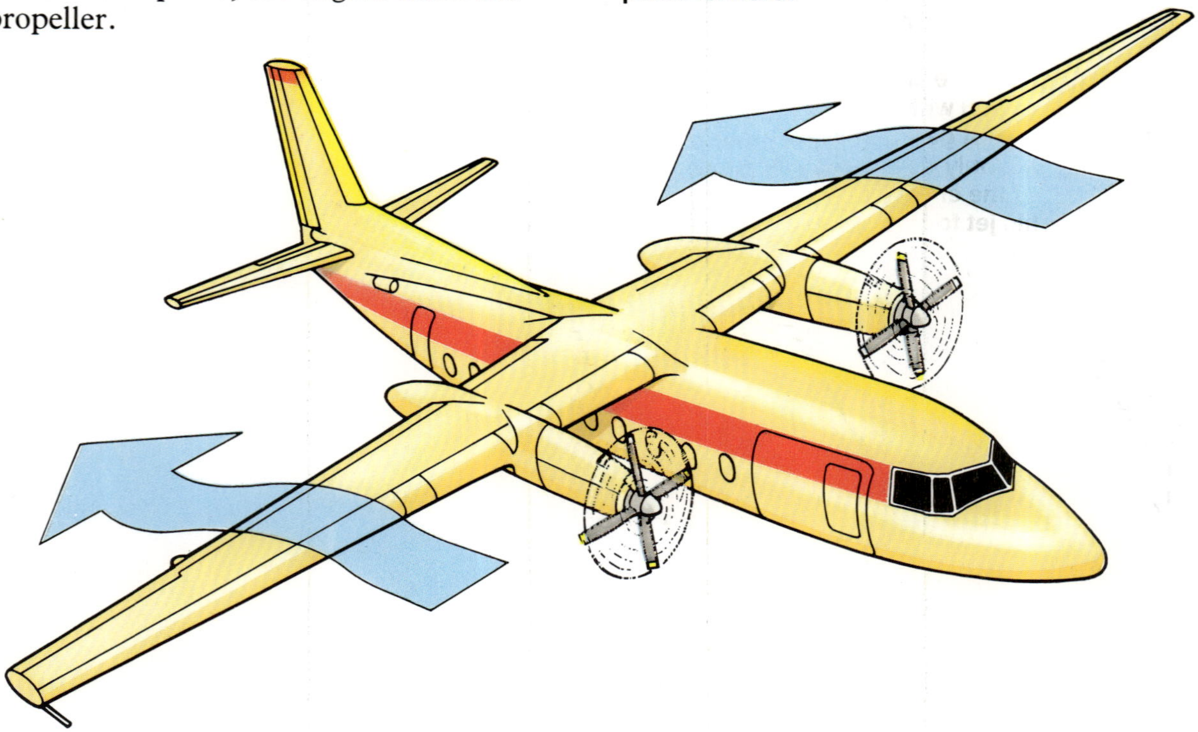

An aeroplane propeller has two or more blades. Each of the blades is slightly twisted. Because of this, the air is driven backwards as the propeller turns. This way, the propeller pulls the plane through the air. The air is swept over the upper surface of the wings. This gives the plane extra lift, as well as thrust.

The engine is cooled by the air as the plane is flying. The propeller engines turn over more slowly than car engines. As a result, they are less likely to break down than car engines. They are more reliable.

Jet power

Jet engines work in a quite different way. They have fewer working parts than other engines, and burn kerosene. This is cheaper than petrol and does not burn so easily.

In a jet engine, air is sucked in at the front. As the air enters the engine it is packed very tight. It is **compressed**. This makes the air become very hot.

The hot air is then mixed with a spray of kerosene. The mixture burns as a very hot flame. The hot gases rush out of the exhaust in a stream. It is this stream of hot gases, travelling very fast, which drives the plane forward.

There are several types of jet engine. One is called the **turbofan**. The Boeing 747, the Lockheed TriStar and the Douglas DC-10 airliners all have turbofan engines.

The four turbofan engines of the Boeing 747 have to be very powerful. With a full load this plane can weigh 370 tonnes. The jumbo flies its 500 passengers through the air at 960 kph.

▼ At the front of a turbofan engine there is a large fan like a propeller. It is made of very many metal blades. They are set close to each other. As this fan spins it sucks in air. Another set of blades packs the air very tight. The air is then mixed with fuel and burned. The very hot gases have to escape. They can only go backwards. They rush out of the engine as a powerful jet. This jet forces the plane forward.

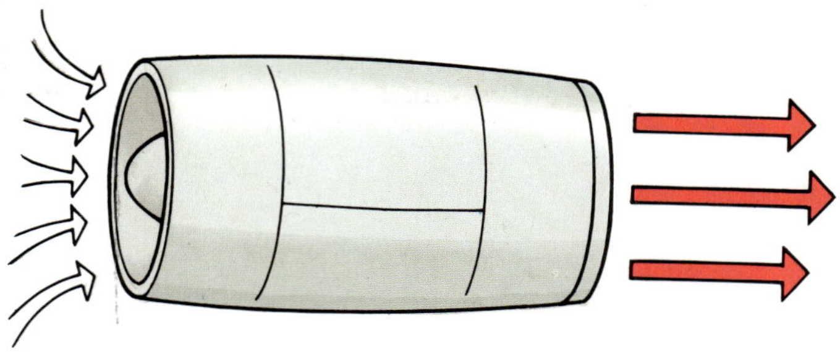

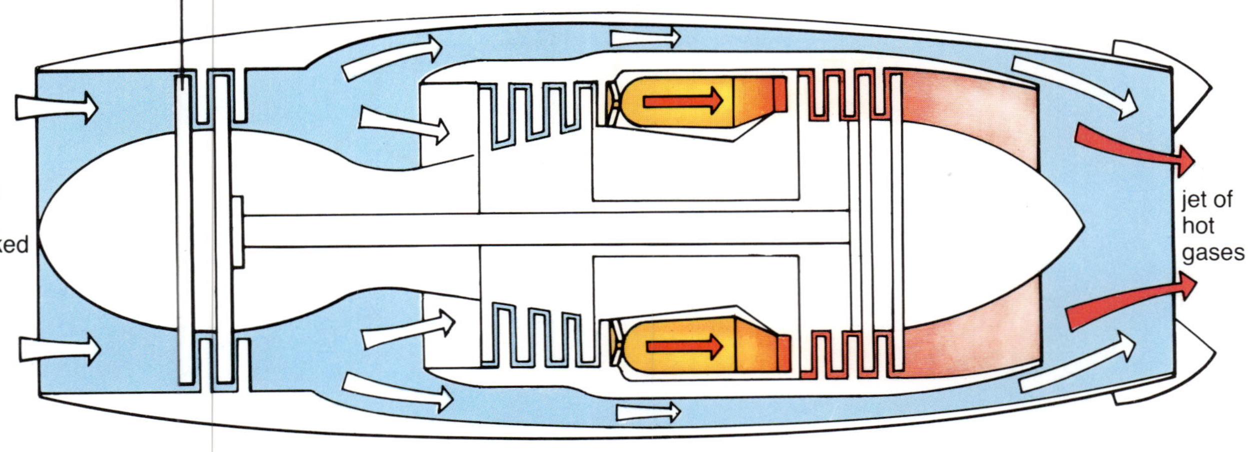

Planes for all purposes

Have you ever been to a small airport where there are very few large planes? Some of these small airfields only have short runways. Sometimes the planes have to take off and land on grass strips.

▼ This plane is a Dassault Falcon 10, made in France. It has two turbofan engines placed near the tail. With these powerful engines it can fly at 915 kph. The Falcon 10 can be used for many purposes.

On a small airfield you often find a great variety of colourful light aircraft. They are used for many different purposes. Some people have their own planes, or share one with friends. There are even air taxis. Then there are club aeroplanes. They are used by people who want to learn to fly.

General purposes

Small jets are often used to carry people from one office to another. Others are used to carry mail and freight. Planes can also be **chartered** for a special journey or visit. These planes are hired, like a taxi or a motor boat. Charter flights often take people to meetings or sporting events.

Special purposes

Some work is easier to do from the air. It could take years to make a map of a forest or a swamp, working on the ground. It is quicker to take photographs from an aeroplane. These photographs sometimes show the faint outlines of buildings that fell down many years ago.

Other special planes are built to help farmers. These are sometimes called 'crop dusters'. They use sprays to kill pests and improve the land. Because of the job they do, these planes have to fly low and slowly.

In the United States planes have been used to spot forest fires since 1919. Special planes have also been built to 'bomb' forest fires with water. They are used to put out fires in Australia and North America. One of these is the Canadair CL-215. It is fitted with floats and wheels. It can take off and land on the ground or on water. Planes like this are called **amphibians**. When a CL-215 goes to fight a fire, it scoops up water from a lake or the sea. It can carry 5000 litres. It bombs the fire with water and goes back to scoop up more. The CL-215 can scoop up its load of water in less than 20 seconds.

A selection of small passenger aircraft

Made by	*Type*	*Country*	*Passengers*	*Speed (kph)*	*Range (km)*
De Havilland	Drover	Australia	8	254	1448
G.A.F.	Nomad	Australia	15	311	1352
De Havilland	Otter	Canada	11	257	1410
Dassault	Falcon 10	France	7	915	3555
Israel Air Industries	Westwind	Israel	10	872	4619
Mitsubishi	MU-2	Japan	9	571	2584
Edgar Percival	EP9	UK	5	235	933
British Aerospace	BAe 125	UK	8	808	4318
Lockheed	Jetstar	USA	10	880	4818
Rockwell	Sabreliner	USA	10	906	3149
Gates Learjet	Learjet 35A	USA	8	859	4234
Beech	Super King Air	USA	13	536	2752
Antonov	AN-2	USSR	14	258	900
Dornier	Skyservant	W. Germany	13	325	1052

Modern airliners

There are airliners for every kind of traveller. Some people from a large company may want to fly in comfort to a meeting. They can use a small jet like the Beech Super King Air. This weighs about 6 tonnes and carries 13 people. It can land on small airstrips.

Wide bodied jets like the Boeing 747 and the Lockheed TriStar have made cheap air travel possible for all of us. The 747 weighs about 370 tonnes with about 500 passengers on board.

Jet airliners have two, three or four engines. The Airbus has two engines. It is a wide bodied jet used mainly for short haul work. It can land and take off on short runways. The Lockheed TriStar has three engines. Two are carried in **pods** under the wing. The third engine is above the tail. The Boeing 747 has four engines.

The distance they travel

The distance that a plane can travel before landing to take on fuel is called its **range**. Some fuel must always be kept in **reserve**. This extra fuel is in case the plane has to change its route, or is slowed by a strong wind. The TriStar is a long range airliner. It can fly 9000 km without a stop. An airliner built in 1930 would have made about 20 stops to take on fuel, over this distance.

▼ The Boeing 747 has an extra large upper deck to carry more passengers. It has four turbofan engines. See how these hang down from the wing in pods.

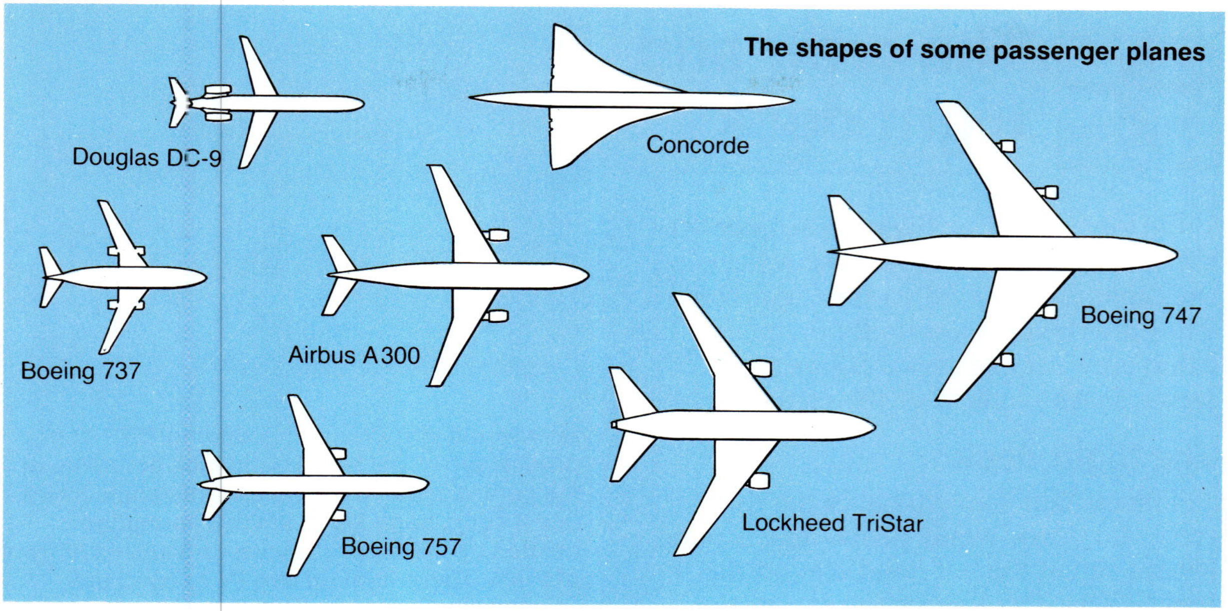

Flaps and spoilers

To take off, an airliner needs as much thrust and lift as possible. When it lands, it needs to increase drag to slow it down. These changes are made mainly by the use of **flaps**.

During take off, the flaps are **extended** from the edges of the wings. This alters the shape of the wings and gives the plane more lift. Once the plane is in the air, the flaps are taken in.

When the plane is about to land the pilot uses flaps. These come down in easy stages. They hang well down from the wing.

Some planes also have **spoilers**. These are extra flaps on the top side of the wings. They lift up during landing and give still more drag. They act as brakes. A large jet touches down at about 250 kph. It has to slow down quickly to stop before the end of the runway.

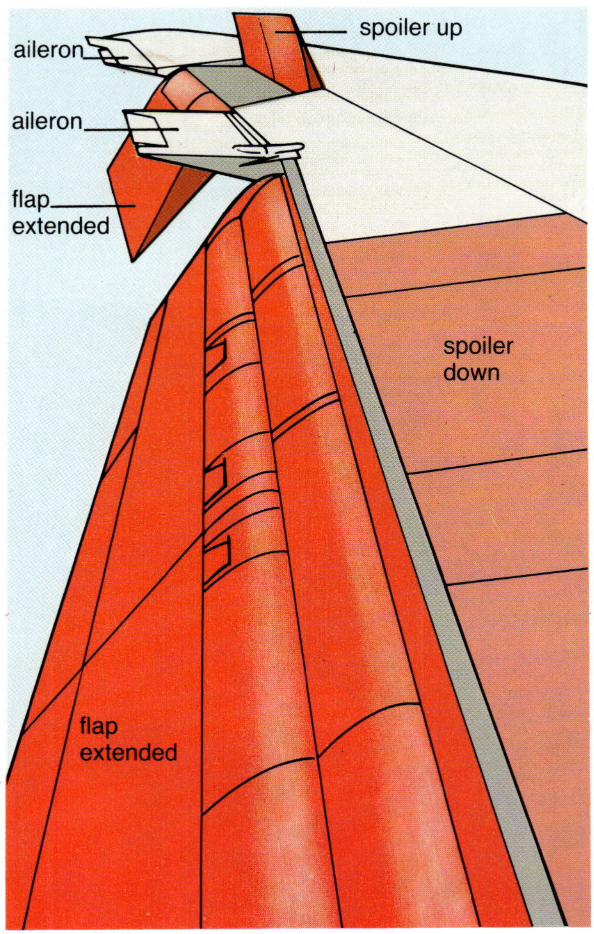

► **On each wing of a plane there are two flaps and two spoilers. The flaps help to give the plane lift. The spoilers rise up and act as air brakes.**

The crew and flight deck

On any passenger flight an airliner carries two kinds of crew. The officers on the flight deck are called the flight crew. They are the people who fly the plane. The cabin crew are the stewardesses and stewards who look after the passengers.

The flight deck

The captain is in charge of the flight crew and of the whole plane. The captain always sits in the left hand seat on the flight deck. The first officer sits in the

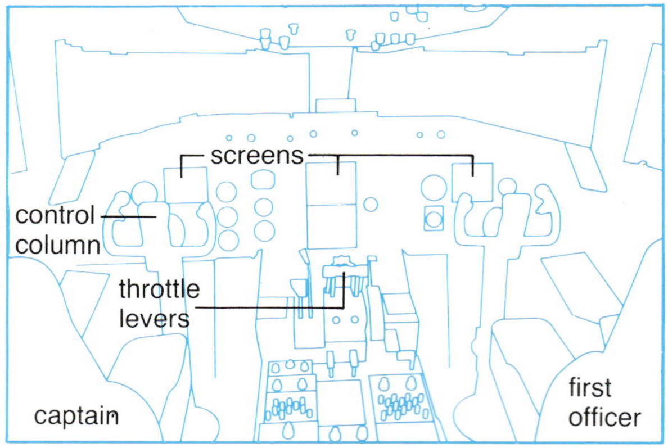

How would you like to fly a Boeing 757? The picture above will help you to pick out some of the controls and instruments. This plane has the latest equipment. Much of the information needed by the crew is shown on screens in front of them. These light up like TV or computer screens.

▲ **The flight engineer sits behind the captain and co-pilot. He has his own set of instruments.**

right hand seat. On large airliners there is also a flight **engineer**, who sits behind the pilot.

The controls and **instruments** are laid out so that either the captain or the first officer can pilot the plane. They do not need to change seats. Dials in front of them show the plane's height, speed and direction. There are two sets of dials. One set can be checked against the other.

In front of each seat is a control column. Between the seats are the engine controls. **Throttle** levers control the power from each engine. Another set of dials shows how each engine is running. The two pilots can easily reach any of the controls they may need to use during the flight.

The flight engineer has another set of intruments. He or she must make sure that the engines are working properly. The captain must be told if too much fuel is being used during the flight.

Training and fitness

Most of the flight crew's work is done for them by instruments and computers. But they must always be ready for an **emergency**. They may have to land in fog. One of the engines might fail. Then the crew must know what to do, and do it fast.

This means that flight crew must be wide awake and fit. There are strict rules that say how long they may fly before taking a rest. They all have regular medical check ups.

Flight crew also have time off for emergency drill. This takes place in a machine called a **simulator**. This has a flight deck which is a copy of a real one. Here the crew can practise dealing with emergencies without using a real plane.

Planning the flight

Every flight is carefully planned. Long before the passengers **check in** at the airport, people are hard at work to make sure that each flight will go well.

The ground staff check that all parts of the plane are working properly. Any faults reported by the last crew to fly the plane are put right. The cabins are cleaned. Food and other supplies for the flight are put on board.

At the flight centre, the **flight plan** is made out. This gives the number of passengers and the weight of freight to be carried. The weight of the fuel is also given. The flight plan says when the flight will leave, and how fast the plane will fly. The route is also worked out. The last item is the flight's ETA – the estimated time of arrival.

Briefing

The flight crew comes **on duty**, which means they start work, about one hour before take off. The captain and crew go to the flight centre. They look at the flight plan and are given the weather report. The captain will need to know what winds are **forecast**. If the plane has to fly against a strong wind, called a **headwind**, the flight may take longer than planned. The plane will use more fuel.

The captain will ask if fog is forecast at the other end of the flight. If it is too foggy to land, is there another airport where the plane can land? Is there enough fuel to get there? The captain may ask for some more fuel to be loaded.

The captain then **briefs** the flight crew. They will be told about the route and any problems they should watch out for.

▼ The captain and his crew report to the flight centre. First they are given the latest weather report. Then they look at the flight plan.

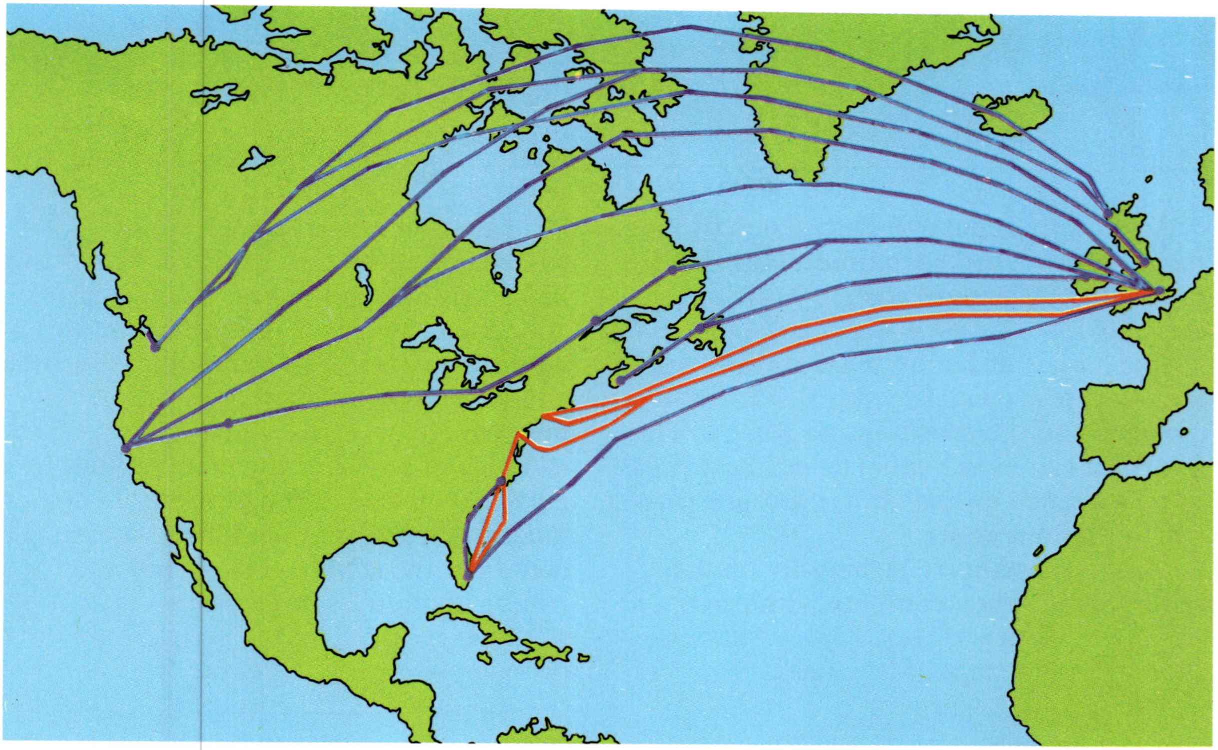

▲ **Planes in flight have to keep well apart. This map of the north Atlantic shows the corridors which planes have to follow. The red lines show the corridors used by supersonic aircraft.**

Pre-flight checks

Then the flight crew goes out to the plane. They begin the pre-flight checks. The passengers are not yet on board. The crew check that all the controls and instruments are working properly. The captain and the first officer do the checks together. They make sure that nothing is missed. The flight engineer checks that the freight has been loaded properly, and that the right amount of fuel is in the tanks.

The captain will also look at the passenger list and the cargo **manifest**. The manifest will say what kind of freight is on board. If there are problems, the flight will be delayed until the captain is certain that things have been put right.

▲ **Before the flight, engineers inspect one of the huge engines. The cover has been raised so that they can see inside.**

Airlines of the world

Airlines fly **regular** flights. They fly on fixed routes. They have **timetables** that list the flights. There are about 500 airlines in the world.

The largest airline in the world is Aeroflot. It is owned by the USSR. Its planes fly all the routes inside Russia. They fly world routes as well. The smallest is Air Fret, a French airline. It has just one plane which flies one route.

Many international airlines fly on the same routes. They **compete** with each other but they have to charge the same price for the same flight. They cannot cut the cost of the ticket to get people to fly on their planes. Instead, they offer better food, or newer films, or more comfortable seats.

The airlines have special ways of painting their planes. They have their own badges or **insignia**. These insignia also appear on the crew's uniforms, and in **advertisements**. You will often see airline advertisements in magazines and newspapers.

You will see 18 of the main airlines listed here. If you look through some old colour magazines, you may find many more. You could cut the advertisements out and collect them in a scrap book.

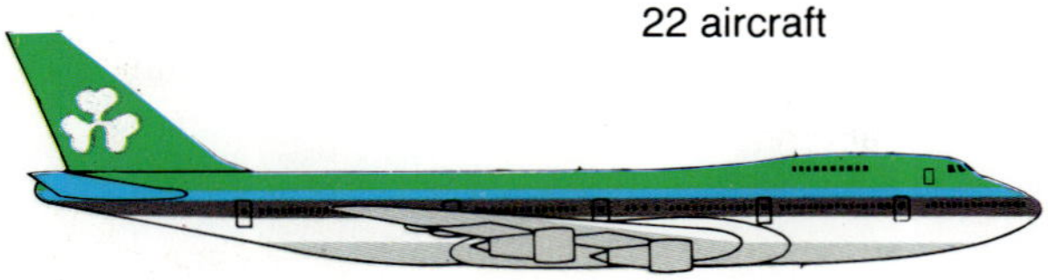

Aer Lingus
Eire
22 aircraft

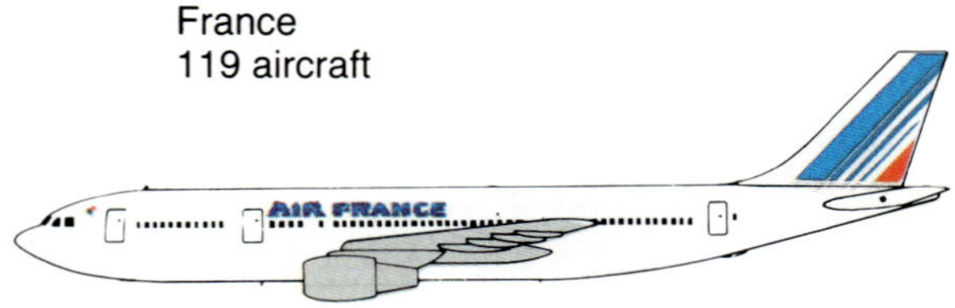

Air France
France
119 aircraft

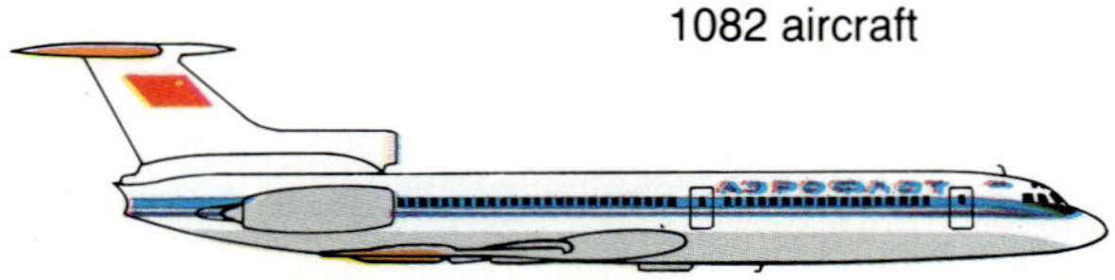

Aeroflot
USSR
1082 aircraft

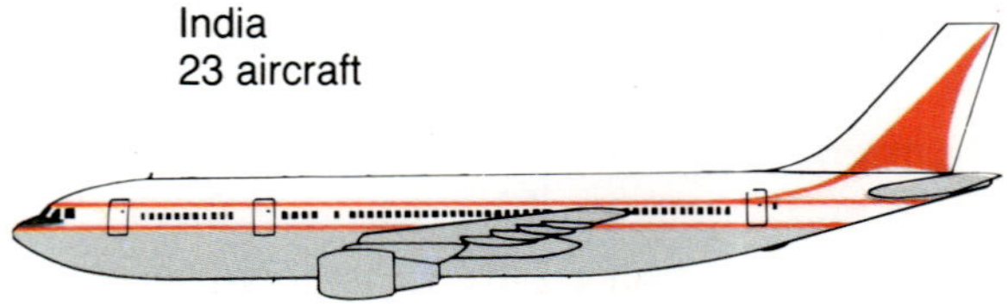

Air India
India
23 aircraft

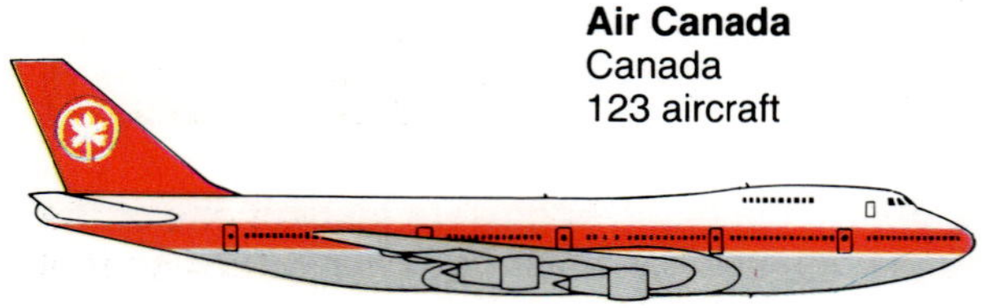

Air Canada
Canada
123 aircraft

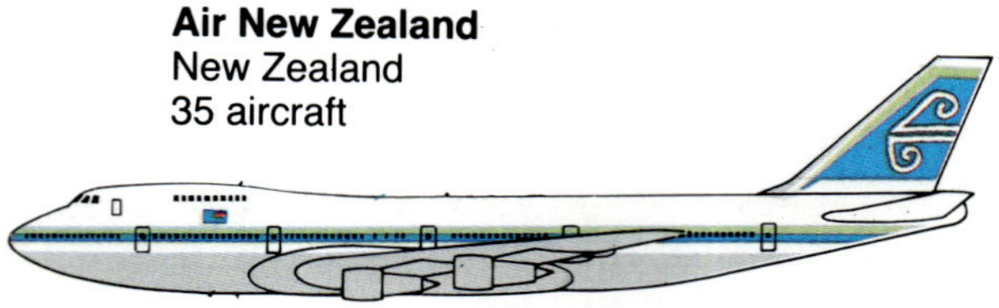

Air New Zealand
New Zealand
35 aircraft

American Airlines
USA
321 aircraft

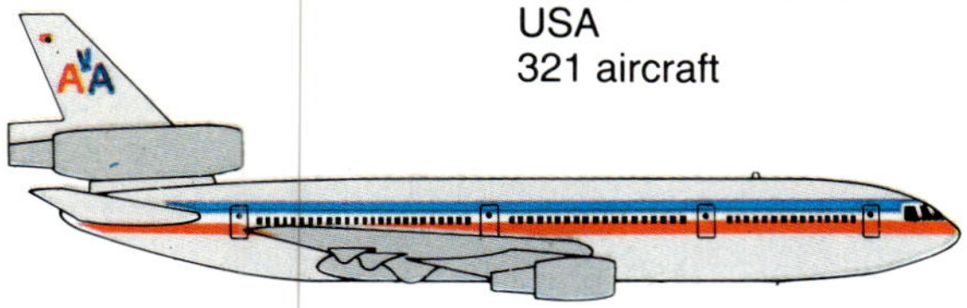

Pan Am
USA
133 aircraft

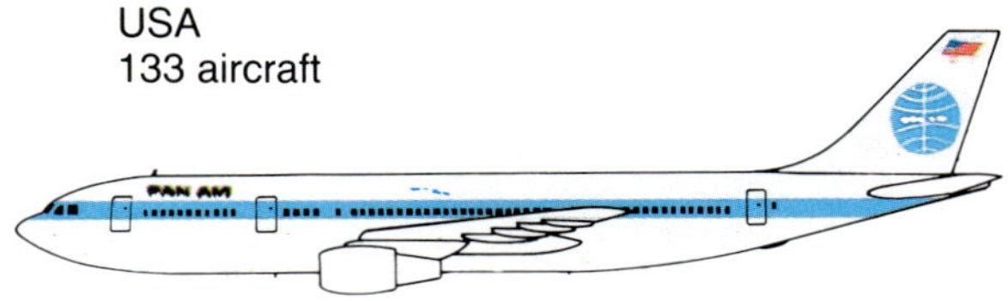

British Airways
United Kingdom
165 aircraft

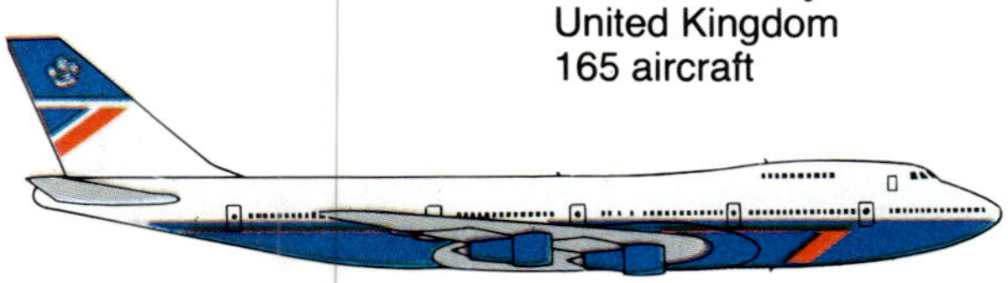

Qantas
Australia
30 aircraft

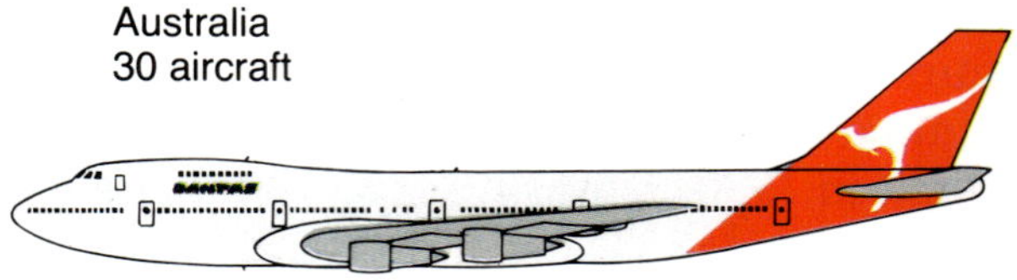

British Caledonian
United Kingdom
27 aircraft

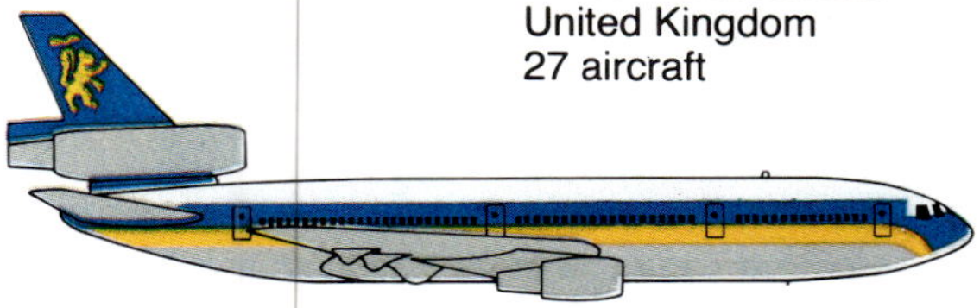

SAS
Sweden/Norway/Denmark
99 aircraft

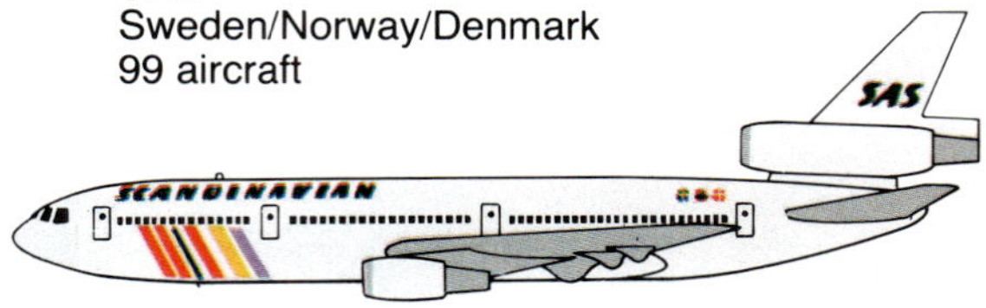

Japan Airlines
Japan
93 aircraft

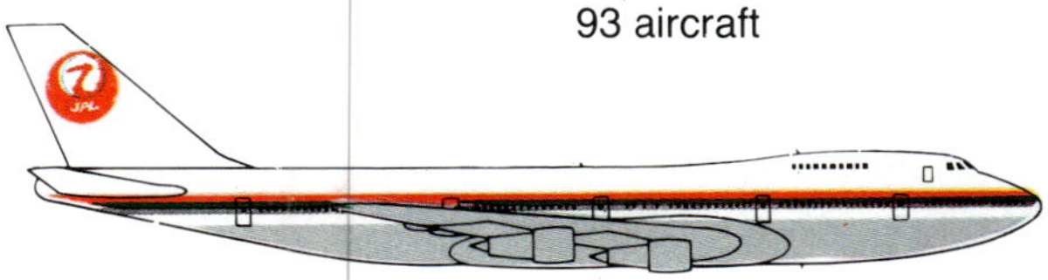

Swissair
Switzerland
57 aircraft

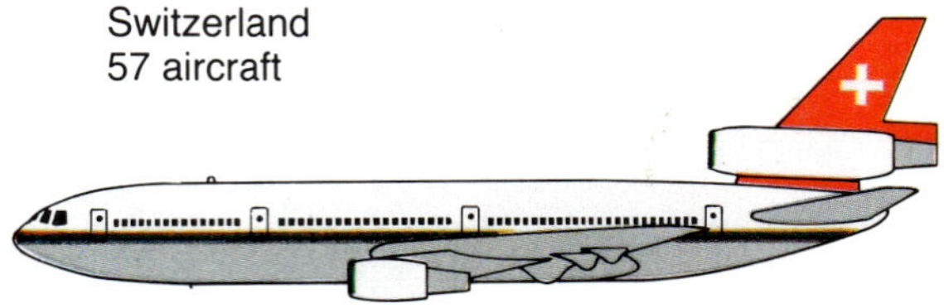

KLM
The Netherlands
55 aircraft

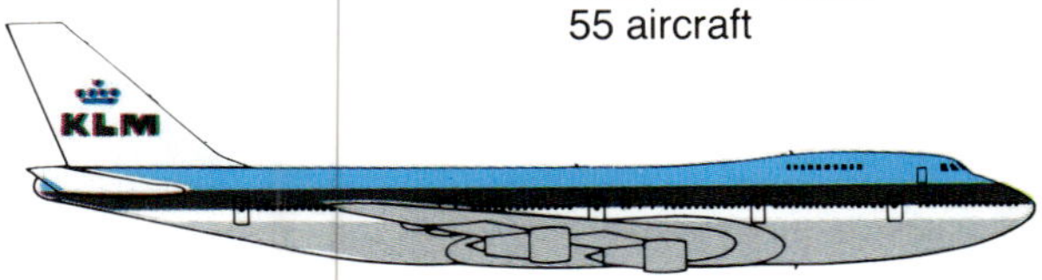

TWA
USA
166 aircraft

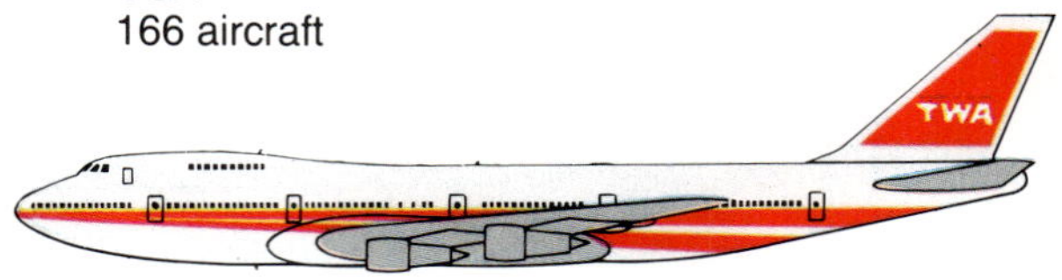

Lufthansa
West Germany
137 aircraft

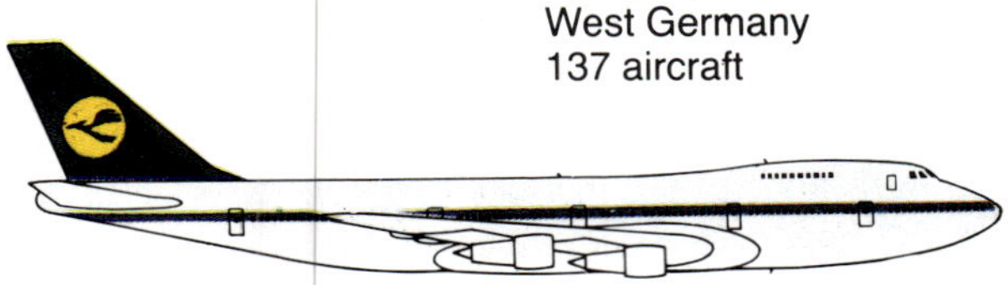

United Airlines
USA
340 aircraft

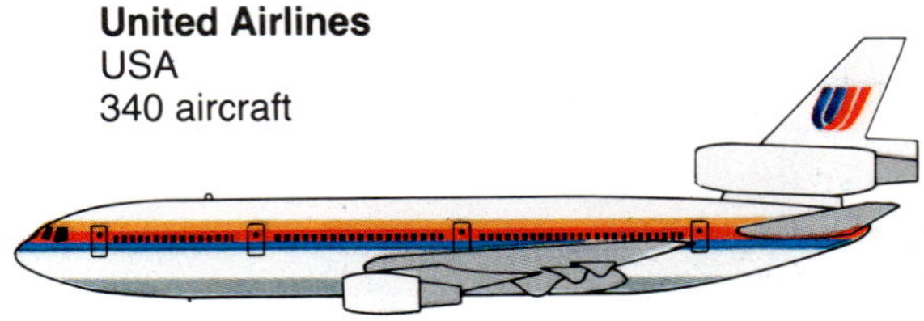

Cabin staff

The job of the cabin staff is to see that passengers have a safe and enjoyable flight. The cabin staff are known as **stewards** and **stewardesses**. The first stewardess was a nurse called Ellen Church. She worked for United Airlines when she made her first flight in 1930. It was from San Francisco to Cheyenne, USA.

Flight duties

One of the cabin staff stands by the door to welcome the passengers aboard. On most flights, people have their own seat

▲ A stewardess welcomes one of the passengers aboard as he steps into the plane. She is wearing the British Caledonian uniform. At some airports passengers board the planes through a covered way. This is a kind of tube connected to the airport building. In this picture the passenger has walked up steps from the ground.

◄ Above the seats there are cupboards to carry light baggage and other items. This British Airways stewardess is helping a passenger to stow his coat and hand baggage. The plane is a Boeing 747.

▲ **During the flight the cabin crew are busy all the time. The Cathay Pacific stewardess is beginning to serve a meal. On a long flight, meals help to pass the time. The boy is playing a board game with his mother.**

numbers on the tickets. Cabin staff show them where to sit. They see that everyone is comfortable, and that hand baggage has been stowed safely.

When all the passengers are in their seats, the cabin staff go through the **safety drill**. They make sure that all passengers put on their seat belts. They point out where the emergency doors are. Before take off, the cabin staff show passengers how to put on a life jacket. There is one under every seat. Life jackets would only be needed if a plane were to crash in water. Above each seat is an **oxygen** mask. This gives extra air if, for some reason, it is needed on the flight.

In flight

Safety is only one part of the cabin staff's job. The other is to look after the passengers during the flight. Light meals are served on most flights. On long flights, the cabin staff will serve two or more full meals. A jumbo jet may have up to 20 cabin staff on board. Looking after about 400 people is hard work.

Some passengers may need special care. If they are old or ill, the cabin staff may have to keep a watchful eye on them. If the flight is bumpy, some people may feel airsick. Babies, too, will need special food. Young children may get bored on a long flight. If so, the cabin staff will try to keep them amused with toys and games.

Training

All cabin staff need to have some **first aid** training. They have to deal with people from different countries. So being able to speak at least one foreign language is useful.

Staff learn their jobs in full size model cabins on the ground. Then they help out on real flights with a senior member watching them. Even the senior staff have more training from time to time to remind them of safety drills.

Being a passenger

Flying can be great fun. But a long flight may seem very slow. The reason for this is quite simple. Most of the time you have to stay in your seat. Sitting still for several hours makes us all want to fidget. Even so, there are plenty of things to do.

▲ At Frankfurt airport in West Germany a Lufthansa flight is about to depart. Passengers are boarding a Boeing 737 through two doors.

Things to do

Once the plane has taken off, you can adjust your seat to make it more comfortable. If you wish, you can stretch out your legs and go to sleep. Near your seat there is a control unit. It has buttons and switches on it. With these you can turn on a reading light – or ring for the cabin staff. You can also plug in a **head-set** and listen to music.

Films are often shown on long flights. The film **sound-track** comes to you on the head-set. This way you do not hear the noise made by the aeroplane engines.

When it is time for a meal you can use a table which unfolds from the seat in front of you. You can use the table when you like or fold it away to give you more room.

Looking out

In a jumbo jet there are more than 150 windows. If you have a window seat you can look out. At night, the lights of towns and cities show up clearly. They twinkle below you. On a clear day the land below is spread out like a map. The plane loses height near the end of the journey. The map gets larger. Soon you start to see signs of life, like trucks and traffic. When you start seeing people the plane is about to land.

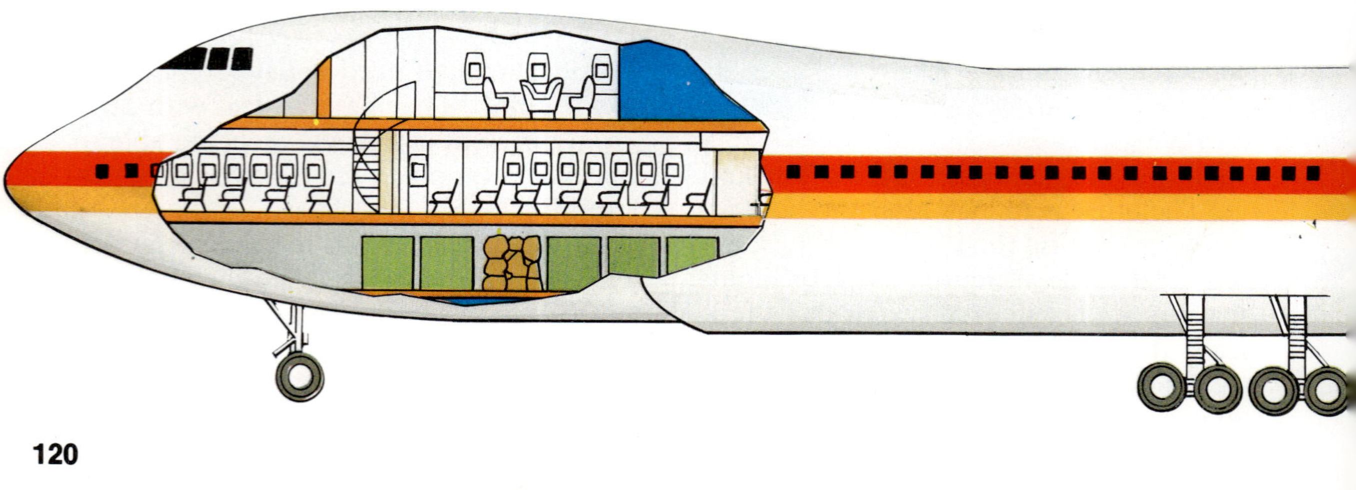

Moving around

The Boeing 747 can carry up to about 500 people. The seats are laid out in rows of ten. In between, there are two **aisles** for walking around. You can take quite a long walk to stretch your legs. When the plane is full it is not so easy. Other people may want to have a walk too.

The cabin of the 747 is very long. It is about 100 metres. Orville Wright's first flight in *Flyer I* was quite a lot less than this. He could have taken off and landed in half the length of a 747.

▲ This is just one of the compartments in a Boeing 747. In each row there are ten seats. There are two aisles between for people to walk around.

▼ The Wright *Flyer I* flew a distance of 40 metres. Compare this with the length of the Boeing 747. How things have changed in less than 100 years!

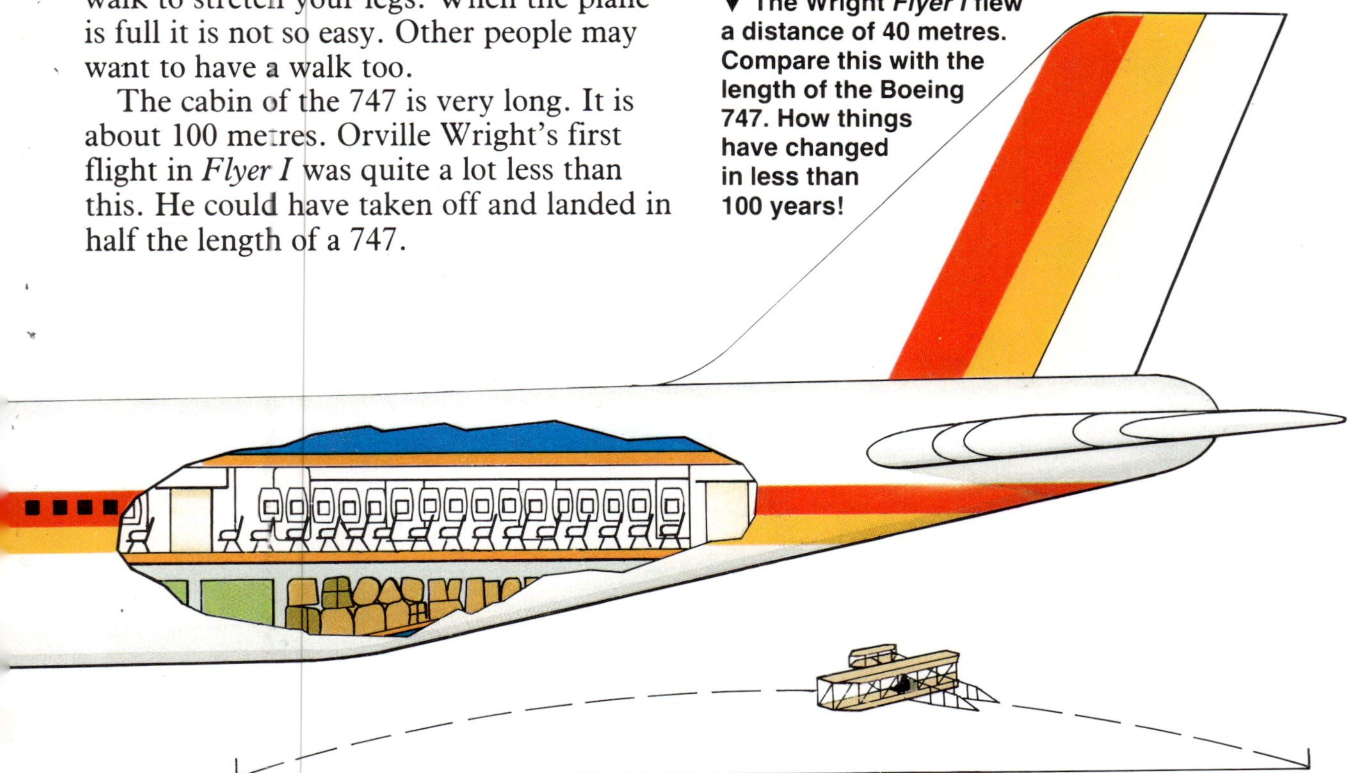

Air cargo

As well as passengers, goods are carried by air. It costs more to send goods by air than by land or sea. But it is far quicker by air.

Goods sent this way are called **air cargo** or **air freight**. Some aeroplanes are used only for cargo, but passenger planes also have cargo **holds**. These are large spaces under the passenger cabin. Sometimes all the seats can be taken out of the cabin. This way there is more room for cargo.

▼ This shows the upper deck of a DC-10. The passenger seats have been removed to carry freight. The floor is fitted with rollers and rails. These make it easier to handle heavy freight. In the small picture you can see pallets on the left. At the other end, a container is being rolled into place.

Loading the cargo

Aeroplanes cost a lot of money. They can only earn money when they are flying. People and cargo must be loaded and unloaded as quickly as possible.

Goods to be sent by air go to the cargo **terminal**. Here there are large **hangars** where the cargo is sorted out for different flights. Goods going to the same place are packed into **containers** or on to **pallets**. Containers are large metal boxes made to fit into the plane's hold neatly. Pallets are flat trays with a net over the top to keep the packages in place.

The cargo is taken out to the plane on trolleys pulled by tractors. Fork lift trucks and lifting platforms are used to lift cargo into the hold. Some planes have rails and rollers in the hold to slide containers into place.

Loading cargo into a plane must be done with great care. Computers are used to make sure that the weight is spread evenly. The cargo must not move about during the flight. Also the plane must not be too tail heavy or nose heavy during the flight. It is too late to find this out when the plane is in the air.

All kinds of cargo

Many different things can be carried by air. Road vehicles or even light aircraft can be carried. A large number of zoo animals are flown about the world. They travel in holds fitted with cages. Racehorses, too, are often carried by air.

The strangest load of all was the space shuttle *Enterprise*. In 1977, a Boeing 747 was used to carry the shuttle 'piggy-back'. The shuttle was then launched in mid-air. This way the scientists could find out how well it would glide back to Earth and land.

◀ The nose of this Boeing 747 freighter lifts up for loading. Containers are moved on rollers to the rear of the cargo hold.

▼ For its first test flight the space shuttle was carried into the air by a Boeing 747. It was launched from a height of 7350 metres.

Safety on the ground

An airport is an exciting place. It has to keep going night and day, every day of the year. Hundreds of flights arrive and depart in one day. Millions of people pass through one airport in one year. Safety on the ground is just as important as safety in the air.

Ground staff

Hundreds of people work on the ground at an airport. Many are there to keep flying safe. Before you board your flight you will meet some of them.

There are strict rules about what you may take on a flight. **Security** staff see that the rules are kept. That is why your hand baggage may be checked by **scanners** before you board your plane. If a buzzer sounds it will be searched. You may also have to pass through a special gateway. If you have anything metal in your pockets, an alarm will sound. You will have to show the staff what you are carrying.

While you wait for your flight, engineers will be checking the plane. They will put right any fault that has been reported by the last crew to fly the plane. If there is anything wrong, the plane will not be allowed to fly. This may cause a delay, but safety is the first rule.

The runways

Ground staff have to check the runways all the time. They look for weak spots and loose objects. These could be dangerous for planes landing and taking off. At some airports birds have to be scared away. They could damage planes taking off and landing.

▼ A passenger passes through the security gate (on the left). If someone is carrying a metal object a buzzer will sound. Baggage is scanned separately (on the right).

▲ A ground engineer checks the nosewheel of a Boeing 747. Landing wheels are fitted in pairs. This reduces the danger if one tyre bursts.

Snow and ice

Snow and ice cause problems at airports. The lightest fall of snow or hail can make a runway dangerous to use. Teams of people work all the time to keep runways clear of snow. They use special trucks to brush or blow the snow away.

Emergency services

Airports have their own police, fire and ambulance services. Teams of firefighters are on standby night and day. The fire engines can go very fast. They can reach a fire in seconds. The fire engines carry foam and powder to put out fires quickly.

▼ Runways must be kept clear at all times. Here you can see ground staff at work with snow ploughs.

Prepare for take off

You can tell when your flight is about to begin. The cabin staff will close the aeroplane's doors. Then one of the staff will go to the front of the cabin and show how the life jackets work. They will point out the emergency doors. They are often coloured red.

There is a warning light to tell you when to fasten your seat belt. It will come on before the plane has started to **taxi** out to the runway. You must keep your belt fastened all the time the light is on.

Up front on the flight deck, the crew will be checking their instruments. There are warning lights and buzzers to tell them if anything is wrong. The captain is in touch with the **control tower** by radio. The crew must not start the engines until the tower gives permission.

▲ From the control tower the controllers can see in all directions. They can speak to every plane by radio.

▼ This DC-10 is ready for take off. It is being pushed out by a powerful tug. Some tugs, like this one, have a driving cab at both ends.

Now you can hear the whine of the engines. One by one they are started up. Tractors are sometimes used to tow planes out of the parking bay. The plane may be towed backwards.

▲ **At Atlanta Airport, Georgia, USA, there is a constant stream of air traffic. The line of planes will have to taxi a long way to reach the head of the runway. Even then, there is more waiting. Each plane has to take its turn. One by one they are cleared by the tower for take off.**

Taxiing

Special wide roads called **taxiways** are used to take planes to the runways. This can take quite a long time. The plane bumps up and down as it rumbles out. Planes are made to fly in the air, not to roll along the ground.

From where you are sitting you may be able to see the wings. Do not worry if they shake up and down. They are made to bend a bit like the wings of a bird. It may be raining outside. A high wind may be blowing. But an aeroplane can take off in almost any weather.

Lining up

At the end of the runway, the plane may have to hold in line for its turn to take off. The captain waits for his orders from the tower. When your flight is cleared for take off, the captain lines up the plane with the centre of the runway.

So far, the engines will have been fairly quiet. Now the crew run up the engines to full power. The noise may surprise you. But sit back in your seat and relax. You are ready for take off.

Taking off

The engines are at full power, but so far the plane is not moving. The captain is holding it on the brakes. Then as the brakes are released the plane rolls forward. It gathers speed very quickly. The captain's eyes are on the centre line of the runway. The first officer watches the instruments and calls out the speed to the captain.

If an engine should fail on take off the captain knows what to do. Up to a certain speed called V1 (*vee one*), the plane can be stopped before the end of the runway. Beyond V1, the plane can still take off, even with one engine out of action. Runways are long enough to give the captain time to make a safe choice.

Take off

At take off speed the captain eases back the control column. This brings the **nose wheel** off the ground. A few seconds later the plane lifts off.

▼ The flight is cleared for take off. With the brakes on, the engines are opened up to full power. Then the brakes are released and the take off begins.

You can feel and see the plane climbing. The cabin slopes up towards the front. As soon as the climb begins, the wheels are taken in. You will hear a rumble as this happens. This is followed by a clunk, as the landing wheel doors close.

You will notice other things as well. If you can see the wings from where you are sitting, you can watch the movement of the flaps. You may find that your ears go 'pop' as the plane climbs. This is caused by the change in air pressure. Sucking a sweet or swallowing will help.

Take off is very noisy. The engines are at full power. Some planes can be heard taking off from a great distance. Soon after take off power has to be cut back. Too much noise would annoy people who live beneath the flight path.

In bad weather, the plane may have to climb through storms until it is above the clouds. As it climbs, the plane may bump and swing. This is due to **turbulence**. Once this turbulence has stopped, the seat belt warning light is switched off. This is to tell you that you can unfasten your seat belt. Now you are really on your way.

▲ This Boeing 747 is shown at the very moment of take off. First the nose is raised and the nosewheel leaves the ground. Then the other 16 wheels leave the ground and the plane is flying.

▼ Look through the window after take off. You can see the wing of the plane. You may see the airport below as the plane turns on to its course.

Above the clouds

During the early part of the flight, the plane goes on climbing. Jets fly at between 6 and 12 km above the Earth. There are two reasons for this. One is that flying 'above the weather' is smoother. The other is that flying high saves fuel. Less thrust is needed to push the plane through the thinner air.

The air inside

Above 4 km, the air is too thin for easy breathing. It is freezing cold, too, colder than at the North Pole. The plane has to make its own **climate** so that people inside the cabin are comfortable.

The cabin is **pressurized**. Air is compressed and pumped into the cabin. This makes the air inside the plane like it is on the ground. Should the pressure system fail you would have to put on your oxygen mask. This rarely happens.

▼ This Boeing 747 is climbing above the clouds.

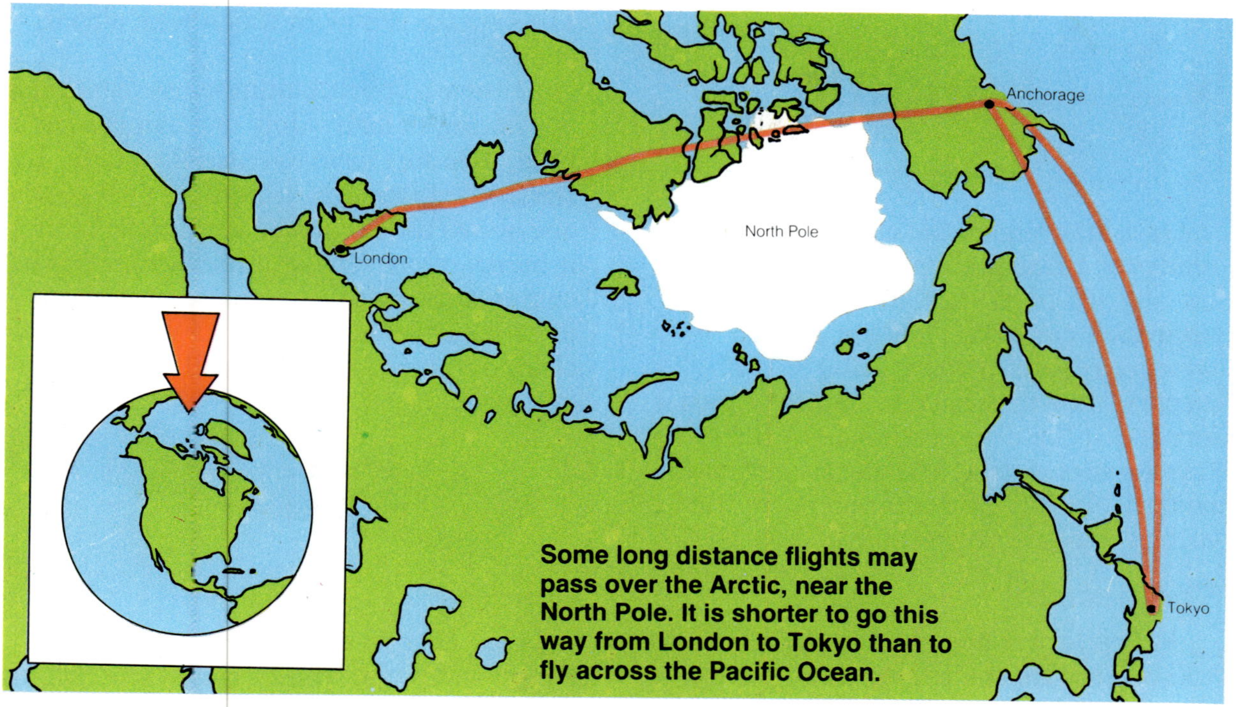

Some long distance flights may pass over the Arctic, near the North Pole. It is shorter to go this way from London to Tokyo than to fly across the Pacific Ocean.

Finding the way

Before take off, the crew knows exactly which route to follow between one airport and the next. There are no road signs in the sky! Instead, there are radio beams. Along the route from one airport to another there are radio stations on the ground. Each one sends out its own strong radio signal. On their **radar** screens the controllers see every plane as a 'blip' of light. A radar set sends out a beam in all directions. This beam bounces back off solid objects like planes. Even a flock of birds may show up on the screen.

When they see the 'blip', the controllers know which plane it is. They can tell which airline it belongs to and where it is going to. Each plane has its own code. This shows up on the screen.

The plane too keeps in touch with each of the radio stations along the route. This way the crew know exactly where they are. Computers are used to make it easy for planes to stay on the flight path.

▲ As the controller watches the screen in front of him he can see the movement of every plane in his area.

Keeping the air safe

Air traffic controllers on the ground are the traffic police of the sky. They tell captains how high and how fast to fly. The controllers make sure that all planes are a safe distance from each other. Planes flying in opposite directions fly at different heights to avoid crashing into each other.

Landing

On a long flight, the crew starts to get ready for landing about 160 km out from the airport. Now they are in touch with **approach control**. They are given a weather report. If there is fog at the airport, they may have to **divert** to another airport. If the cloud is very low, the captain may decide to make an **automatic** landing. In this case computers are used to bring the plane down safely.

The descent

At first, the descent is very gradual. You will notice that the engines are quieter. Some way out from the airport, the final descent begins. The seat belt lights go on. The plane loses height quite quickly.

The captain is now in touch with airport control.

At busy airports a number of planes may be waiting to land. Only one can land at a time. The rest have to enter the **stack**. In a stack, the planes fly around an oval course, one above the other. As your plane circles it **banks** often. You will notice changes in engine noise as this happens. Each plane joins the stack at the top. As your plane is cleared to land, the others all move down one place.

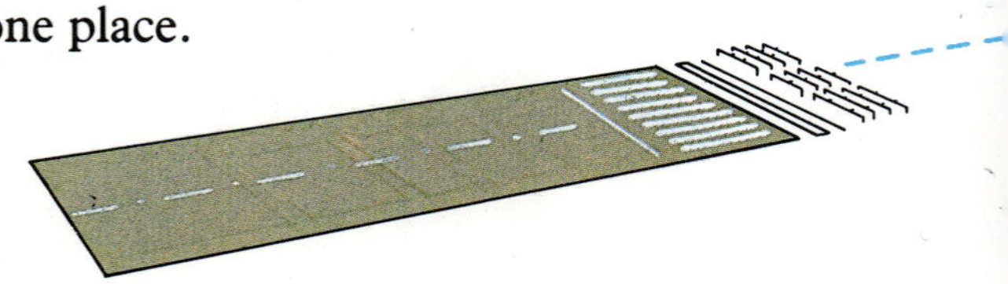

Landing

In the final approach, the captain lines the plane up with the runway. The landing wheels come down with a clunk. The flaps come out further. The captain aims for the markers at the near end of the runway. Between the plane and the runway are other sets of markers. The captain knows how high the plane should be as it passes over each set.

▼ This plane is just about to land, controlled by the automatic pilot. The captain does not need to touch the controls.

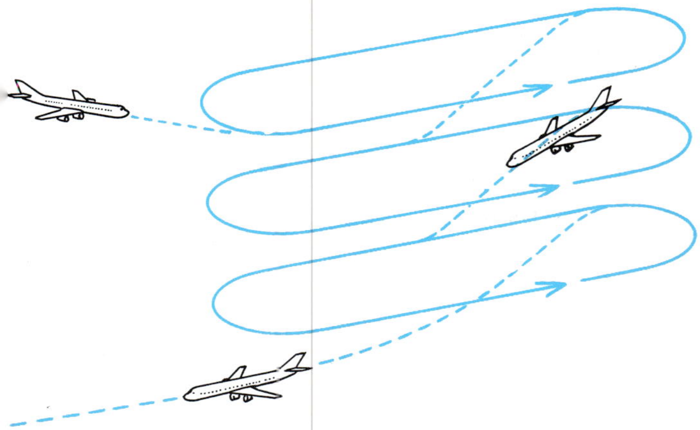

▲ **When a plane joins the stack at the top, it flies around on an oval course. The planes move down one place each time the bottom plane goes in to land.**

▲ **The flarepath lights help the pilot to land, even in daytime. They can be seen through thin cloud. The nearest lights in the picture are the approach lights. They are like car fog lamps. They point towards the planes as they come in to land. This helps the pilots to fly down the centre line of the runway.**

Just before touching down, the plane's nose is lifted slightly. The power is cut back. The flaps are now fully out. You can feel a bump and a rumble as the plane touches down. Then there is a roar as the engines go into **reverse thrust**. This helps to slow the plane down. You may feel the wheel brakes going on and off as the plane slows to a halt.

The plane then taxis slowly to the terminal. You have to keep your seat belt on until the plane has stopped and the engines die down. Then it is all bustle in the cabin. The passengers collect their things and fill the aisles. They line up to leave the plane. The doors are opened and the flight is over.

▼ **Steering a large plane on the ground is tricky. Marshallers make signs with bats or lights to help the pilot steer.**

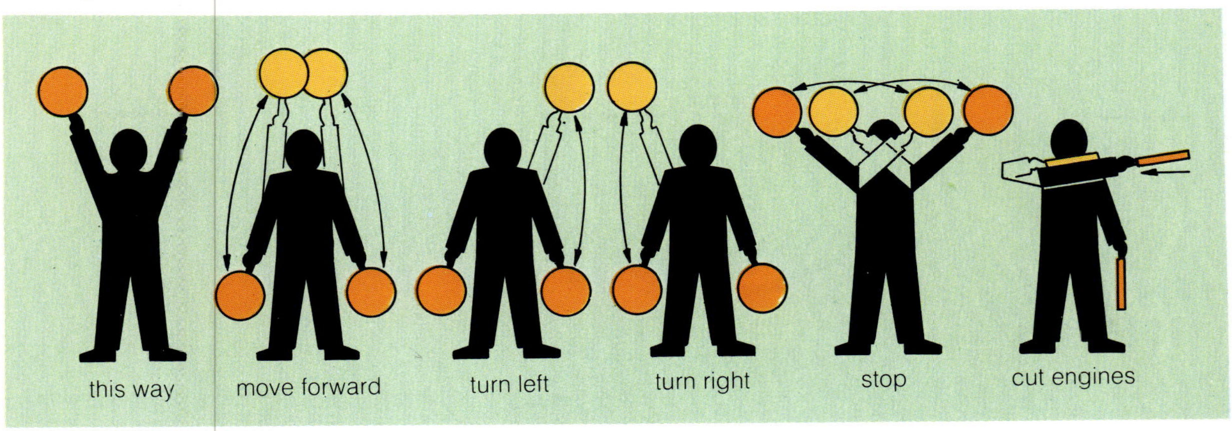

Supersonic flight

When a plane is flying it squashes the air around it. The air waves that it makes spread out in all directions. They are like the waves from a stone thrown into a pool.

But if the plane flies at the speed of sound something strange happens. The air waves cannot spread out fast enough. They build up into a **barrier** – a wall of air. It is known as the sound barrier. Ordinary planes cannot stand the shock of this. They would break up or go into a spin.

The speed of sound is about 1200 kph at sea level. Higher up the speed of sound becomes less. Planes built to fly faster than sound are called **supersonic**. The speed of sound at any height is known as **Mach** 1 (*Mac one*).

Planes that fly faster than the speed of sound have a special shape. The nose must be pointed and the wings tapered. That is why Concorde is shaped like a paper dart.

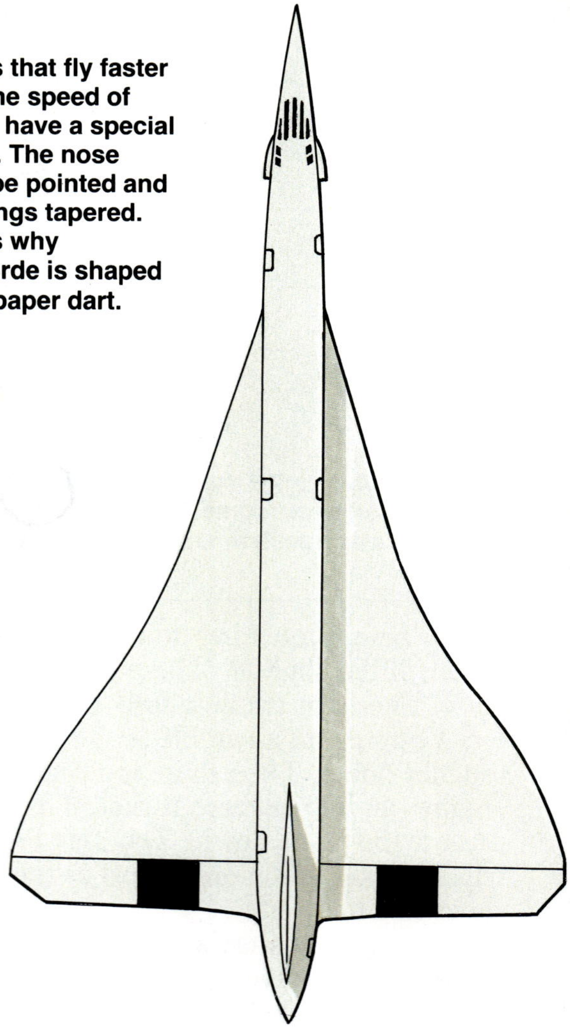

▼ When a plane flies faster than the speed of sound it squashes the air in front of it. This makes a shock wave. At the same time a loud noise like thunder is heard on the ground below.

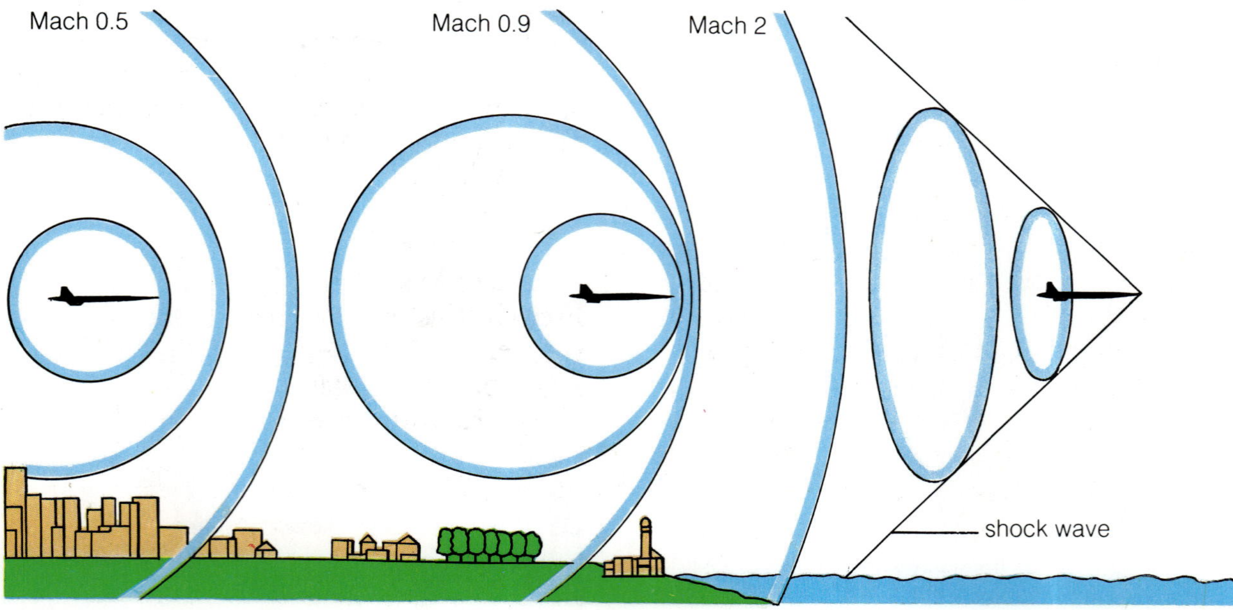

▲ The nose of Concorde is slightly lowered for take off. It comes back gently as the plane starts climbing. The nose is dropped down even more for landing. This helps the captain to see the runway.

Concorde

The first supersonic airliner was the Concorde. It went into service in 1976. Concorde is designed to fly through Mach 1 without harm. Its wings are **tapered**. They are swept back to pass through the barrier easily. Also, the nose is pointed for the same reason. It can be moved up or down. When it is down the captain has a better view of the runway. Concorde flies about 16 km above the Earth. Its speed is more than 2100 kph.

At one time people thought that supersonic flight would be the air travel of the future. No one thinks that now. When a plane breaks through Mach 1, the shock wave makes a loud boom that can be heard below on Earth. The noise can be loud enough to break glass. It can damage buildings and frighten people. So planes can only fly at supersonic speeds over the sea.

That is not the only problem. Very powerful engines are needed to reach these high speeds. They burn a huge amount of fuel. But Concorde can only carry 128 people. This makes it very costly.

The future

Concorde was built by the British and French. Russia also built a supersonic airliner, the TU-144. It is not likely that any more will be built.

An ordinary airliner can cross the Atlantic in five or six hours. Concorde takes three or four. Those who fly on Concorde have to pay much more money for their flight. Most people choose to pay less and take an hour or so longer.

Looking ahead

What kinds of planes will we travel in 20 years from now? Some will be much the same as those of today. The Boeing 747 may still be in use. But there will be some new planes. What will they look like?

For one thing, they will probably be no bigger. Anything much heavier would damage the runways. Aeroplanes will certainly be quieter, for the sake of those who live near airports.

New fuels

Airliners of the future will have to use less fuel. In the years ahead they may burn a different kind of fuel. The world's supply of oil is running short. The search is on to find other types of fuel for planes to use.

The Lockheed company has **adapted** a TriStar to use the gas **hydrogen**. It is loaded and carried as a liquid. In flight it is changed into a gas.

After the year 2000 people may want the excitement and speed of supersonic flight. If they do, then these designs by artists may well be the shape of things to come. The plane above would use hydrogen as a fuel. The design below is for a different kind of plane altogether. It could fly above the Earth on the edge of space. There it might reach a speed of Mach 30.

New shapes

Aeroplanes need large wings to give lift for take off. At cruising height less lift is needed. 'Swing Wing' planes can fold their wings back once they are in the air. This makes them go faster and use less fuel. The wings swing forward again for landing.

Boeing designed a 'Swing Wing' airliner some years ago. It was planned to fly 6500 km at 2900 kph. This plane would carry 350 passengers. However, it was going to cost too much to build. Because of this, Boeing had to give up the idea. It seems that the shape of aeroplane wings may stay the same for many years to come.

▼ This plane is also an artist's design for the future. It would be able to fly from Los Angeles to Tokyo in 2 hours 18 minutes.

New airports

Many short haul aeroplanes may use a new kind of airport, called a STOLport. STOL stands for 'Short Take Off and Landing'. Planes using STOLports will have to be able to climb or descend very quickly. The runways will be short. STOLports could be built in the middle of cities instead of outside them. This would save the passengers a lot of time. Today, people often take longer to get to an airport than they spend in the air.

The future of air travel depends upon what people want. The men and women who design and build aeroplanes will come up with new ideas. We can be sure of one thing. People who travel by air in the years to come will be given what they want.

SPACE TRAVEL

John Mason

Introduction

What would it be like to be fired like a bullet from a huge gun? That is how the French writer Jules Verne thought that people would first go into space. In his book *From the Earth to the Moon*, written in 1865, Jules Verne was writing about the future. In his story a huge gun was pointed up to the sky. From this gun, three space travellers were blasted away from the Earth at vast speed. They sped to the Moon in a **spacecraft** shaped like a cone. When they came back to the Earth from the Moon they splashed down in the sea. They were picked up quite unharmed.

Space travel now

A little over 100 years later, the Jules Verne story came true. On 21 July 1969, the first people landed on the Moon's rocky surface. They were **launched** from Florida, USA, just as Verne had said in his book. When they returned to the Earth, the **astronauts** splashed down safely in the sea.

In the last 25 years, people have started to travel in space. In the next 100 years there may be colonies in space. People from the Earth may live and work on space stations. Spacecraft launched from the Earth would take people and supplies to the space station. The spacecraft would then return to the Earth.

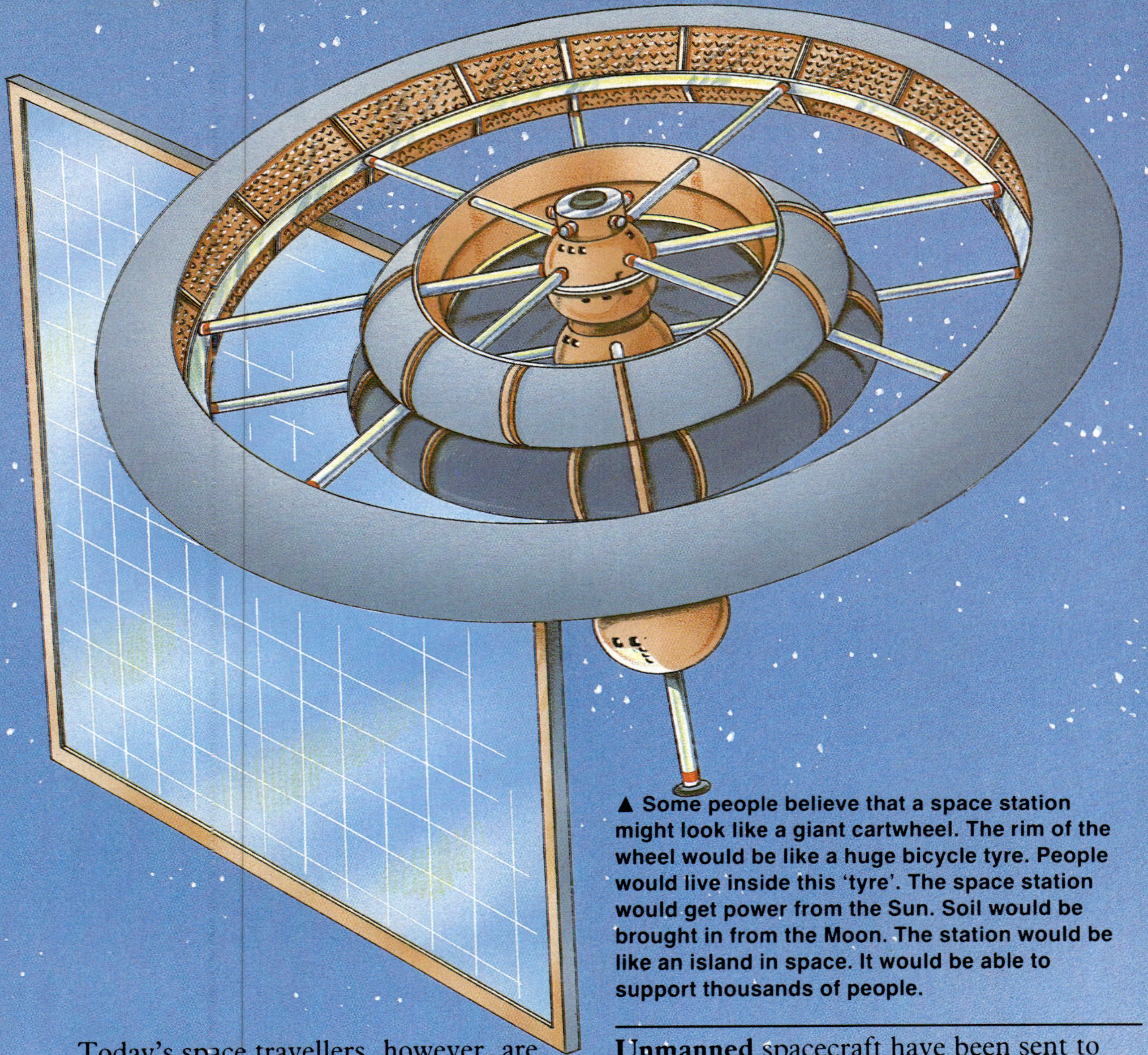

▲ **Some people believe that a space station might look like a giant cartwheel. The rim of the wheel would be like a huge bicycle tyre. People would live inside this 'tyre'. The space station would get power from the Sun. Soil would be brought in from the Moon. The station would be like an island in space. It would be able to support thousands of people.**

Today's space travellers, however, are not fired from a gun. The sudden jolt of the gun firing would kill them. Spacecraft are launched from the Earth by **rockets**. When it is fired, a rocket starts slowly. Bit by bit, it gains speed. As it rises into the air, it goes faster and faster. Soon it leaves the Earth altogether. It heads off into outer space. Space travel is no longer a dream or a story. It is now a reality.

The future

In just 25 years space travel has made great progress. The first **manned** flights into space led to landings on the Moon. **Unmanned** spacecraft have been sent to **probe** the depths of outer space, far beyond our Moon. These **robot** spacecraft have travelled vast distances.

What does the future hold for space travel? The next step will be to build a manned station in space. It may look like the one shown here. From space stations, rockets will be sent to worlds far beyond the Earth. People will search for things we need on Earth, such as metals and **fuels**.

Maybe, in the distant future, people will go out from the Earth to set up **colonies** in space. They may have to do this if the Earth becomes too crowded.

The Earth and space

The Earth is covered by a blanket of air. This is called the **atmosphere**. You cannot see the air, but you can feel it. If you move your hand quickly to and fro you can feel the air.

All the air in the atmosphere presses down upon you. This is called **air pressure**. The greatest pressure is at ground level. If you travel up through the atmosphere in a balloon, things change. The higher up you go, the lower the air pressure becomes. As you get higher, the air gets thinner and it becomes more difficult to breathe. There is no air at all when you reach empty space.

The air we breathe is made up of a number of different gases. Together, these gases make up the Earth's atmosphere. The most important of these gases is oxygen. All animals and plants need oxygen to stay alive. The air gets thinner and there is less oxygen as we climb away from the Earth. Fifty kilometres above the Earth, the atmosphere gradually disappears altogether.

Beyond the atmosphere

In space, there is no air of any kind. We call this a **vacuum**, which means empty. Whenever a spacecraft comes back to Earth from space it has to **re-enter** the atmosphere. The spacecraft does this at very great speed. It gets very hot as it rubs against the air. The spacecraft has to be protected by a **heat shield**. Without this it would soon burn up.

There are tiny bits of dust in space. Some of these enter the Earth's atmosphere. They are very quickly burnt up. As the bits of dust burn, we can see them briefly as streaks of light in the night sky. They are called **meteors**, or shooting stars.

The pull of the Earth

If you throw a ball up into the air, it will reach a certain height. Then it will fall down again. Throw the ball up faster and it will go a bit higher. Things fall to Earth because they are pulled by the **force of gravity**. This force keeps our feet on the ground. The Earth, the Sun, the Moon and the stars all have their own gravity.

Leaving the Earth

If you could throw a ball into the air at a speed of 40 000 kph, it would never fall down to Earth again. The Earth's gravity would not be strong enough to pull it back. The ball would escape into space. The speed of 40 000 kph is called the Earth's **escape velocity**.

The air is made up of millions of tiny parts all moving around at high speed. They are not moving fast enough to escape from the Earth's gravity, so the Earth keeps its atmosphere.

▼ When you throw a ball into the air, it comes down again some distance away. If you throw it harder, it goes higher and lands further away from you. If you could throw the ball at 40 000 kph, it would escape into space.

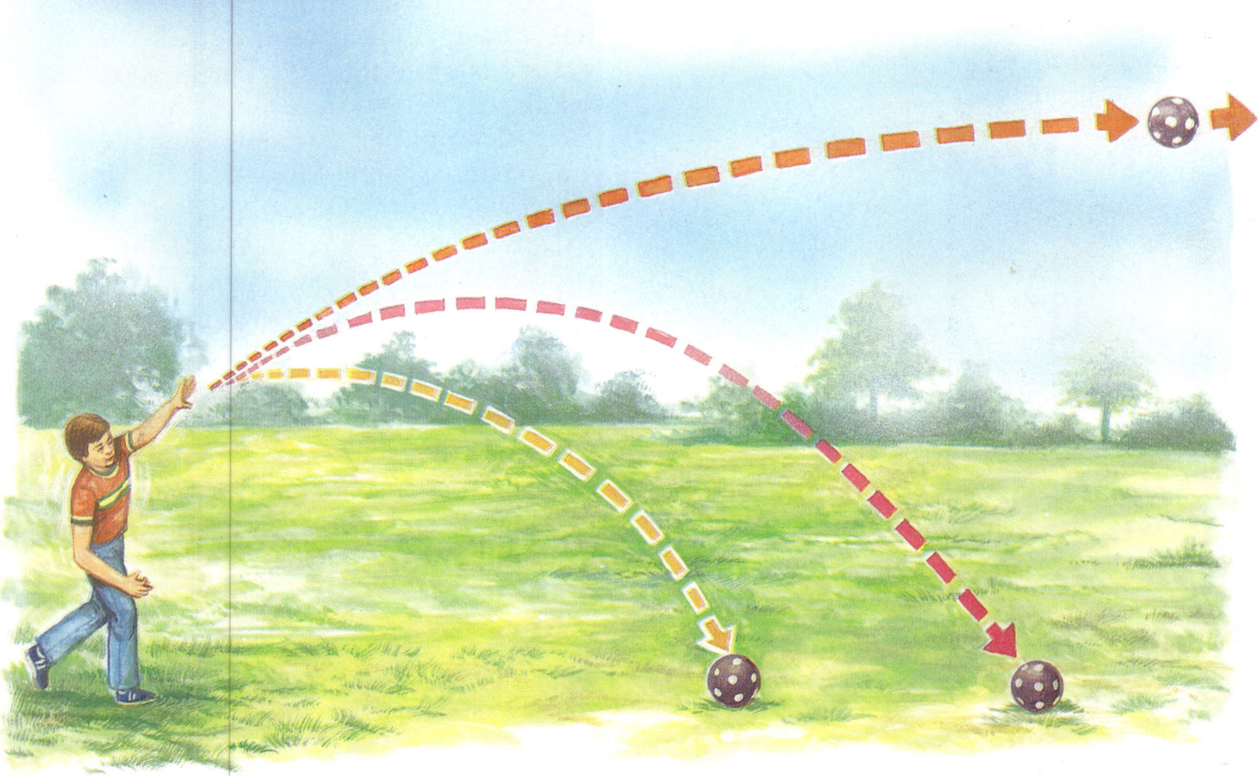

Using rockets

A spacecraft has to travel upwards at 40 000 kph to escape into space. A spacecraft has to start slowly, and build up speed until escape velocity is reached.

Balloons and aircraft only work when they are surrounded by air. They need air to support them, and to give them **lift**. Aeroplane engines also need air to make them work. Planes would not work in space, where there is no air. A Russian teacher, Konstantin Tsiolkovskii (*see-ol-kof-skee*), thought about the kind of power which a spacecraft would need to escape from Earth. In 1895, he found the right answer, which was to use rockets. Tsiolkovskii did not build a rocket. It was not until 1926 that an American, Robert Goddard, launched the first successful rockets.

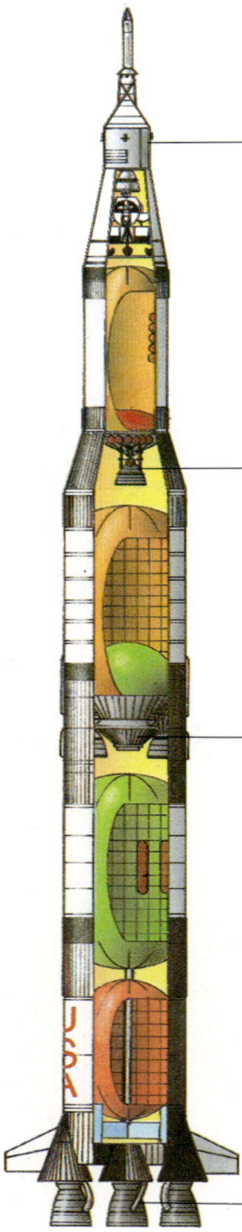

How rockets work

Think of a firework rocket and how it works. It is a hollow tube filled with **gunpowder**. The tube is closed at one end. The gunpowder is lit at the other end of the rocket. It burns very quickly and makes a large amount of hot gas. The gas rushes out through the open end of the rocket. What happens? The action of the gas going one way thrusts the nose of the rocket the other way. This is called a **reaction**.

The gunpowder is the firework rocket's fuel. This gives the power to make the rocket rush into the sky. The gunpowder soon burns out, so the rocket falls back to Earth. It would be no good using gunpowder as a fuel for a space rocket. Gunpowder burns far too quickly.

Liquid fuels are used instead. They have names like kerosene, hydrazine, hydrogen and oxygen. Two of these liquids are carried in separate tanks. The two liquids are pumped through different pipes to meet each other. When they mix, they react violently. Hot gases come rushing out. The rocket soars into space. Liquid fuels can go on being used for much longer than gunpowder. They give much more **thrust**.

◄ Saturn V was the most powerful rocket ever built. It was 111 m in height. The Apollo spacecraft which Saturn V had to launch was only three metres in height.

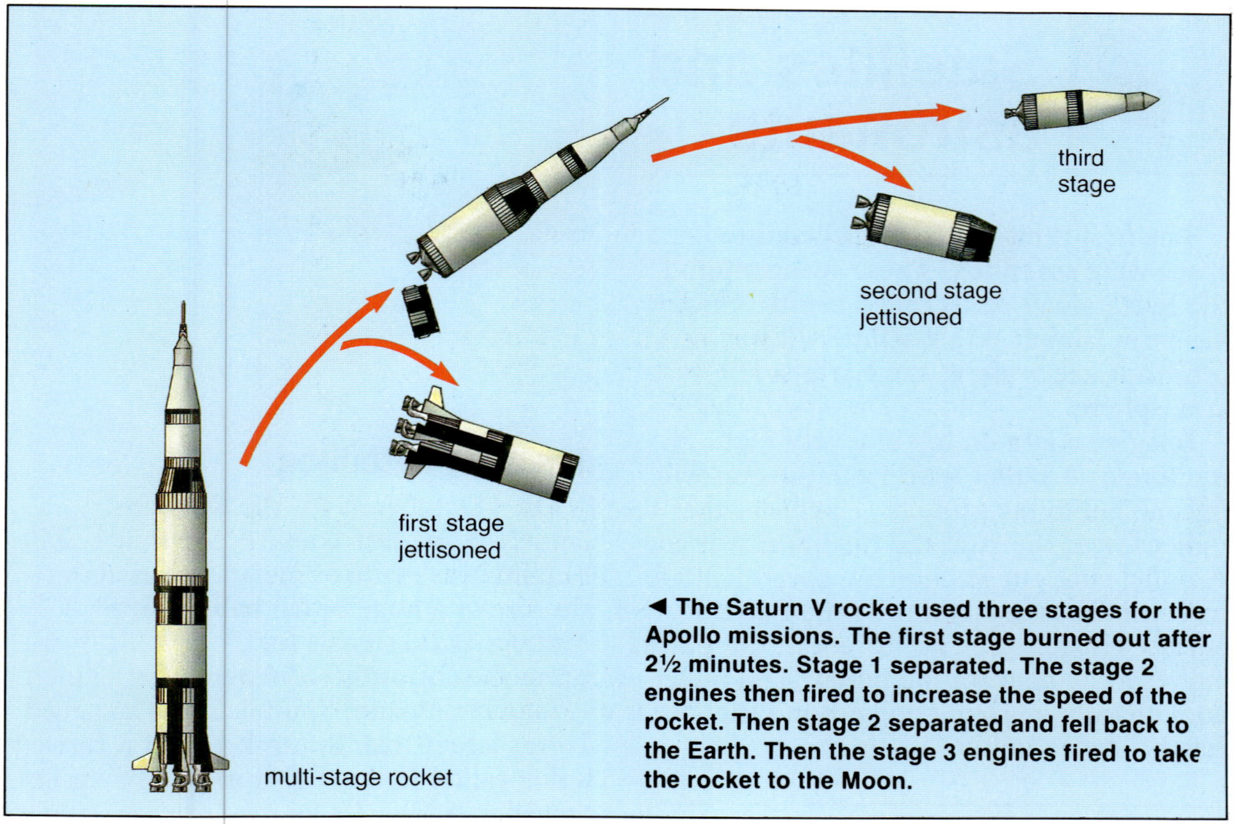

◄ The Saturn V rocket used three stages for the Apollo missions. The first stage burned out after 2½ minutes. Stage 1 separated. The stage 2 engines then fired to increase the speed of the rocket. Then stage 2 separated and fell back to the Earth. Then the stage 3 engines fired to take the rocket to the Moon.

Multi-stage rockets

The thrust from one rocket is not enough to reach escape velocity. More thrust can be made by using two or more rockets, one on top of the other. This is known as a **multi-stage rocket**. The huge first stage of the rocket gives the thrust to launch the whole rocket from the ground. Soon its fuel is used up. This stage of the rocket is **jettisoned**, and drops away. The next stage goes on into space, using another rocket engine.

Three stages are used for a Moon rocket, like the American Saturn V. The astronauts are carried in the **command module** on top of the third stage.

► The Saturn V engines produce massive thrust at the moment of lift-off from the launch pad. The first stage has to lift itself, the other two stages, and the spacecraft. The five engines of the first stage give a thrust of 3500 tonnes.

Satellites and astronauts

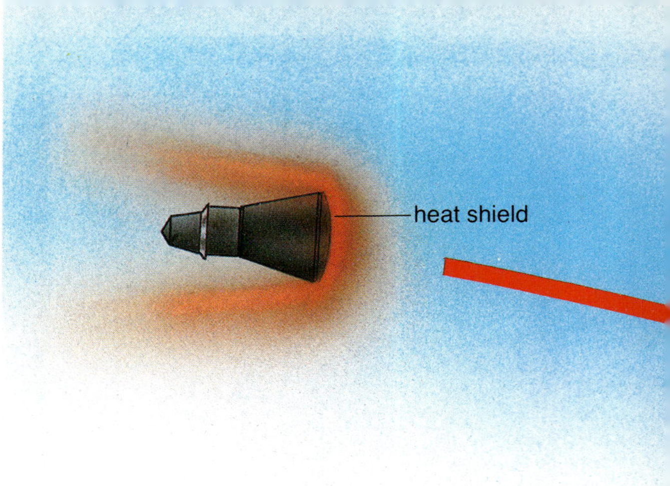

The first things to be launched into space were **satellites**. These swing around the Earth along paths called **orbits**. Once it has been launched, a satellite will stay in orbit if it keeps above the Earth's atmosphere.

Imagine a gun on top of a very high mountain. A bullet fired from the gun will in time fall to the ground. The faster the bullet leaves the gun, the further it will go. A bullet shot out at immense speed will travel so far that it will miss the Earth's surface altogether. The surface of the Earth curves away beneath the bullet. The bullet goes on falling around and around the Earth, like a satellite.

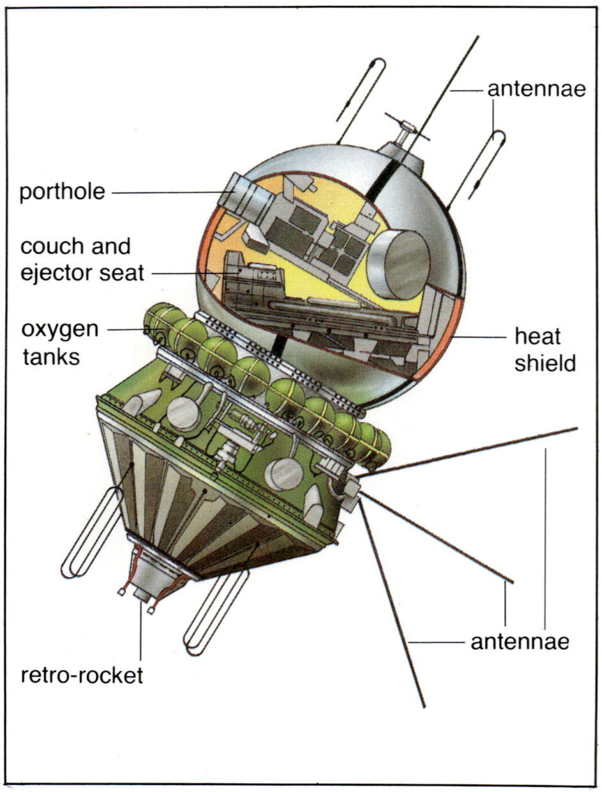

The first satellites

On 4 October 1957, the Russians launched the first satellite, Sputnik 1. The satellite was made of metal. It was about the size of a large beach ball. Sputnik 1 sent out radio signals for 21 days. It burnt up in the atmosphere 96 days after launch.

One month later Sputnik 2 was launched. It was larger than Sputnik 1, and it carried a dog called Laika, the world's first space traveller. Sadly, Laika died in space. On 31 January 1958, America joined the 'space race' with the launch of Explorer 1.

Russians in space

By now, men and women were being trained for flights in space. The Americans were called astronauts, the Russians were called **cosmonauts**. The first man in space was Yuri Gagarin. On 12 April 1961, he completed one orbit of the Earth in Vostok 1. Four months later Gherman Titov in Vostok 2 completed 16 orbits in about 25 hours.

The first woman in space was also a Russian, Valentina Tereshkova. In June 1963 she completed 48 orbits in Vostok 6.

◀ Vostok 1, the first manned spacecraft, carried Yuri Gagarin into space. It was in the shape of a sphere, slightly over two metres across. Vostok 1 went into space on top of the last stage of its rocket. It circled the Earth once.

Americans in space

The first American in space was Alan Shepard. On 5 May 1961, his spacecraft Freedom 7 reached a height of 190 km, but failed to get into orbit. He landed safely in the sea 490 km east of the launch site. On 20 February 1962, John Glenn became the first American in orbit. He took about five hours to orbit the Earth three times in Friendship?

When the spacecraft re-entered the atmosphere there were worries that the heat shield had broken away. All went well however, and Glenn splashed down safely in the sea. These flights were part of Project Mercury.

▼ **The spacecraft was still travelling at a high speed after re-entry. Its parachutes opened to slow the spacecraft to a safe speed so splashdown could take place.**

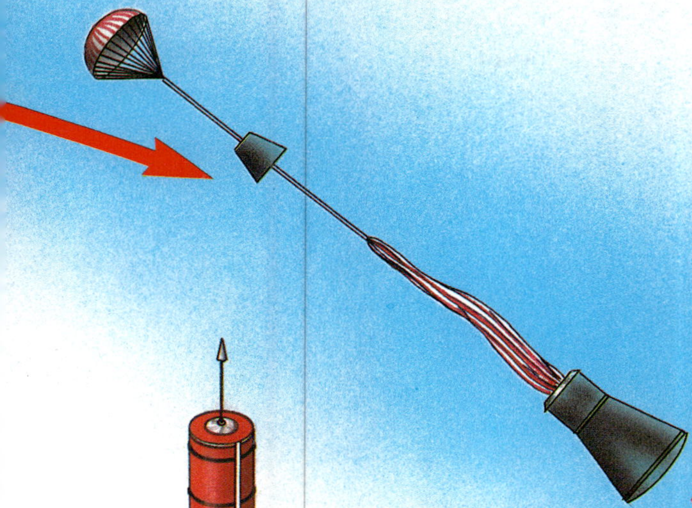

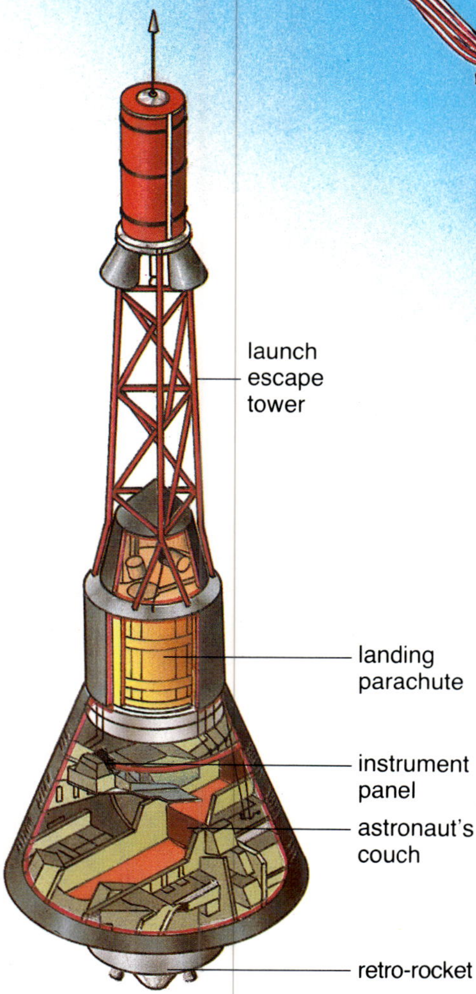

▲ **The Mercury spacecraft was shaped like a cone. It re-entered the Earth's atmosphere at a speed of 40 000 kph. As the spacecraft slowed, the heat shield became red hot.**

Working in space

In 1961, President John F. Kennedy made a promise to the world. He said that America would land a man on the Moon before 1970 and bring him home again. At that time, nobody knew how astronauts would cope with living and working in space.

Feeling gravity

When a car makes a fast start you feel you are being pushed back into your seat. You are thrown forward when the car brakes. You feel **G-forces**, or the force of gravity, when these things happen. On Earth we feel a force of 1G, due to the pull of gravity.

During a rocket launch an astronaut feels a force of up to 7G. It might be more than 11G on **re-entry**. These G-forces make the body feel extremely heavy. The astronaut may be unable to see or think properly.

Weightlessness

After Glenn's flight, Project Mercury went on with other flights. During these flights the crews spent most of their time in orbit. When a spacecraft is in orbit, the crew have no feeling of weight. This is called **weightlessness**. Strange things happen with weightlessness. If you hold a cup and then let it go, it will not fall. You cannot pour liquids. Things will float about if they are not fixed down.

▶ The three astronauts were weightless in space for 84 days during the Skylab 4 mission. In this experiment, Edward Gibson appears to be holding up his fellow astronaut Gerald Carr with only one finger.

▲ Ed White floats into space connected to the spacecraft by an eight metre lifeline. He wears an oxygen pack on his chest for breathing.

▼ In this picture Ed White is outside the spacecraft, holding the space gun. He fires this gun to move about in space.

Walking in space

The next series of space flights were called Project Gemini. The spacecraft were made to carry two people. In June 1965, Ed White stepped outside his Gemini 4 **capsule**. His space walk lasted 21 minutes. This was first tried by Russian cosmonaut Alexei Leonov three months earlier.

While he was outside, Ed White moved around. He used a small hand-held gun which fired a jet of gas. By firing the jet one way, he would move the other way. As Ed White turned the gun on and off, he could move around. More space walks were made. They showed that astronauts could work outside a spacecraft if they needed to.

During the Gemini flights, two spacecraft were joined together in orbit. This was called **docking**. This showed that two spacecraft could be brought close to each other in space and joined together. The Gemini flights went on until November 1966.

Target – the Moon

The Earth is our home in space. It is part of the **solar system**. This is made up of just one star (the Sun), nine **planets** and thousands of smaller **bodies**. The Sun is just one small star out of the millions we can see in the sky. The Earth is a planet, and all the planets move around the Sun. The Sun gives out huge amounts of heat and light all the time. The planets shine because they **reflect** the light of the Sun.

The Moon shines in the same way as the planets. It has no light of its own. The Moon is Earth's closest neighbour. It moves around the Earth at a distance of about 370 000 km. The Sun is 400 times further away from us.

Seas and mountains

The Moon is a strange place. It has no atmosphere and no water, so nothing lives or grows there. With a small telescope you can see dark patches on the Moon. These patches are called seas although there has never been any water in them. You can also see deep valleys snaking their way across the Moon's surface.

There are large mountain ranges on the Moon. The tallest, the Leibnitz range, is a little higher than Mount Everest, the tallest mountain here on Earth.

Craters

On the Moon, there are hundreds of circular markings called **craters**. The craters are a bit like shallow saucers in the surface. The Moon is covered with them. Some craters are vast, like Bailly which is 295 km across. Others are just tiny holes. The large craters have outer walls. These are not very steep. Some people think the craters were caused by **meteorites** hitting the Moon's surface. Others think they were caused by **volcanoes**.

The surface of the Moon

At one time people thought that the surface of the Moon was covered in a thick layer of dust. Now we know that the surface is quite firm. If you stood on it you would sink in no more than two centimetres.

The Moon is smaller than the Earth, so it has less gravity. This is why it has lost all of its atmosphere. People on the Moon weigh only one-sixth of their weight here on Earth. A person weighing 75 kg on Earth would weigh only about 13 kg on the Moon.

◀ This close-up view of a full Moon was photographed from the Apollo 11 spacecraft on its journey homeward. The seas show up as dark areas.

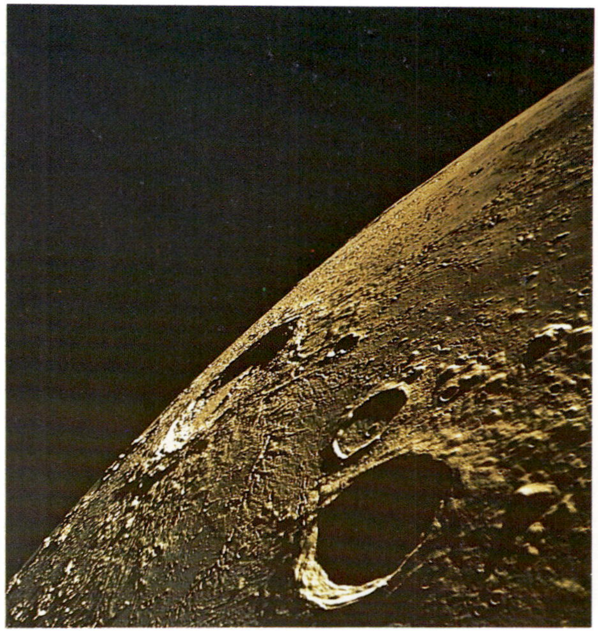

▲ This picture of the crater Copernicus was taken during the second Moon landing.

▼ This picture shows how high a girl would be able to jump if she were on the Moon. The girl could jump six times higher than she would be able to on the Earth.

Closer to the Moon

The Americans called their plan to land people on the Moon the Apollo project. Scientists needed photographs of the Moon's surface to help find good sites for the Apollo spacecraft to land. They planned a series of unmanned flights close to the Moon. A flight close to a body in space is known as a **probe**.

Lunar probes

The Ranger project was set up. There were nine unmanned flights altogether. The first six were failures. The last three Ranger flights took many thousands of very good photos before crashing into the Moon. These were the first close-up views of the surface of the Moon.

▼ The picture shows how orbiters and probes were launched from the Earth and put into orbit around the Moon.

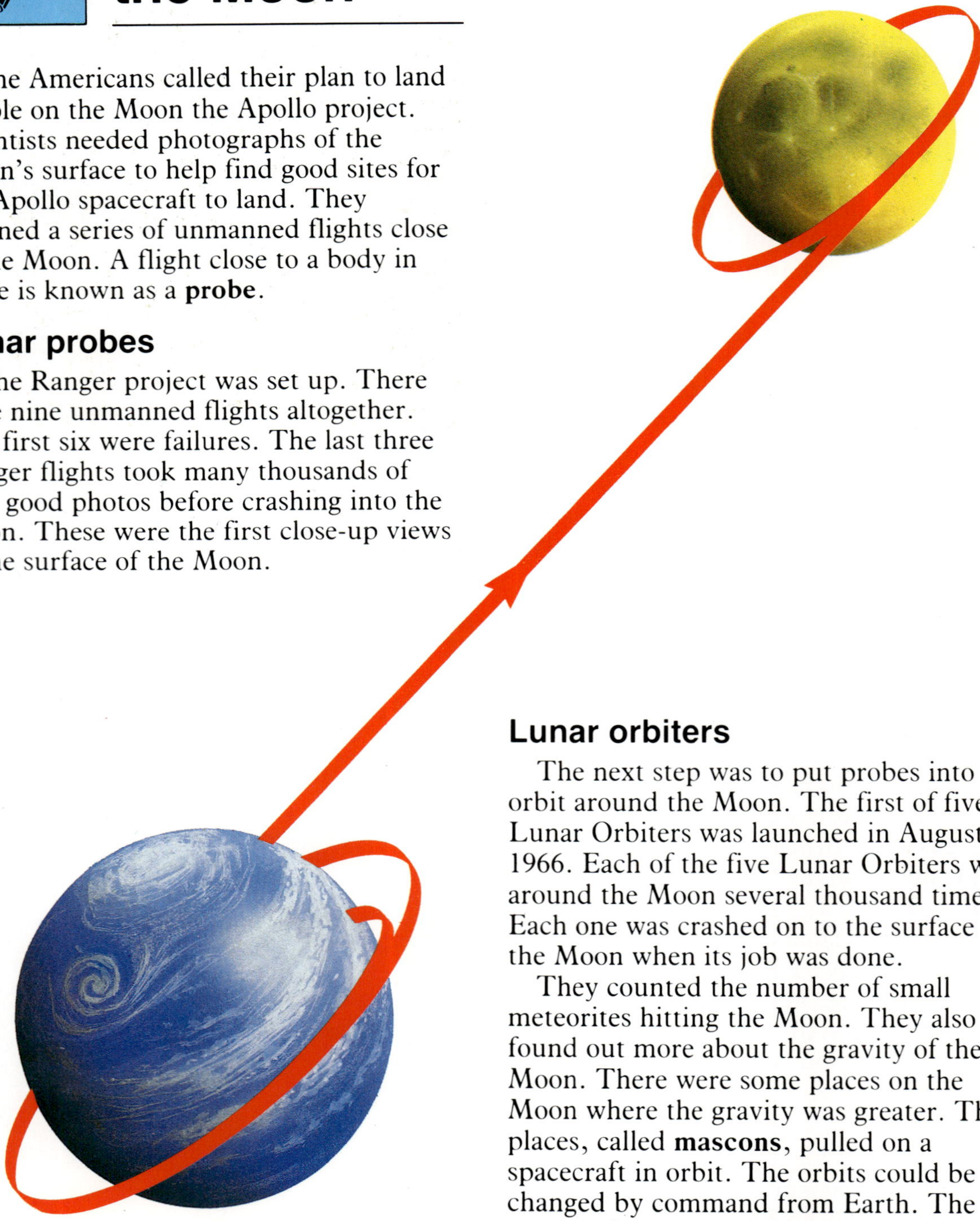

Lunar orbiters

The next step was to put probes into orbit around the Moon. The first of five Lunar Orbiters was launched in August 1966. Each of the five Lunar Orbiters went around the Moon several thousand times. Each one was crashed on to the surface of the Moon when its job was done.

They counted the number of small meteorites hitting the Moon. They also found out more about the gravity of the Moon. There were some places on the Moon where the gravity was greater. These places, called **mascons**, pulled on a spacecraft in orbit. The orbits could be changed by command from Earth. The spacecraft could go as close as 40 km above the Moon's surface.

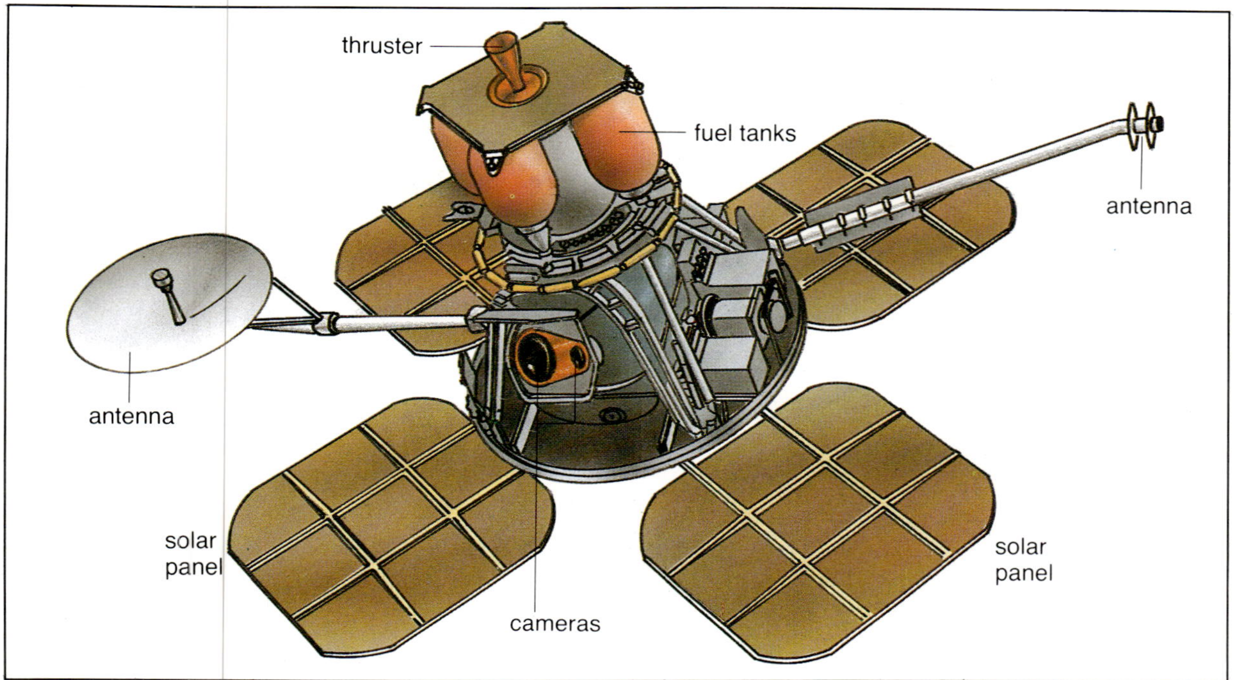

▲ **The Lunar Orbiter carried two cameras. One camera was used for close-up shots, the other for views. The cameras were powered by solar panels. The pictures were sent by radio antenna to Earth. The Orbiter carried a small thruster to point the spacecraft in the right direction.**

Photos were taken of things on the Moon as small as one metre across. The first lunar atlas was built up from the Orbiter photos. This atlas included the far side of the Moon, which is always hidden from Earth. Like the Earth, the Moon turns on its **axis**. The Moon makes just one turn in 27⅓ days. This is the same as the time it takes to orbit the Earth. This is why we only see one side of the Moon.

Russian probes

The Russians also sent probes to the Moon. Luna 1, in January 1959, was the first spacecraft to leave Earth and head off into space. Luna 1 passed within 6000 km of the Moon, and then it went into orbit around the Sun. This type of flight is called a **fly-by**. Luna 2 was crash-landed on the Moon. Luna 3 took the first photos of the far side of the Moon.

► **The far side of the Moon was photographed during the Apollo 10 mission. We never see this side of the Moon from Earth.**

Robots on the Moon

The United States and the USSR had both sent probes to the Moon. They had received many good pictures of the surface. The next step was to be much more difficult.

The aim was to land a spacecraft on the Moon without damaging it. This is called a **soft-lander** probe. As the spacecraft is pulled towards the Moon, **retro-rockets** are fired towards the surface of the Moon. They slow down the spacecraft so that it can land gently.

These spacecraft are robots. They are controlled by computers, and will do what they are told.

▼ The Lunokhod moonwalker worked very well. 'Eyes' in the form of television cameras showed people on Earth where it was going.

The race to the Moon

The United States had one target – to land a man on the Moon. The USSR meanwhile kept on with their Luna probes. In February 1966, Luna 9 made the first **soft-landing** on the Moon. TV pictures were sent back to Earth. Luna 9 did not sink into the dust. The Apollo team then knew that the first man on the Moon would be able to walk.

The USSR made many more Luna probes. Luna 16 brought back soil samples to Earth in September 1970.

The Lunokhod 'moonwalker'

Two years after the first Americans landed on the Moon, the USSR launched Luna 17. It carried the Moon's first moving robot, Lunokhod 1. This moonwalker had a circular body two metres across, with a lid which could be opened and closed. It had eight wheels. A team on Earth could control it.

The moonwalker could climb slopes and weave in and out of craters. It was not easy to drive. In 11 months it crawled 10 km over the surface, taking samples of soil.

Lunar Surveyor

The United States soft-landed five probes on the Moon between June 1966 and January 1968. The Surveyors did not go into orbit before landing. Retro-rockets were fired for 40 seconds when the spacecraft were 96 km above the Moon. At 40 km above the Moon the speed of the spacecraft was down to 400 kph. Then smaller rockets were fired. The probe landed at about 12 kph.

Surveyors had three legs, with large feet. They each carried a scoop so that they could dig holes in the lunar soil. Each carried a TV camera, and thousands of pictures were sent back. The way was now set for the Apollo Moon landings.

The Surveyor probes could not move around but they did valuable work. They were able to show that a manned Moon landing would be possible.

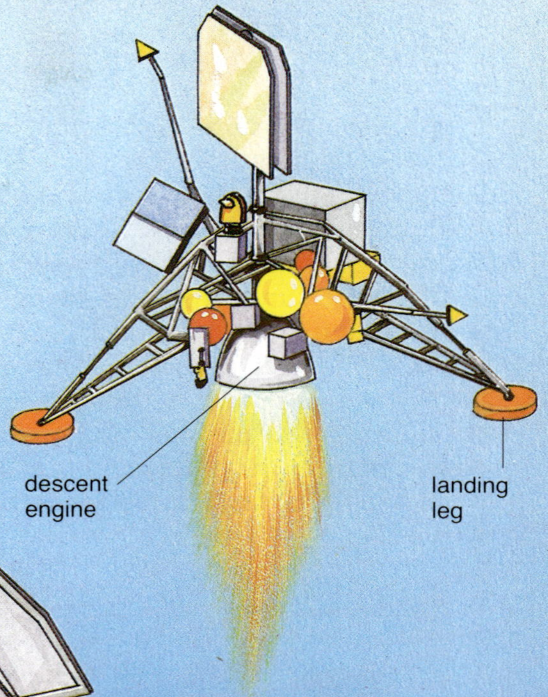

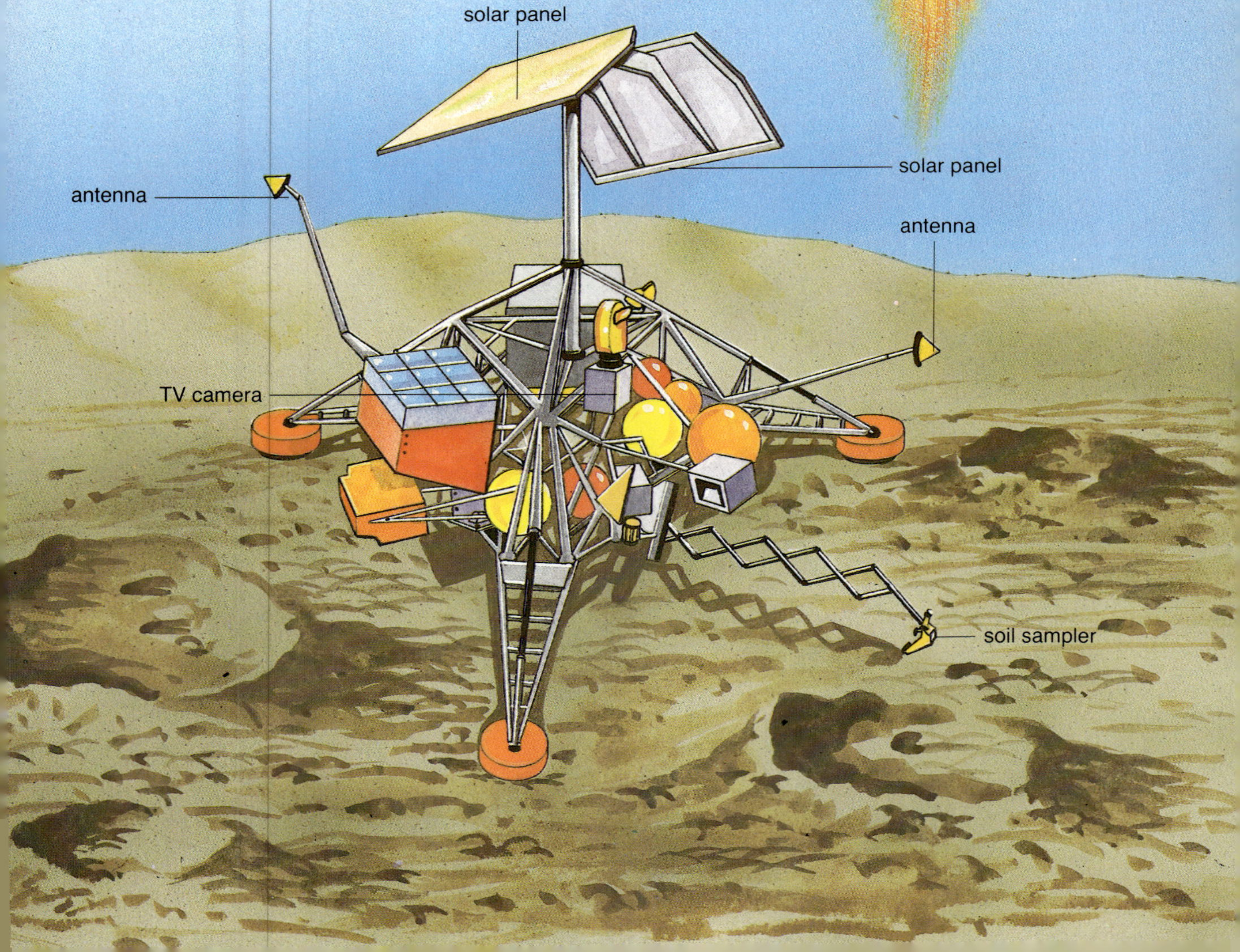

Living in space

In space there is no air to breathe, no food to eat and no water to drink. It is either scorching hot in the rays of the Sun, or bitterly cold in the dark. In space, an astronaut needs a **spacesuit** to protect the body and a **life support system** to give air, food and water.

Inside a spacesuit or spacecraft, air is made to push on human bodies just as it does on Earth. The air must be **pressurized**. The **air pressure** inside is the same as it is on Earth, even when there is space outside.

▼ **This picture was taken inside Skylab. It shows science astronaut Owen Garriott at work.**

Inside the spacecraft

The astronauts wear easy clothes inside the spacecraft. They do not need spacesuits. The life support system supplies the air at just the right pressure. It also keeps the air fresh. The air is pumped through **air filters**. These soak up the poisonous gas **carbon dioxide** which we breathe out.

To stop air leaking from the spacecraft, people enter and leave it through an **airlock**.

Some electricity is also needed. This is made by **fuel cells**. These are used to make power for the instruments and to form water. The water is used for washing, cooking and drinking. Little water is needed for washing. In the weightlessness of space, water clings to the skin. The wash basin has a fan to suck water away. **Suction** and an air draught are used to get rid of body wastes.

Outside the spacecraft

Outside the spacecraft, astronauts have to wear spacesuits. The suit has several layers of plastic and metal to protect the body. Over the top is a sealed suit. The suit and the helmet are filled with oxygen at the right pressure.

The astronauts carry a small life support system in a backpack. They can bend their arms and legs easily. They use a **manned manoeuvring unit**, or MMU, for moving around. It has 24 small **thrusters**. These squirt jets of gas like little rockets so that the astronaut can move around.

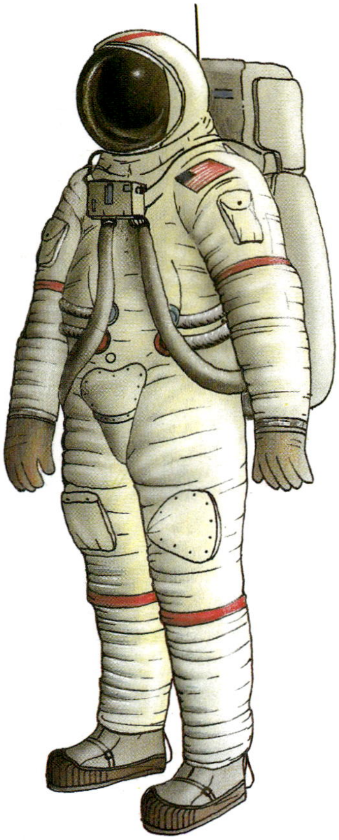

◀ **The spacesuit protected the astronaut in space. It was made of 15 layers of plastic. The astronaut carried a life support system on a back pack.**

▼ **The first person to use the MMU for moving about in space was Bruce McCandless II. The MMU is shaped like a chair, and is worn as a backpack. The astronaut is able to control each of the 24 small thrusters as he sits in the 'chair'.**

Mission Control

Every space launch is called a **mission**. Each mission is normally controlled from one place on the Earth. The Apollo flights to the Moon were controlled in two main parts. The launch rocket and the Apollo spacecraft were put together at the Kennedy Space Centre in Florida, USA. This has two areas – the Vehicle Assembly Building (VAB), and the Launch Control Centre (LCC) nearby. As soon as a spacecraft is launched, the flight is controlled from the Mission Control Centre (MCC) in Houston, Texas.

The VAB is one of the largest buildings in the world. Clouds can gather inside if the doors are left open. It is 160 metres high. Inside, a complete Saturn V rocket can be put together on its mobile launch platform. It is taken to the launch pad on a giant caterpillar tractor.

This picture shows Apollo 13 and its Saturn V rocket on the mobile launch platform. The huge caterpillar tractor under the platform is taking the rocket from the VAB. It is on the way to the launch site which can be seen in the distance.

The launch

The whole rocket is checked out once it is on the launch pad. Nine hours before launch the liquid fuel is pumped aboard. Two hours 40 minutes before launch the astronauts enter the command module of the Apollo spacecraft.

In the final moments of the launch, the voice of LCC can be heard giving the **countdown** ...'10,9,8,7,6,5,4,3,2,1, zero ... all engines running ... lift-off, we have lift-off'. The LCC hands over to the MCC. 'Houston, this is launch control: all engines are looking good'. While the countdown is in progress all the systems are watched by teams of scientists. If anything goes wrong, the countdown is stopped. Lift-off is delayed until the fault is put right. Then the countdown is re-started.

In space

After lift-off, a team of flight directors at MCC make decisions on every part of the mission. Each flight director wears a set of headphones, and watches a TV screen. A very large screen in front of the rows of desks shows pictures of the astronauts.

All the spacecraft systems are checked the whole time by computers at Houston. These 'talk' to the computers on the spacecraft. In this way, if a problem occurs it can soon be put right.

► The launch of Apollo 11. The Saturn V rocket burns 15 tonnes of fuel per second at lift-off.

▼ This photograph shows the flight directors at work at the Mission Control Centre. Each director has a special job to do.

The Apollo programme

CM	**Command Module** Control centre and living quarters
SM	**Service Module** Contains main rocket engine
CSM	**Command and Service Module** Command Module plus Service Module
LM	**Lunar Module** For descent on to and ascent from Moon
SLMA	**Spacecraft Lunar Module Adaptor** Links Apollo spacecraft to rocket

A very powerful rocket was built for the Apollo Moon landing programme. It was called the Saturn V. A three-man spacecraft would be launched on the top of this giant rocket.

A complete Apollo spacecraft is 25 m tall. It consists of several parts.

The Spacecraft Lunar Module Adaptor links the Apollo spacecraft to the rocket during lift-off. It surrounds and protects the Lunar Module. The Service Module is a 7½ m cylinder. It cannot be entered by the astronauts.

After the launch, the Apollo spacecraft and the upper stage of the rocket enter Earth's orbit. Then the motors of the upper stage are fired again. The astror are on their way to the Moon.

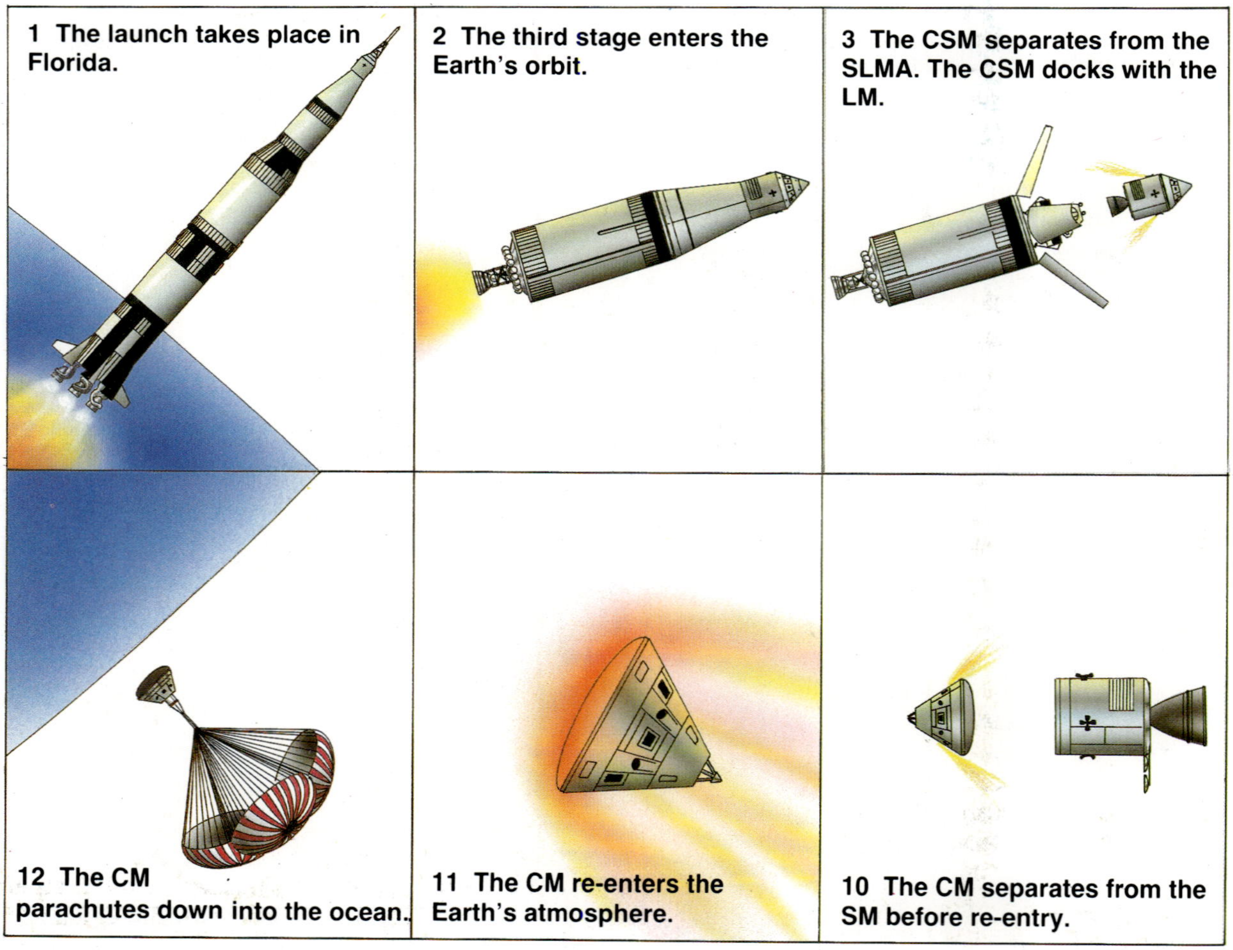

1 The launch takes place in Florida.

2 The third stage enters the Earth's orbit.

3 The CSM separates from the SLMA. The CSM docks with the LM.

10 The CM separates from the SM before re-entry.

11 The CM re-enters the Earth's atmosphere.

12 The CM parachutes down into the ocean.

The landing

The Command and Service Module separates from the SLMA. Then, the CSM is turned around, and **docks** with the LM. The CSM and LM head off for the Moon. When the CSM and the LM orbit the Moon, one astronaut stays in the CSM while the other two astronauts get into the LM. The LM separates from the CSM and then it descends to the surface of the Moon.

There are two parts to the LM. One is the descent stage and the other is the ascent stage. The main engine is used in the descent stage to bring the LM smoothly down on to the surface. The LM has four legs with large feet for landing gently on the Moon.

The return

The descent stage is the launch platform when the time comes for the two astronauts to leave the Moon. The ascent stage has its own engine to lift the LM back to the CSM waiting in orbit above them. The CSM and LM then dock. The astronauts crawl through the docking tunnel linking the two spacecraft.

Then the LM is jettisoned and the three crew return to Earth in the CSM. The CM separates from the SM shortly before re-entry into the atmosphere. The SM drops away and burns up. The CM is protected by the heat shield on re-entry. Parachutes are opened and it splashes down gently into the ocean.

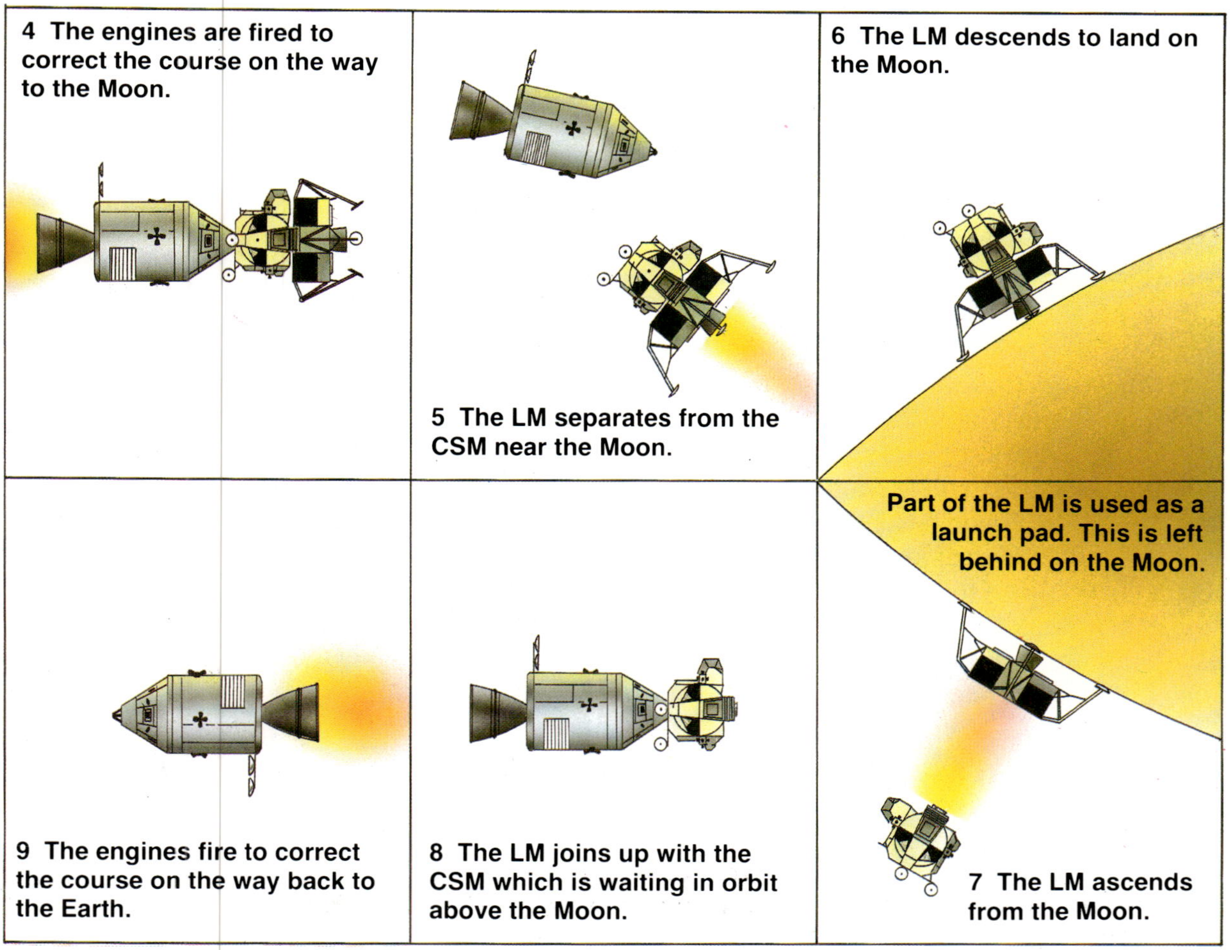

4 The engines are fired to correct the course on the way to the Moon.

5 The LM separates from the CSM near the Moon.

6 The LM descends to land on the Moon.

Part of the LM is used as a launch pad. This is left behind on the Moon.

7 The LM ascends from the Moon.

8 The LM joins up with the CSM which is waiting in orbit above the Moon.

9 The engines fire to correct the course on the way back to the Earth.

Men on the Moon

By 1969, everything was ready for the historic flight of Apollo 11. There were three astronauts, Neil Armstrong, Edwin 'Buzz' Aldrin and Michael Collins. The launch took place from Cape Kennedy on 16 July 1969. All went very well on the first stage of the flight. On 19 July, the CSM and the LM, named *Eagle*, started to orbit the Moon.

On 20 July, Armstrong and Aldrin crawled through the docking tunnel into the LM. Collins remained alone in the CSM. The two spacecraft separated on the thirteenth orbit around the Moon. The engine on *Eagle* was fired and it descended towards the Moon.

The landing site chosen for Apollo 11 in the Sea of Tranquillity was seen to be covered with large rocks. Armstrong took over **manual control** of the LM. He found a flat area clear of rocks.

The Eagle has landed

Armstrong brought the *Eagle* smoothly down on to the Moon. More than 500 million TV viewers throughout the world heard Armstrong tell Mission Control in Houston 'The *Eagle* has landed'. Mission Control anxiously replied 'We're breathing again — thanks a lot'.

Keen to walk on the Moon, the astronauts put on their spacesuits. Then they opened the hatch. Neil Armstrong backed carefully out of the LM. He climbed slowly down the ladder. As he placed his left foot on to the dusty lunar soil, with millions of people listening, he said 'That's one small step for a man; one giant leap for mankind'. It was Monday 21 July 1969.

▲ This photograph was taken by Michael Collins from Apollo 11's CSM. It shows the LM on its way to the Moon.

▼ 'Buzz' Aldrin descends the ladder of the LM to join Neil Armstrong.

▲ Aldrin sets up scientific experiments in front of the LM while Armstrong photographs him.

▼ The Apollo mission is over. The CM has splashed down safely in the Pacific Ocean. The astronauts are shortly to enter a health centre on the recovery ship.

Aldrin joined him 18 minutes later. They spent 2½ hours on the surface. There was plenty of work to do. They tried walking, running and even a sort of bouncing 'kangaroo hop'. They set up an American flag. A **plaque** was unveiled on the LM's descent stage, which was to be left behind on the Moon. It read 'Here men from planet Earth first set foot upon the Moon, July 1969, AD'.

Armstrong and Aldrin collected moon rocks. Then they placed a box on the Moon's surface containing messages from most of the world's leaders. They also left a package of scientific **experiments**.

The return to Earth

Then the time came for them to return to Earth. The ascent stage of the LM blasted off from the Moon. It docked with the CSM 3½ hours later. There was much jolting while they were docking, but there was no damage. Armstrong and Aldrin joined Collins in the CM. The LM was left behind.

The SM's rocket motor was fired and the spacecraft returned to Earth. The CM splashed down in the Pacific Ocean on Thursday 24 July. They had travelled 1½ million km, and were only 30 seconds late.

More Moon landings

The second mission to the Moon was Apollo 12. The launch in November 1969 took place during a thunderstorm. Shortly after lift-off, the Saturn V rocket was struck by lightning. The spacecraft's electrical system was out of action for a while, but everything was found to be working.

The crew of three, Charles Conrad, Richard Gordon and Alan Bean set off towards the Moon. Conrad and Bean made the Moon landing. Their mission was very difficult. They had to land in the Ocean of Storms, close to the place where Surveyor 3 landed in April 1967. They had to bring back to Earth the TV camera, the scoop and other parts of Surveyor.

The LM landed only 183 m from Surveyor. Conrad and Bean were on the Moon for 31½ hours. They removed the parts from Surveyor and made two moon walks totalling 7½ hours. They collected 34 kg of moon rock and set up some experiments. The return trip to Earth went well.

▼ The Apollo spacecraft was made up of three parts, or modules. The crew sat in the CM during launch and landing. The SM carried the engines, and the air and water supplies. The CM and the SM together were known as the CSM.

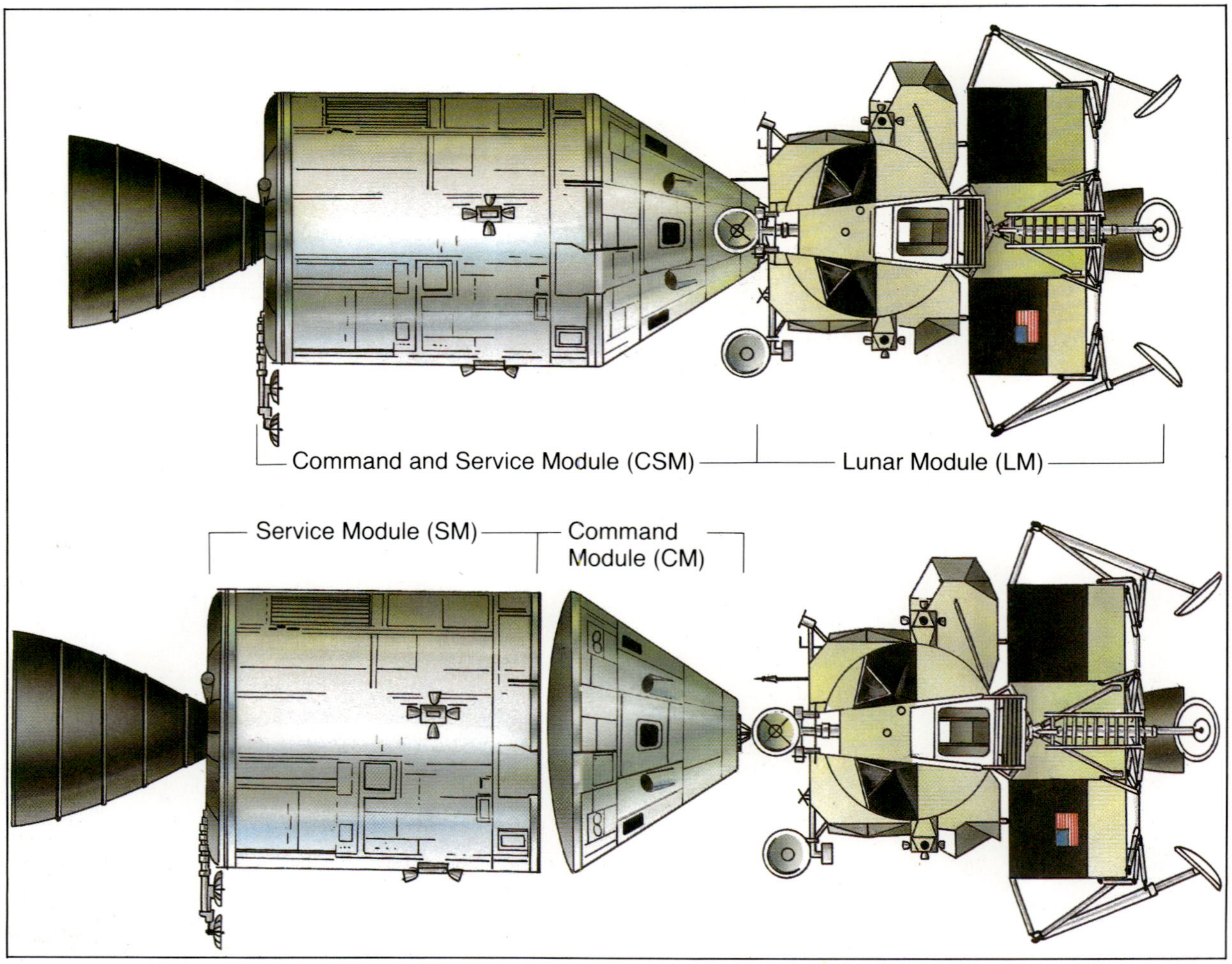

The LM was seven metres high when its four legs were extended. It had a roof hatch for docking with the CM, as well as a front hatch for getting out on to the surface of the Moon.

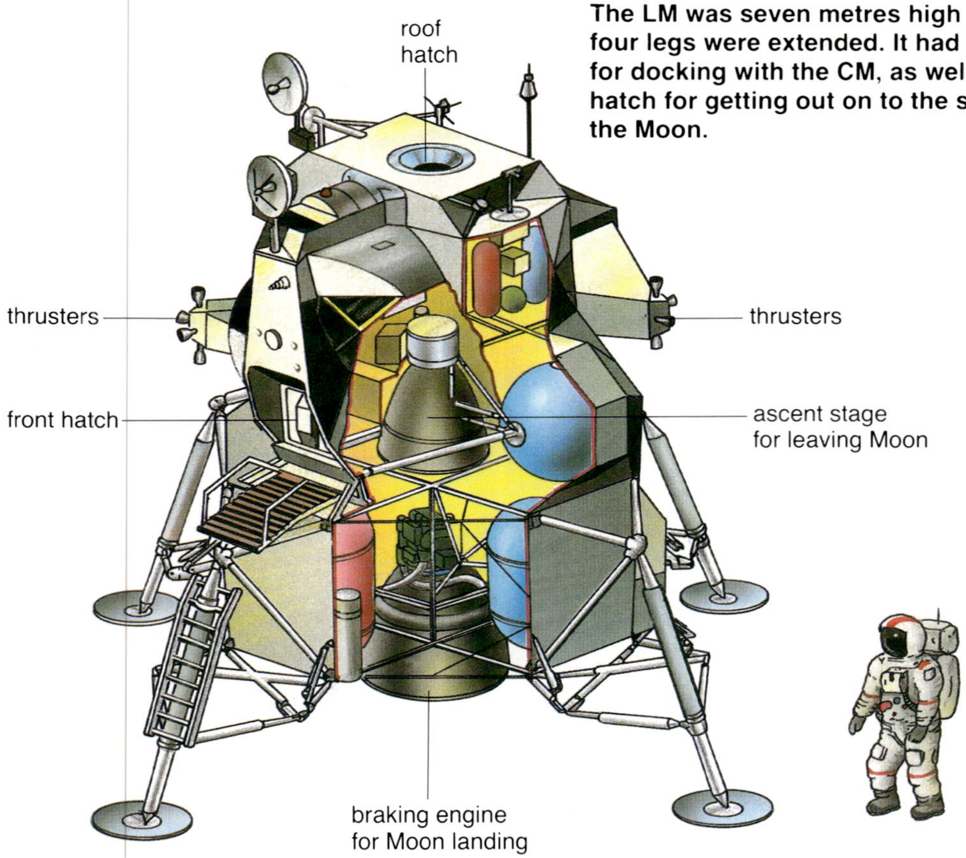

Apollo 13

The next mission, Apollo 13, went wrong. On the way to the Moon, an explosion in the fuel tanks of the SM put the spacecraft out of action. The mission became a 3½-day space rescue drama. The landing on the Moon could not take place.

The spacecraft was swung around the Moon and headed straight back to Earth. The three crew, Jim Lovell, Jack Swigart and Fred Haise, used the LM as a lifeboat to tow the crippled spacecraft home. They had to use the LM's life support system, rocket motor and fuel because the SM had been damaged. The SM and LM were jettisoned before re-entry. Finally, the CM splashed down safely in the sea.

Apollo 14

The third Moon landing, Apollo 14, was led by Alan Shepard, America's first man in space in May 1961. Now, ten years later, his fellow crew were Stuart Roosa and Edgar Mitchell.

The Moon landing went very smoothly. Shepard and Mitchell touched down only 27 m from target. They made two moon walks, each lasting 4 hours 40 minutes. They collected 44 kg of moon rock and soil. On one walk, they took a small hand cart with them for collecting rock.

Alan Shepard ended his moon walk by playing golf with two balls he had brought with him. The return flight to the Earth went very well.

The last missions

The last Apollo missions carried out useful scientific work. Apollo 15 was launched in July 1971. It was the second longest mission, lasting over 12 days. The three crew were David Scott, Alfred Worden and James Irwin.

The LM landed on 30 July 1971. Touch down was close to Hadley Rille, a deep valley running across the Moon's surface. The astronauts did three moon walks on the surface, totalling over 18 hours.

The Lunar Rover

Apollo 15 was the first mission to carry the Lunar Roving Vehicle, or LRV. This was a four-wheeled car weighing 209 kg. It had a top speed of 17 kph and a range of 92 km. It could carry two crew and their equipment, plus a load of 127 kg. It was used on the last three Apollo flights.

The LRV bounced about in the Moon's low gravity. The drivers said it was a real 'bucking bronco'. They had to use seat belts. They covered 28 km in the LRV and collected 78 kg of moon rock.

▼ This photograph was taken on the Apollo 15 mission. It shows the LRV in the foreground. The LM is seen in the background.

▲ **The LRV was used to explore the Moon. The antenna, shaped like an umbrella, sent signals to the Earth.**

◄ **Dr Jack Schmitt stands beside a huge rock during the final Moon mission.**

Apollo 16

Like Apollo 15, Apollo 16 was a great success. The three crew were John Young, Ken Mattingly and Charles Duke. The landing took place about 250 m from target. Young and Duke drove 27 km in the LRV and brought back 98 kg of moon rock. John Young drove the LRV at top speed in circles, skidding the wheels to test their grip. The return to Earth went well.

Apollo 17

Apollo 17 was launched in December 1972. It was the best of the Moon missions. The crew were Eugene Cernan, Ronald Evans and Dr 'Jack' Schmitt.

Cernan and Schmitt were on the surface for 75 hours, and spent 22 hours outside the LM. They collected 113 kg of moon rock, including some orange lunar soil. The two men travelled a total of 35 km in the LRV.

After the two astronauts had docked with the CSM, it stayed in lunar orbit for two more days. They spent this time mapping the far side of the Moon. When they returned to Earth, the astronauts splashed down in the Pacific. In this last Apollo mission, they had travelled nearly 2.4 million km in space.

Space stations

The idea of a space station orbiting above the Earth has long been a dream of science fiction writers. Earth and outer space can be easily watched from a space station. It can also contain workshops for scientists.

▼ This picture shows Skylab with an Apollo spacecraft docked. The orbital workshop was 15 m long, and about seven metres wide.

Salyut space stations

The Russians have achieved much with the Salyut space stations. Teams of cosmonauts have stayed in these stations for several months at a time. The first Russian space station, Salyut 1, was launched in April 1971. A Soyuz spacecraft docked at one end of Salyut 1. After 2800 orbits it burnt up in the atmosphere, in October 1971.

Later Russian space stations were larger than Salyut 1. A Soyuz spacecraft could dock at both ends. The total weight was then over 25 tonnes and the length over 21 m. In 1982, two cosmonauts stayed aboard Salyut 7 for nearly seven months.

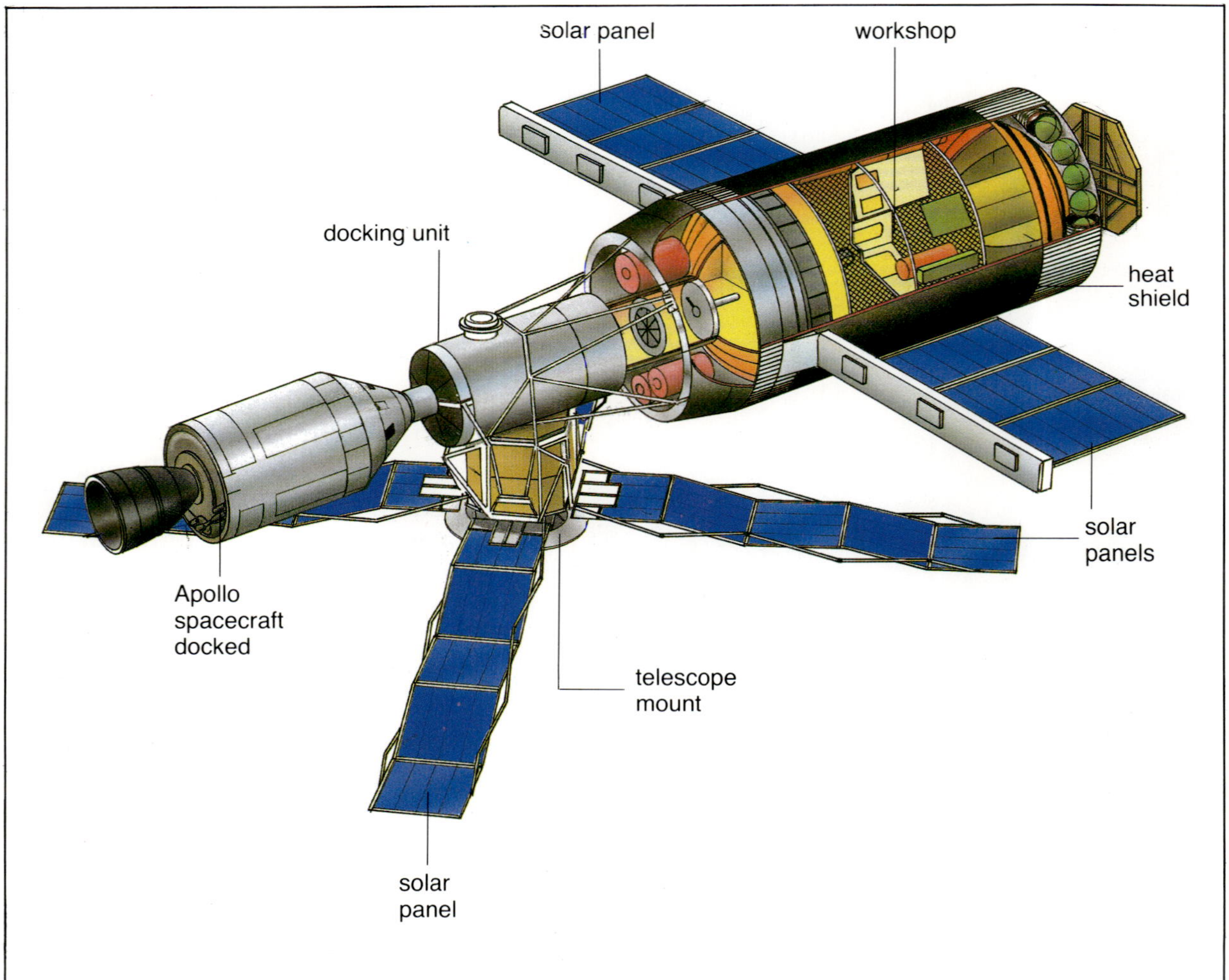

Skylab

The American Skylab space station was the first large space station which could be visited by different teams. It was launched by the Saturn V rocket on 14 May 1973. Skylab was visited by three Apollo crews. They lived and worked in it for periods of 28, 59 and 84 days.

There were problems when Skylab was launched. Several parts were shaken to pieces and a heat shield was torn away. There were two huge **solar panels** for making electricity. One was torn off, and the other was damaged. Inside Skylab the heat became fierce. It seemed that no one could survive inside it.

However, 11 days after the launch, the first crew, 'Pete' Conrad, Joseph Kerwin and Paul Weitz arrived. They worked tirelessly to repair the broken parts. A sunshade was used to cool the station. One solar panel was repaired and set up. The power came on. At the end of their 28-day mission the crew had completed most of their work.

▲ Skylab is seen in orbit after repairs had been carried out. Only one wing-like solar panel remained. The 'sunshade' was used to keep the space station cool. The cross-shaped solar panels supplied power for the eight telescopes on board Skylab.

The third Skylab crew showed signs of strain from overwork on their 84-day mission. Weightlessness and the lack of room in the space station can cause health problems and make astronauts irritable.

After long periods in space human bones can become brittle with lack of use. The heart slows down as it does not have to work so hard. These things can make astronauts ill in space, or when they return to Earth after a long flight.

The Skylab missions helped doctors find out how crews can stay fit and healthy when they work in space for a long time.

◀ These two Skylab crewmen have strapped their feet to the floor. This keeps them from floating about in the experiment area of the orbital workshop.

Probes into space

The American Surveyor and Orbiter probes to the Moon had been successful. Why not have probes to the planets? Scientists want to find out more about the planets. They want to study what they are made of. They would also like to know if Earth is the only planet where there is any kind of life.

Probes to the planets

Venus and Mars are the closest planets to Earth. Venus is a very difficult planet to explore. It is surrounded by thick clouds of very poisonous gases. On the surface, it is extremely hot. The pressure of the Venus atmosphere would crush a human being to death. Robot probes have been sent to Venus and landed successfully. The robots were built to stand up to these conditions.

The planet Mars

Mars is a much easier planet to study. Between 1965 and 1969, Mariners 4, 6 and 7 flew by Mars and sent TV pictures back to Earth. Mariner 9 was the first probe to orbit Mars. It discovered huge volcanoes on the surface, and an immense swirling dust storm.

▼ Viking 2 landed on Mars in September 1976. Photographs taken from the lander showed the surface of Mars to be a red, stony desert. There were no signs of life.

Vikings 1 and 2 reached Mars in 1976. Their task was to study the atmosphere and surface, and look for signs of life. Each probe was in two parts. A soft-lander took pictures on the ground, scooped up soil and looked for life. No life was found. An orbiter circled the planet and mapped it.

Recently, robot probes have been sent to the more distant planets, Jupiter, Saturn and Uranus.

Halley's comet

Robot probes have also been sent to look at small bodies in the Sun's family – the **comets**. These are icy snowballs no more than 10 km across. They orbit between the planets on long paths. These paths are close to the Sun at one end of the orbit and far away from it at the other end.

The most famous is Halley's comet. It comes near the Sun every 76 years. In March 1986, five probes were sent to study this comet in detail. The European Giotto probe had to fly by the icy **core** of the comet at 68 km per second, missing it by 500 km. Its purpose was to take many photos and to make new discoveries.

▲ In 1981, Voyager 2 passed close to the giant planet Saturn on its way to a meeting with Uranus in January 1986. It will then fly on to reach the distant planet Neptune in August 1989. This picture shows Dione, one of Saturn's ten moons.

▼ This artist's impression shows the Giotto probe passing through Halley's comet on 13 March 1986. The probe was planned to pass within 500 km of the comet's centre.

The Space Shuttle

The Space Shuttle is the first real **spaceplane**. It takes off like a rocket and goes into orbit around the Earth. It has wings, and on return to Earth it glides to land on a long **runway**. The Shuttle can be used again and again.

The main part is the Shuttle Orbiter. It carries the crew and cargo into space. At launch, the Orbiter sits on a launch pad pointing up into space like a rocket. Alongside the Orbiter is a huge fuel tank. It is called the External Tank, or ET. This holds liquid oxygen and hydrogen. At lift-off these fuels are pumped into the Orbiter's three main rocket engines. To give extra thrust at launch there are also two thinner tanks alongside the Orbiter on the launch pad. These are Solid fuel Rocket Boosters, or SRBs. They work like huge firework rockets.

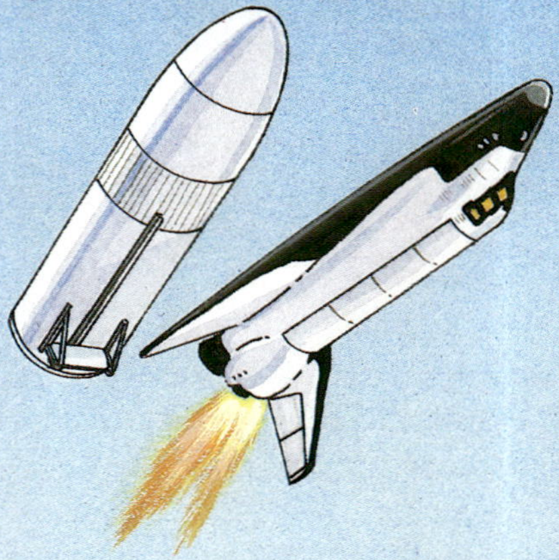

The empty ET drops away.

The SRBs separate and parachute into the sea to be recovered.

The Space Shuttle at life-off.

The launch

When the countdown reaches zero the main engines roar. The Orbiter, with its ET and two SRBs, lifts off from the launch pad. After about two minutes the SRBs burn out and they drop away. They parachute into the sea. There the SRBs are picked up by ships to be used again. The speed of the Shuttle increases until it reaches a height of about 120 km. Then the main engines shut down. The empty ET is dropped into the sea. Two other rocket engines on the Shuttle take over. They are called the Orbital Manoeuvring System, or OMS, engines.

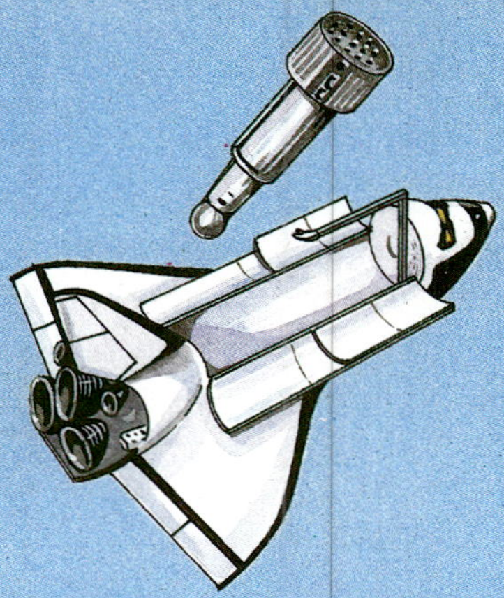

The Space Shuttle in orbit with its cargo bay doors open. It is seen launching a satellite.

In orbit

These engines give the Shuttle its final thrust and 45 minutes after launch it is in Earth orbit. A second 'burn' of the OMS engines puts the Orbiter into a near circular orbit about 280 km above the Earth. It stays at this height during the flight, travelling at 27 800 kph. The cargo bay doors are opened and work begins.

The Shuttle lands on a 4½ km runway. A parachute is used to bring it to a standstill.

The Shuttle re-enters the Earth's atmosphere at the end of the mission.

The return to Earth

When it is time to return to Earth, the OMS engines are fired forward like retro-rockets. This slows the Orbiter and it leaves its orbit. It enters the Earth's atmosphere at about 26 500 kph. The heat shield beneath the Shuttle glows red-hot with the fierce heat of re-entry. Special tiles on the Shuttle protect the crew and the spacecraft. The Orbiter slows down as it reaches the lower part of the atmosphere. It glides in to land. The wheels are lowered just before touch-down. It lands on a very long runway at about 350 kph, and then rolls to a stop. The Shuttle flight is over.

The Space Shuttle glides in to land as the atmosphere slows it down.

Inside the Shuttle

The Shuttle crew live in a pressurized cabin. This keeps the air inside the same as it is on Earth. The Orbiter has two levels – an upper flight deck, and a lower main deck where the crew live. The **cockpit** of the flight deck is just like the cockpit of an airliner. There are two seats side-by-side in the cockpit. The flight commander sits on the left. The co-pilot is on the right. In front of them is an **array** of instruments. There are also three TV screens. These show information about the Shuttle's control system.

Controlling the Shuttle

There are five computers on the Orbiter. These computers can do 325 000 sums each second when they are working together. Computers control the Shuttle most of the time. The whole spacecraft is controlled from the flight deck. The pilot uses foot pedals to move the Orbiter's **rudder**. Pistol-grip controls are used to tip the Shuttle's nose up and down and to roll it from side to side. Small gas jets, called thrusters, are used to make these movements. These fire like little rockets.

While the Shuttle is in space, there is continuous **communication** between the Orbiter and Mission Control. Radio and TV signals go back and forth. There are four systems on the Orbiter to handle them.

▲ This is the flight deck of the Shuttle. The pilot and the co-pilot each have a set of instruments so that either of them can fly the Shuttle.

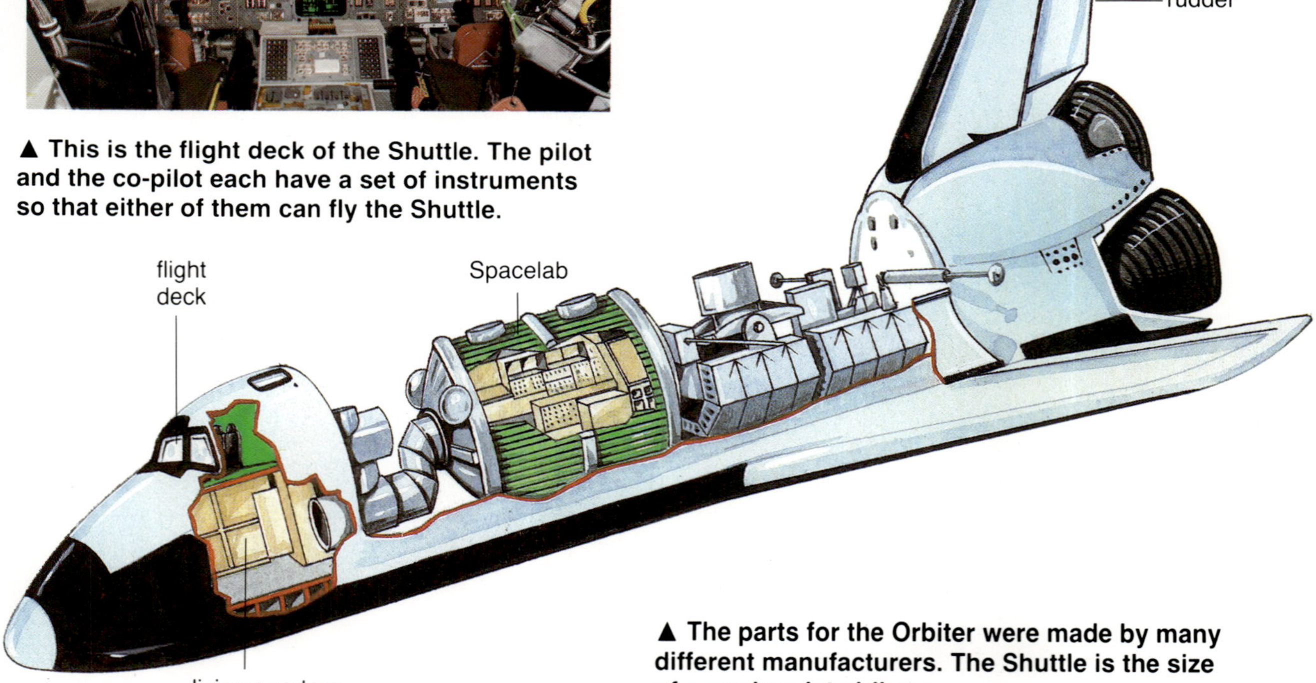

▲ The parts for the Orbiter were made by many different manufacturers. The Shuttle is the size of a modern jet airliner.

► This photograph of the Shuttle's cargo bay was taken from inside the cabin during its second mission, in November 1981. Boxes of experiments can be seen in the foreground.

Living quarters

Below the flight deck a hatch leads down to the main living quarters for the crew. There is very little space. There is a galley for cooking, a small wash basin and a toilet. Opposite are the sleeping quarters. Nearby are lockers for storage. The astronauts take plenty of exercise in the living quarters to keep fit. Behind the living quarters is an airlock. The crew enter and leave the Shuttle through this. Spacesuits are put on inside the airlock.

The cargo bay

Behind the two decks is the massive cargo bay. It is over 18 m long and nearly 5 m across. It is bigger than a large railway carriage. It can carry a total load of 30 tonnes. This might be the weight of two or three satellites. A number of smaller loads can also be fitted in the cargo bay. These include research projects from schools and universities. The cargo bay has two huge doors which open when the Shuttle is in orbit.

The Shuttle at work

▼ The manipulator arm is used to handle the Shuttle's payloads. The arm is over 15 m long.

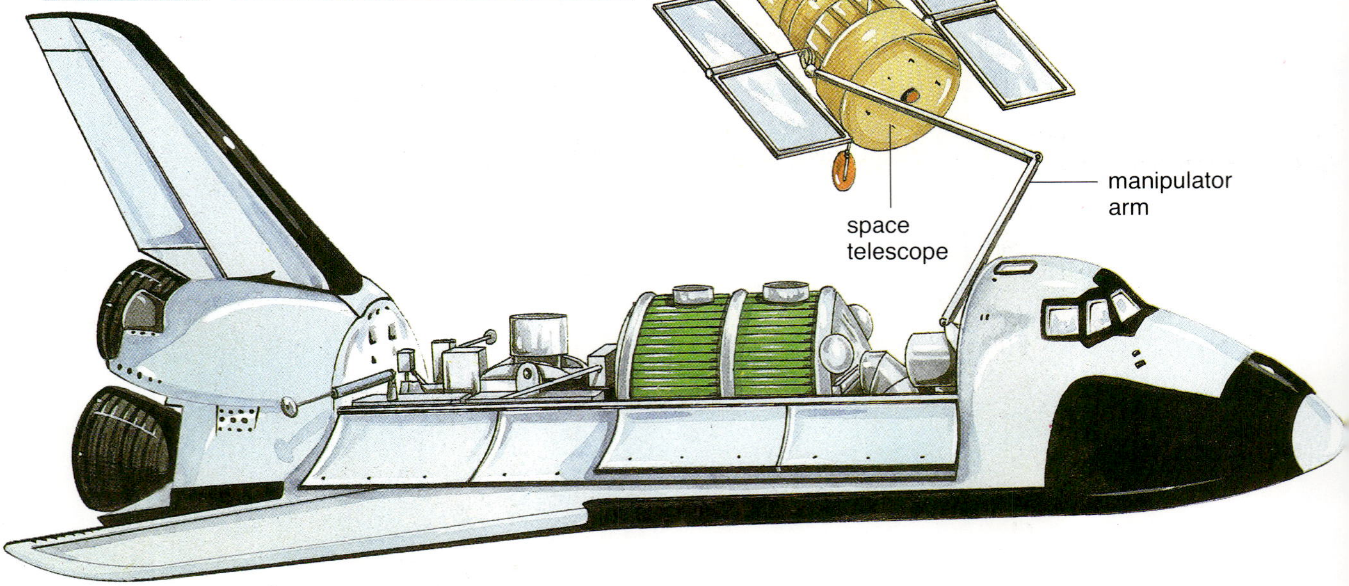

The crew of the Shuttle do not feel very high G-forces at lift-off and re-entry. This means that healthy men and women can go into space on the Shuttle with less space training. The Shuttle commander and the co-pilot however are highly trained astronauts and pilots.

In addition to the astronauts there are scientists on board. They carry out experiments or operate **payloads**. These people do not need to enter the cargo bay. They can see and control what is happening from a **console** at the rear of the flight deck. A window looks on to the cargo bay.

Handling satellites

From the console, a satellite can be launched and then tested in orbit. A faulty satellite can be brought back into the cargo bay. Simple repairs can be carried out there by astronauts in spacesuits. More difficult repairs have to wait until the Shuttle gets back to Earth.

Objects in Earth orbit have no weight. Lifting them does not need any effort. They only have to be moved with care. To move satellites into and out of the cargo bay there is a long **manipulator arm**. This is worked by **remote control** from inside the Orbiter. The manipulator arm is over 15 m long. It is jointed so that it can be moved like a human arm. On the flight of the Shuttle *Challenger* in June 1983, America's first woman in space, Dr Sally Ride, controlled the arm.

► Dr Sally Ride was the first American woman in space. She is seen here in charge of an experiment during the flight of *Challenger*. One of her duties during the mission was to operate the manipulator arm.

► Spacelab fits inside the Shuttle's cargo bay. It can be used to test metals and medicines in space.

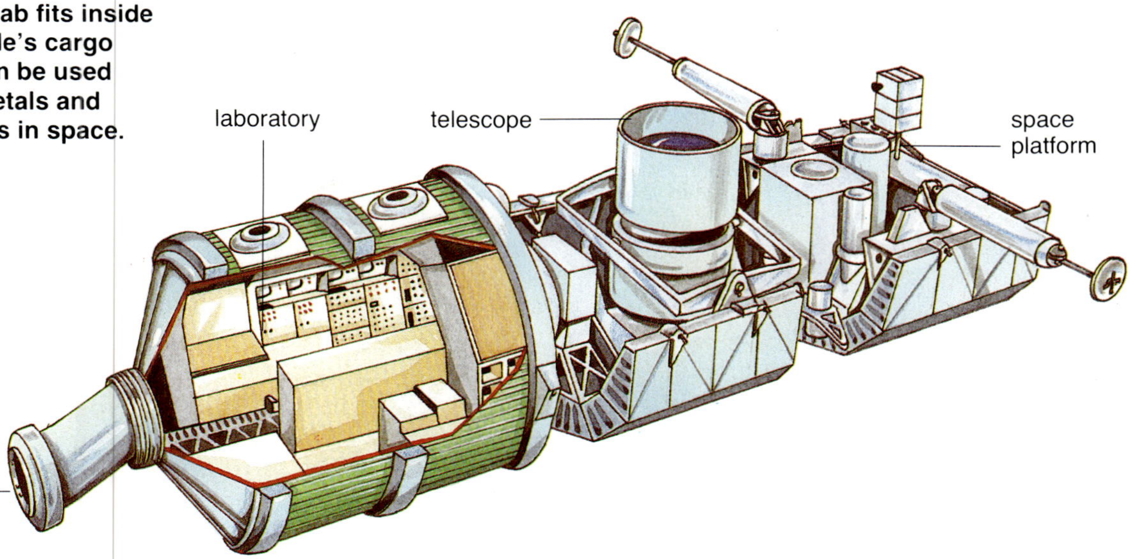

Spacelab

One special payload carried by the Shuttle is the European Spacelab. This made its first flight on *Columbia* in November 1983. Spacelab is a **laboratory** where scientists can work. It is pressurized, so that people can wear normal clothes inside it. Scientists enter it through an airlock from the Orbiter. Spacelab also carries a special rack for experiments which need to be kept outside in the vacuum of space.

The Space Telescope

The Shuttle will also be used to launch the Space Telescope. Astronauts will be able to see things more clearly through the Space Telescope. In space, it will be free from Earth's atmosphere. It will be possible to see things more clearly than from Earth. The Space Telescope will see seven times further into deep space than ever before. Scientists will find objects 50 times fainter than is possible from Earth and might even see planets in orbit around other stars.

► There are plans to carry a large space telescope in the Shuttle. It will be able to see much further into space than can be done from the Earth.

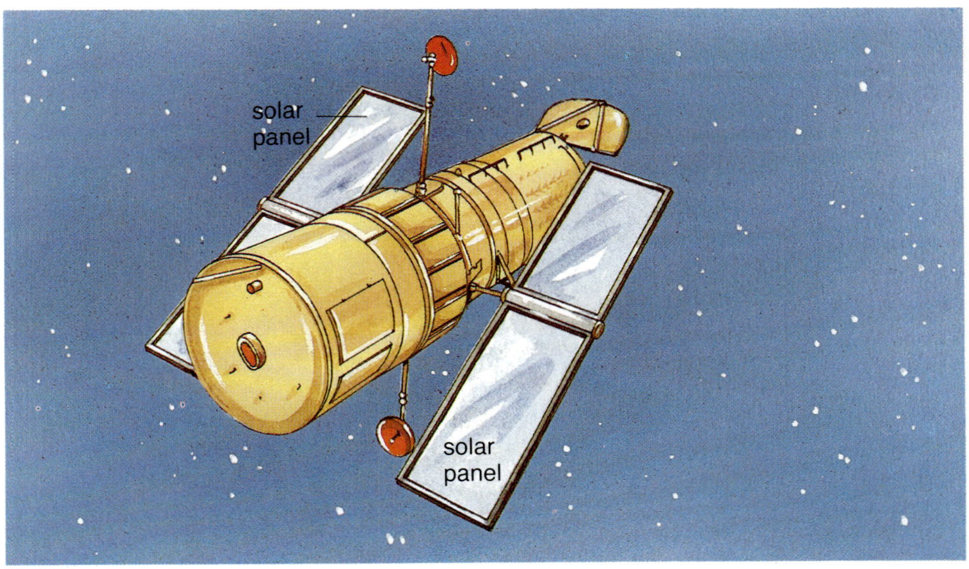

Future space stations

The next big step in space will be to set up a space station in orbit around the Earth. Crews will go there to carry out special jobs. They will return to Earth when their work is done. People will travel to the station in a space capsule or by Shuttle. Several countries plan to build spacecraft life the Shuttle over the next ten years.

Using a space station

When spacecraft dock with the space station, people will enter it through an airlock. The space station has its own life support system. This supplies fresh air and water. It also gets rid of waste. New supplies of food and other things are brought by Shuttle from Earth when they are needed. The space station has places for working and sleeping. People can take exercise when they want to.

A space station will have many uses. It is a fine lookout for watching the Earth and the stars. Scientists can study the Earth's atmosphere, land and oceans. They can

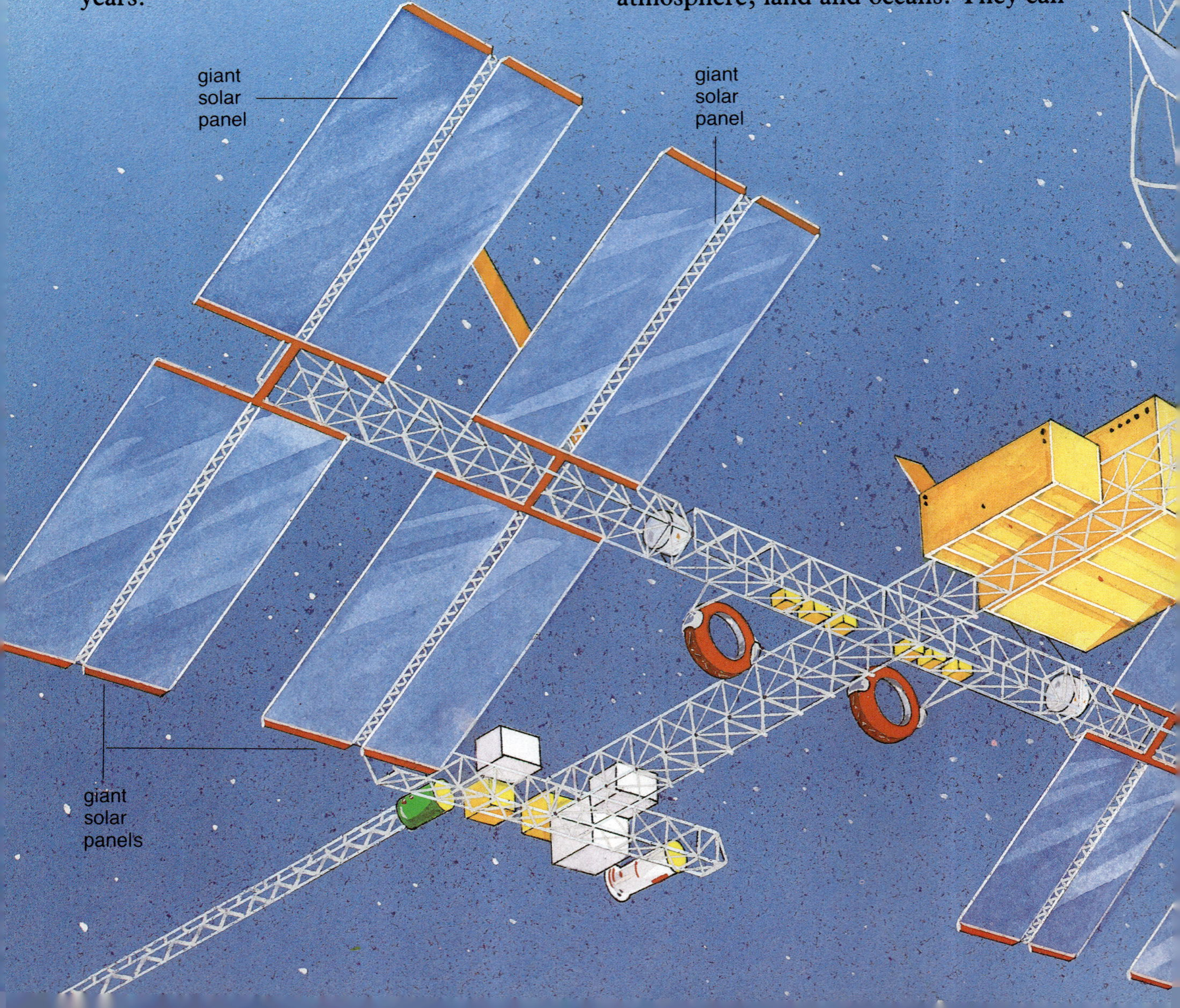

watch the health of forests and crops. They can look for new places to drill for oil.

A space station will contain special workshops. Many things can be made in space which cannot be made on Earth. People could make medicines for the sick, or new metals for building machines. One day there might be complete factories in space.

Giant space stations

Giant space stations may also be used to gather the Sun's rays. The energy would be beamed down to Earth. Special power stations on Earth would store it. This might give us the fuel we need when all the coal, oil and gas on Earth are used up.

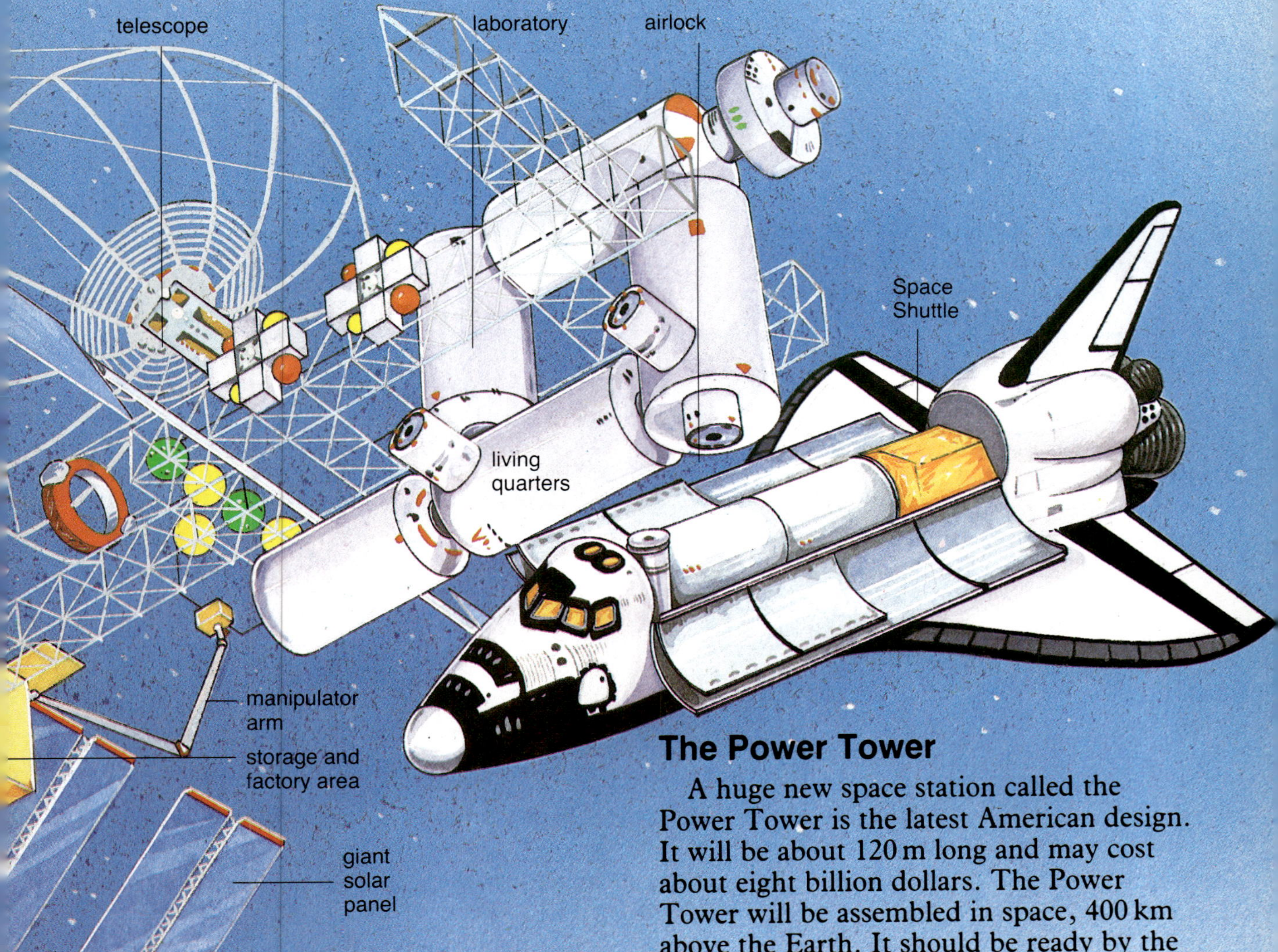

▲ **Our world may run very short of fuel during the next 50 years. The Power Tower in space might help to solve this problem. Huge reflectors on the Power Tower would beam the Sun's rays to power stations on the Earth.**

The Power Tower

A huge new space station called the Power Tower is the latest American design. It will be about 120 m long and may cost about eight billion dollars. The Power Tower will be assembled in space, 400 km above the Earth. It should be ready by the mid-1990s.

In the distant future, space stations may be used as space ports. From here space ships will depart for the Moon. They may even leave for more distant bodies like the planet Mars.

Colonies in space

Fifty years ago no one would have believed that people would land on the Moon or travel through space. Today it is very difficult to say what will happen in fifty years time.

Lunar base

The first stage might be the building of a lunar base. The Moon's surface is firm enough to carry a building. Of course, there would be problems. The Moon has no atmosphere. Also, it is very hot by day on the Moon, and bitterly cold at night. All supplies for the lunar base would have to be sent from Earth.

It is unlikely that work would start on the base before the year 2000. The lunar base would probably have a number of **inflatable** domes. There might be one large dome to live in. There would be others nearby for use as workshops.

It might even be possible to grow plants inside the lunar base. As the size of the base increased, there would be more men and women working there. Large lunar bases making up a colony of several hundred people may be on the Moon by the year 2025.

A colony on Mars

Mars has a very thin atmosphere. It has clouds, weather and seasons. Mars may well be the next place to be visited after the Moon. The air on Mars, however, is poisonous to humans. A life support suit would always be needed. Living and working on Mars would always be difficult. The first bases on Mars would be no larger than those on the Moon. A small colony might be set up on the planet Mars by the year 2025.

Colonies of the future

We cannot tell what the future holds for colonies in space. The Moon and Mars are possibilities. Apart from these two, there are no other places in the solar system where colonies could be built. Only if the Earth became too crowded would we need colonies at all. Our own planet Earth has all we want, if we can learn to plan our future.

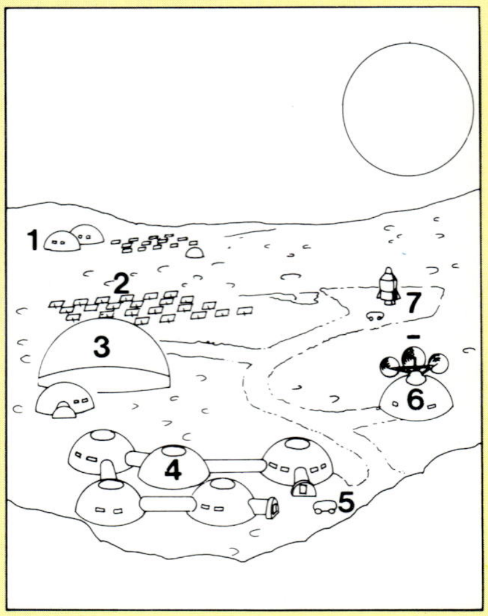

A lunar mining colony of the year 2025

1. Area where rare minerals are mined for use on Earth.
2. Solar panels for collecting energy from the Sun's rays.
3. Lunar garden. Vegetables grow in chemical 'soil' beneath a clear plastic dome.
4. Living quarters beneath inflatable domes for mineworkers, scientists and astronauts.
5. Lunar vehicle for carrying goods and people.
6. Base headquarters and command centre. From here, movements of spacecraft and lunar vehicles are controlled by radio. Base can also speak to Earth.
7. Landing area and launch pad for lunar modules.

Glossary

acacia: the name of a group of small trees and shrubs found in warm countries
adapt: to alter or change something to suit a different purpose
advertisement: a printed announcement offering goods or services for sale or hire
aerofoil: the curved shape of a plane's wing. It is almost flat underneath and curved on top
agger: a chalk or clay bank on which the Romans built their roads
aileron: a hinged surface at the back of a plane's wing. It is moved up and down to help a plane turn
air cargo: the goods carried by an aircraft
air filter: an object which cleans the air. It removes or filters poisonous gases and dust from the air
air freight: the goods carried by an aircraft
airline: a company which provides flights from place to place. The flights are listed in a timetable
airlock: a sealed chamber with special doors. It allows people to enter or leave a spacecraft without the air leaking into space
air pressure: the way in which the layers of air press down on you. The greatest air pressure is felt at ground level. The higher up you go, the less air there is and the lower the air pressure becomes
aisle: a passage for walking between rows of seats
amphibian: a plane that can land or take off from land or water
approach control: the group of people who are in charge of plane movements near an airport
aqueduct: a channel built to carry water
arch: something built in the shape of a curve over an opening. Arches are used to support bridges
array: a number of objects or instruments laid out so that they can be seen easily
articulated: describes a large truck with a trailer which is jointed between the tractor unit and the trailer
astronaut: a person who has been trained to go into space
atmosphere: the layer of gases that surrounds a planet. The Earth's atmosphere is the air
attendant: a person who looks after the needs of passengers on trains
autobahn: the German name for a road specially built to carry fast motor traffic
automatic: describes a machine that works on its own without human aid
autoroute: the French name for a road specially built to carry fast motor traffic
autostrada: the Italian name for a road specially built to carry fast motor traffic
axis: an imaginary straight line around which a body such as the Earth spins or rotates
axle: a wooden or metal rod which joins two wheels
bank: to tilt the wings and turn a plane in the air
banked: built up so that it slopes upwards on bends
barge: a flat-bottomed boat built to carry cargo on rivers and canals
barrier: something which separates one thing from another
barrow: a hand-cart with one or two wheels. A wheelbarrow
battery: a store for electricity, consisting of two or more cells
beam wind: a wind blowing across a ship as it moves forward
becalmed: unable to move at sea because there is no wind
biplane: a plane with two sets of wings, one wing above the other
body: an object in space such as the Earth, stars or any piece of matter however large or small
bomber: a plane specially made to carry bombs
botany: the study of plants
bow: the front end of a boat or ship
bridge: the raised section from which the captain controls the ship
brief: to give facts and instructions
bulk carrier: a large ship which carries a loose dry cargo, like grain
bulkheads: the steel walls which divide up the decks and hold of a ship
buoy: a floating marker which shows shipping lanes or warns of sunken wrecks
business: the work that people do, often buying or selling
canal: a water channel built by people across land to connect two stretches of water
capsule: the front part of a spacecraft containing the crew and the passengers. The capsule can be separated from the rest of the spacecraft
caravel: a light, fast ship with two square sails and one lateen sail at the stern
carbon dioxide: a gas found in the air. We breathe in oxygen and breathe out carbon dioxide
cargo: goods carried by ship
carrack: a large, three-masted, trading ship
carriage: a wheeled vehicle for carrying people, usually drawn by horses, also a railway passenger vehicle

cathedral: a large and important church
cedar: a kind of large evergreen tree whose wood was used for shipbuilding
channel: a narrow stretch of water deep enough for ships to use
chariot: a light, two-wheeled cart drawn by one or more horses. Chariots were used by the Romans for war and for racing
charter: to hire a plane to a group of people for a special flight. Charter flights are often used for holiday trips
charts: maps used by sailors
chauffeur: a person whose job is to drive a car for someone
check in: to report at an airport with ticket and baggage before a flight. You report to the check in desk
climate: the usual weather conditions found in an area. Climate differs from one area to another
clinker built: a method of building the hull or shell of a ship in which each plank of wood overlaps the one below it
clipper: a long, narrow sailing ship built for speed. Clippers carried people and cargo over long distances
coaster: a small ship carrying goods, used for short voyages near the coast
cockpit: the place where a pilot sits to fly a plane. The word is mainly used for light planes
colony: a group of people who leave their original home and settle in another place
comet: a small icy body in the solar system. A comet sometimes has a long 'tail' which we can see from the Earth. The tail is made of dust and gases. These reflect light from the Sun
command module: the control centre and living quarters of a manned spacecraft
communication: information or news sent from one place to another
commute: to travel daily to and from work
compete: to try and do better than someone else
compress: to pack very tight. Air can be compressed
console: an instrument panel from which machines can be operated
container: a large metal box for carrying cargo
container terminal: a port or part of a port where containers are loaded and unloaded
continent: one of the large land masses on Earth. There are seven continents
contract: an agreement, usually written, detailing a number of items. Contracts are made between two people
control column: the lever used by a pilot to make a plane go up or down, and left or right in the air
control tower: the tall building at an airport where orders are given to all planes at the airport
conveyor belt: a moving track which carries cars or other things from one part of a factory to another
core: the centre of an object
cosmonaut: the Russian name for an astronaut, a person who has been trained to go into space
countdown: the counting aloud of the number of seconds before a spacecraft is launched
crater: a bowl-shaped hollow. There are many craters on the surface of the Moon
crowsnest: a look-out position at the top of the mainmast. From the crowsnest a sailor can see land or ships far away
cutting: a wide passage cut through a hill for a road or railway
deckhouse: a building on deck, near the stern, to protect the crew
derrick: a crane on the deck of a ship, used to lift cargo in and out of the hold
design: the way something is made or built and how it looks
dhow: an Arab boat with one lateen sail
diesel: a type of engine that burns heavy oil. The diesel engine was invented by Rudolf Diesel
displacement: the amount of water forced out of place when an object is put into the water
divert: to change course. Planes sometimes have to divert and land at another airport because of fog
dock: to bring together two spacecraft or two parts of a spacecraft
domed: rounded at the top
drag: the force that slows down a plane as it flies through the air
dumb barge: a flat-bottomed boat, without an engine, built to carry cargo on rivers and canals. Dumb barges are often pulled or pushed by barges with engines or tugs
economy: the careful use of something, such as fuel, to avoid wasting it and to save money
embankment: a bank of earth on which railways and roads are built
emergency: an unexpected danger
empire: a number of countries under one ruler
engineer: a person who builds roads, railways and other large works. An engineer also looks after engines and machines
escape velocity: the speed an object needs to reach in order to escape from the pull of gravity
exit: the way out from a road or building

experiment: a test to try out an idea. People carry out experiments when they want to find out more about something
explosive: gunpowder or other material used to blow something up
extended: pushed out. The flaps are extended before landing
fare: the price of a ticket for a journey
feeder: a road or railway line which feeds traffic on to larger or more important roads or railway lines
figurehead: a carved wooden figure fixed on the bow of a ship
first aid: quick help for someone who is injured or ill
fittings: small parts which are fixed on to something larger. A door handle is a door fitting
flange: the raised edge on the inside of a railway wheel
flaps: moving parts fitted to the rear edge of plane wings. They help to slow a plane down for landing
flight plan: the written details which show where a plane is going, how long the flight will take, and other important facts
flint: a kind of stone which is hard but splits easily
fly-by: a path that takes a space probe close to a body in space. The probe does not land on the body or go into orbit around it
flyover: one road carried over another road
foil: a thin metal strip, shaped like a ski or a fin of a fish
following wind: a wind blowing from behind a ship which helps it to move
force of gravity: the invisible force which pulls things towards the Earth, or other bodies. Gravity makes objects fall and gives them weight
ford: a shallow place in a river where people or vehicles can cross
forecast: a statement about what is expected to happen in the future. It is not always certain to be true
forecastle: a raised deck at the bow of a ship. Forecastles were built to protect the crew from attack
formula: a class of racing car
freight: the goods carried by any from of transport
freighter: a ship carrying goods, powered by an engine
friction: the rubbing of one surface against another surface. Friction slows things down
fuel: a material burned in engines to provide power for movement
fuel cell: a special device used on a spacecraft to make electricity
galley: a ship first built by the Greeks and Romans. Later, galleys were used as warships
G-force: the force felt when something is speeding up or slowing down. The force of gravity, or G-force, throws you forward when a car brakes
glider: a plane without an engine
gravel: small stones
gunpowder: a mixture that produces a lot of gas when it is set alight
hangar: a large building where planes can stand or be repaired. Cargo can be stored in a hangar
hang glider: a glider where the pilot hangs underneath the wing
head-set: headphones which fit over the ears
headwind: a wind blowing against a plane in flight
heat shield: a thick layer of special material on the outside of a spacecraft. It protects the spacecraft from the great heat when it re-enters the Earth's atmosphere. During re-entry the heat shield glows red-hot
highwayman: a man on a horse who used to stop travellers and rob them
hold: the place where goods and baggage are stowed during flight
horizon: the distant line where the sky and the sea or land appear to meet
hovercraft: a type of ship which moves above the surface of the sea on a cushion of air. It is driven by propellers in the air
hull: the main body or shell of a ship
hydrofoil: a type of ship with foils which skim the surface of the water. It is driven by a propeller beneath the water
hydrogen: a gas which is very light and burns easily
inflatable: an object which can be made bigger by pumping air or gas into it. A balloon is an inflatable object
inland waterway: a river or canal used by boats
insignia: signs or badges by which things are known. Airlines have insignia on their planes and uniforms
instrument: a dial like a clock-face which gives information, for example, about engines and speed
inventor: a person who makes something quite new
jettison: to throw something away that is no longer needed. To let something go so that it falls away
juggernaut: the name given to a large road truck
junction: the place where roads or railway lines join
keel: the long piece of wood or metal which runs along the bottom of the hull and is the backbone of a ship
kerosene: an oil fuel used in jet engines
laboratory: a building or room where scientists work and carry out experiments
lateen: a triangular sail
launch: to blast off a spacecraft

levitation: lifting above the ground
life support system: equipment that supplies astronauts with air to breathe. It also supplies food and water
lift: the force needed to get a spacecraft or aircraft into the air, and to keep it from falling. The launch of a rocket is often called 'lift-off'
liner: a ship carrying passengers that makes regular voyages at fixed times
lock: a stretch of a canal with gates at each end. It is used to enable ships to go 'uphill' or 'downhill'
locomotive: an engine which pulls a train
long haul: a long distance flight by an airliner
longship: a long, narrow ship built by the Phoenicians and the Vikings. It was used for exploring and as a fighting ship
luxury: very great comfort
Mach: a measure of flying speed. The speed of sound is Mach 1. Twice the speed of sound is Mach 2, and so on
maglev: a new kind of train which does not have wheels. Maglev is short for magnetic levitation, which means lifted above the ground by magnets
magnet: a piece of iron or steel made to attract or repel another piece of iron
maiden voyage: the first journey by a new ship
mainmast: the tallest mast on a ship, usually in the middle of the ship
manifest: the list of freight carried on a flight
manipulator arm: a kind of crane used in space to move objects about. Its joints are a bit like the human arm
manned: containing or controlled by people. A manned spacecraft contains astronauts
manned manoeuvring unit (MMU): a piece of equipment used by astronauts to move around in space. It is like a large L-shaped backpack and is attached to the astronaut
manual control: the control or movement of a vehicle or machine by a person
mascon: an area of dense rock just below the Moon's surface. It increases the Moon's gravity in that area, affecting the orbit of spacecraft around the Moon
mass production: a way of making things in a factory where each worker does the same job time after time
meteor: a small piece of material in the solar system. It is quickly burned up if it enters the Earth's atmosphere from space
meteorite: a large meteor that has not totally burned up in its fall through the atmosphere. It falls as a piece of hard rock
mission: a journey with a purpose. Also the name given to a space launch
model: a particular design of something made by one manufacturer. New models of cars are made each year
motorway: the British name for a road specially built to carry fast motor traffic
multi-stage rocket: a large rocket made up of several separate rockets one on top of the other.
network: a system of roads or railways that join each other
nose wheel: the wheel at the front of a plane
nuclear power: the power produced by the heat made when atoms are split
on duty: at work
orbit: the path of one body, like a planet or satellite, around another body. The Earth moves in orbit around the Sun
outback: part of a country, such as Australia, which is far away from towns
oxygen: a gas in the air which we need for breathing
pallet: a flat tray of wood. Goods are stacked and carried on a pallet
patrol: a regular voyage or flight. Patrol boats are often used to watch for icebergs, changes in the weather or smugglers
payload: the part of the load on an aircraft or spacecraft which is carried in return for payment of money by the owner
pike: a long pole with a pointed metal tip, once used in battle
pilot: a captain who takes charge of a ship entering or leaving harbour (ii) a person who flies a plane
pitch: to plunge up and down in the sea. A ship pitches when the waves hit it at the bow of the ship
planet: a body in space which moves in orbit around a star like the Sun. Planets have no light of their own. They reflect the light of the Sun
plaque: a metal plate with a message on it. Plaques are used to mark important events
Plimsoll line: the line painted on the side of a ship. When the ship is fully loaded, the water level touches the line
pod: a seed-shaped container. Aeroplane engines hang from the wings in pods
pollute: to spoil something. When oil is spilt from a ship it pollutes the water and can kill fish and birds
port: the left hand side of a ship
powered: using an engine
prairie: a large area of grassland without trees
pressure: the action of one thing pressing against another

pressurize: to alter the air inside the cabin of a plane or a spacecraft. This makes it the same as the air on the ground
probe: an unmanned spacecraft sent to examine something more closely
probe, to: to look closely at something
production line: the part of a factory where machines and workers put things together in stages
propeller: a propeller is made of two or more twisted blades. As it turns, it pulls a plane or ship forward
propeller shaft: a shaft driven by a ship's engine and carrying the propeller
radar: a way of finding the position of an object. Radio waves are sent out. When they meet an object, they bounce back to the radar set
ram: a heavy piece of wood fixed to the bow of a warship and used to sink an enemy's ship
range: the distance a plane can fly without running out of fuel
reaction: an action which has come as a result of something which has happened earlier. When fuel in a rocket is burned, a jet of gases is sent out of the back. The reaction is for the rocket to be pushed forward and upwards
reeds: dried stalks of plants found in marshy places
re-enter: to come back into the Earth's atmosphere at the end of a space voyage
reflect: to throw back. It usually refers to a beam of light. We see the Moon because it reflects the light of the Sun
regular: at fixed times, say every day or every week
reliable: sure not to go wrong
remote: far away from other people and places
remote control: the control of something from a distance, usually through radio or electric signals
reserve: to keep back in case of need
retro-rocket: a rocket used for slowing down a spacecraft. It fires in the opposite direction to the main rocket engines
reverse thrust: a way of slowing a jet plane down on landing. The hot gases from the engine are made to go forward instead of backward
robot: a machine that can perform tasks automatically without help from people
rocket: a device, shaped like a cylinder, used to launch a spacecraft. Its fuel burns and produces a continuous jet of hot gases. These gases are sent out of the back of the rocket and propel, or push, the rocket forward or upwards
roll: to sway from side to side. A ship rolls when the waves hit the side of the ship
round ship: a cargo ship first used by the Phoenicians
route: the way to get from one place to another. Routes are shown on maps and plans
rubble: broken bricks and stone
rudder: a hinged flat piece of wood or metal used to steer boats or planes
runway: a long, straight track for planes to take off and land on. Runways are often made of concrete
safety drill: a set way of doing things in case something should go wrong
sailcloth: a strong woven cloth used to make sails
saloon: a public room on a train or a ship where any passenger can sit in comfort
satellite: a small body in orbit around a larger body in space, such as a planet. The Moon is the Earth's satellite. Manmade satellites circle the Earth. They are often used to send TV and radio signals and for weather forecasting
satellite: an object that people have launched into space, which sends signals back to Earth
scanner: a machine which can check people and baggage for metal
security: looking after safety
sedan chair: a covered, box-like chair for one person which is carried on poles by two other people
shaft: a long handle or pole which is used to carry or pull something along
short haul: a short distance flight by an airliner
simulator: a training machine on the ground which imitates flight in the air
sledge: a vehicle with wooden or metal runners instead of wheels
soft-lander: the sort of space probe which can land on the surface of another body without damage
soft-landing: bringing down a spacecraft gently on to the surface of a moon or planet so that it is undamaged
solar panel: a large, flat area, or panel, that contains many solar cells. Each solar cell collects energy from the Sun's rays and turns it into electricity
solar system: the Sun and the nine planets, including the Earth, which move around it in orbit.
solo: alone, or by one person
sound-track: a strip along one side of a reel of film on which speech and music is recorded
spacecraft: a manned or unmanned vehicle designed to travel into space
spaceplane: a special kind of spacecraft which is also able to act like an aeroplane. The Space Shuttle is an example of a spaceplane. It takes off upwards like a rocket but after re-entry glides in to land like an aeroplane on a long runway
spacesuit: a specially made suit of clothing, including a helmet, worn by astronauts in space

spoilers: extra flaps on the wings of a plane that act as brakes
spring: a metal strip or coil. It bends gently up and down and reduces the shock when a vehicle moves over bumps in a road
stack: planes flying around and around at different heights above and below each other. Planes stack when they are waiting to land
stage: a part of a journey when a plane stops at an airport to take on more fuel
starboard: the right hand side of a ship
stern: the rear end of a ship
sternwheeler: a type of paddle steamer with one paddle wheel at the stern
steward: a man who looks after passengers on a flight
stewardess: a woman who looks after passengers on a flight
stowaway: a person who travels on a plane or ship without paying for a ticket
streamlining: giving something smooth lines so that it moves through air easily
suction: the removal of air from a container so that air or liquid can come in to fill the gap
supersonic: faster than the speed of sound
tacking: sailing on a zig-zag course
tanker: a ship built to carry liquids in bulk
tapered: thin and pointed at the tip or edge
taxi: to move a plane along the ground
taxiway: the roads used by planes when they move on the ground
terminal: the airport building where planes arrive or depart
throttle: the lever which alters the speed of an engine
thrust: the force which is used to drive a plane or spacecraft forward and upwards
thruster: an object with a small opening which allows a jet of gas to escape from it. It works like a rocket. As the gas rushes out, the thruster moves in the opposite direction
tilt: to slope or lean
timetable: a list of places that planes, trains or buses travel to. It shows the times of departure and arrival
toll: the amount of money charged for the use of a road or bridge
toll road: a road which can be used only if money is paid
tractor unit: the front part of an articulated truck. It contains the engine and the driver's cab
trail: a road or track across wild country
trestle: a wooden or metal criss-cross framework that supports a road or railway bridge
trimmed: moved from side to side to catch the wind
turbine: a shaft with many curved blades on it
turbofan: a type of jet engine which has a fan inside it
turbulence: weather that makes flights bumpy
turnpike: a toll road
underpass: a road which passes underneath another road
unmanned: not containing people
vacuum: an empty space
viaduct: a long, high bridge which carries a road or a railway across low ground or a valley
villa: a large house built by the Romans with outbuildings and farm land nearby
volcano: a cone-shaped hill or mountain with a large opening or crater at the top, through which liquid rock, hot gases and ash are forced out under great pressure from below
voyage: a long sea journey
weight: how heavy something is
weightlessness: the sensation of having no weight

Index